C-593   CAREER EXAMINATION SERIES

This is your
PASSBOOK for...

Plumbing Inspector

Test Preparation Study Guide
Questions & Answers

COPYRIGHT NOTICE

This book is SOLELY intended for, is sold ONLY to, and its use is RESTRICTED to individual, bona fide applicants or candidates who qualify by virtue of having seriously filed applications for appropriate license, certificate, professional and/or promotional advancement, higher school matriculation, scholarship, or other legitimate requirements of education and/or governmental authorities.

This book is NOT intended for use, class instruction, tutoring, training, duplication, copying, reprinting, excerption, or adaptation, etc., by:

1) Other publishers
2) Proprietors and/or Instructors of "Coaching" and/or Preparatory Courses
3) Personnel and/or Training Divisions of commercial, industrial, and governmental organizations
4) Schools, colleges, or universities and/or their departments and staffs, including teachers and other personnel
5) Testing Agencies or Bureaus
6) Study groups which seek by the purchase of a single volume to copy and/or duplicate and/or adapt this material for use by the group as a whole without having purchased individual volumes for each of the members of the group
7) Et al.

Such persons would be in violation of appropriate Federal and State statutes.

PROVISION OF LICENSING AGREEMENTS – Recognized educational, commercial, industrial, and governmental institutions and organizations, and others legitimately engaged in educational pursuits, including training, testing, and measurement activities, may address request for a licensing agreement to the copyright owners, who will determine whether, and under what conditions, including fees and charges, the materials in this book may be used them. In other words, a licensing facility exists for the legitimate use of the material in this book on other than an individual basis. However, it is asseverated and affirmed here that the material in this book CANNOT be used without the receipt of the express permission of such a licensing agreement from the Publishers. Inquiries re licensing should be addressed to the company, attention rights and permissions department.

All rights reserved, including the right of reproduction in whole or in part, in any form or by any means, electronic or mechanical, including photocopying, recording, or by any information storage and retrieval system, without permission in writing from the Publisher.

Copyright © 2025 by
National Learning Corporation

212 Michael Drive, Syosset, NY 11791
(516) 921-8888 • www.passbooks.com
E-mail: info@passbooks.com

PASSBOOK® SERIES

THE *PASSBOOK® SERIES* has been created to prepare applicants and candidates for the ultimate academic battlefield – the examination room.

At some time in our lives, each and every one of us may be required to take an examination – for validation, matriculation, admission, qualification, registration, certification, or licensure.

Based on the assumption that every applicant or candidate has met the basic formal educational standards, has taken the required number of courses, and read the necessary texts, the *PASSBOOK® SERIES* furnishes the one special preparation which may assure passing with confidence, instead of failing with insecurity. Examination questions – together with answers – are furnished as the basic vehicle for study so that the mysteries of the examination and its compounding difficulties may be eliminated or diminished by a sure method.

This book is meant to help you pass your examination provided that you qualify and are serious in your objective.

The entire field is reviewed through the huge store of content information which is succinctly presented through a provocative and challenging approach – the question-and-answer method.

A climate of success is established by furnishing the correct answers at the end of each test.

You soon learn to recognize types of questions, forms of questions, and patterns of questioning. You may even begin to anticipate expected outcomes.

You perceive that many questions are repeated or adapted so that you can gain acute insights, which may enable you to score many sure points.

You learn how to confront new questions, or types of questions, and to attack them confidently and work out the correct answers.

You note objectives and emphases, and recognize pitfalls and dangers, so that you may make positive educational adjustments.

Moreover, you are kept fully informed in relation to new concepts, methods, practices, and directions in the field.

You discover that you are actually taking the examination all the time: you are preparing for the examination by "taking" an examination, not by reading extraneous and/or supererogatory textbooks.

In short, this PASSBOOK®, used directedly, should be an important factor in helping you to pass your test.

PLUMBING INSPECTOR

JOB DESCRIPTION
Under general supervision, performs technical work in the inspection of plumbing installations, repairs or alterations to ensure conformance to code, standards, plans or specifications; may operate a motor vehicle; performs related work.

EXAMPLES OF TYPICAL TASKS
Inspects and tests installations and repairs of plumbing and fire sprinkler systems to ensure adherence to codes, standards, plans and specifications; inspects piping, stand pipes, sprinklers and stand pipe installations, and house sewer connections; inspects vacuum cleaning and pumping systems and cafeteria and kitchen equipment for compliance with specifications. Witnesses smoke tests and tests on water, air or gas piping, ranges, space heaters and appliances. Investigates complaints, when requested by the public or contractors, of violations of the plumbing code or illegal plumbing practices. Examines plans of proposed installations for compliance with code requirements, departmental rules and regulations. Studies drawings to obtain details for inspections. Prepares reports of inspections. May supervise and train Apprentice Inspectors (Plumbing). May operate a motor vehicle. May issue summonses.

TEST
The multiple-choice test may include questions on plumbing practices, systems, materials, fittings, tools and equipment; reading and interpreting of plans and specifications; arithmetic calculations; plumbing and sanitary codes; inspection procedures; dealing with the public; safety; record keeping; and other related areas.

HOW TO TAKE A TEST

I. YOU MUST PASS AN EXAMINATION

A. WHAT EVERY CANDIDATE SHOULD KNOW

Examination applicants often ask us for help in preparing for the written test. What can I study in advance? What kinds of questions will be asked? How will the test be given? How will the papers be graded?

As an applicant for a civil service examination, you may be wondering about some of these things. Our purpose here is to suggest effective methods of advance study and to describe civil service examinations.

Your chances for success on this examination can be increased if you know how to prepare. Those "pre-examination jitters" can be reduced if you know what to expect. You can even experience an adventure in good citizenship if you know why civil service exams are given.

B. WHY ARE CIVIL SERVICE EXAMINATIONS GIVEN?

Civil service examinations are important to you in two ways. As a citizen, you want public jobs filled by employees who know how to do their work. As a job seeker, you want a fair chance to compete for that job on an equal footing with other candidates. The best-known means of accomplishing this two-fold goal is the competitive examination.

Exams are widely publicized throughout the nation. They may be administered for jobs in federal, state, city, municipal, town or village governments or agencies.

Any citizen may apply, with some limitations, such as the age or residence of applicants. Your experience and education may be reviewed to see whether you meet the requirements for the particular examination. When these requirements exist, they are reasonable and applied consistently to all applicants. Thus, a competitive examination may cause you some uneasiness now, but it is your privilege and safeguard.

C. HOW ARE CIVIL SERVICE EXAMS DEVELOPED?

Examinations are carefully written by trained technicians who are specialists in the field known as "psychological measurement," in consultation with recognized authorities in the field of work that the test will cover. These experts recommend the subject matter areas or skills to be tested; only those knowledges or skills important to your success on the job are included. The most reliable books and source materials available are used as references. Together, the experts and technicians judge the difficulty level of the questions.

Test technicians know how to phrase questions so that the problem is clearly stated. Their ethics do not permit "trick" or "catch" questions. Questions may have been tried out on sample groups, or subjected to statistical analysis, to determine their usefulness.

Written tests are often used in combination with performance tests, ratings of training and experience, and oral interviews. All of these measures combine to form the best-known means of finding the right person for the right job.

II. HOW TO PASS THE WRITTEN TEST

A. NATURE OF THE EXAMINATION

To prepare intelligently for civil service examinations, you should know how they differ from school examinations you have taken. In school you were assigned certain definite pages to read or subjects to cover. The examination questions were quite detailed and usually emphasized memory. Civil service exams, on the other hand, try to discover your present ability to perform the duties of a position, plus your potentiality to learn these duties. In other words, a civil service exam attempts to predict how successful you will be. Questions cover such a broad area that they cannot be as minute and detailed as school exam questions.

In the public service similar kinds of work, or positions, are grouped together in one "class." This process is known as *position-classification*. All the positions in a class are paid according to the salary range for that class. One class title covers all of these positions, and they are all tested by the same examination.

B. FOUR BASIC STEPS

1) Study the announcement

How, then, can you know what subjects to study? Our best answer is: "Learn as much as possible about the class of positions for which you've applied." The exam will test the knowledge, skills and abilities needed to do the work.

Your most valuable source of information about the position you want is the official exam announcement. This announcement lists the training and experience qualifications. Check these standards and apply only if you come reasonably close to meeting them.

The brief description of the position in the examination announcement offers some clues to the subjects which will be tested. Think about the job itself. Review the duties in your mind. Can you perform them, or are there some in which you are rusty? Fill in the blank spots in your preparation.

Many jurisdictions preview the written test in the exam announcement by including a section called "Knowledge and Abilities Required," "Scope of the Examination," or some similar heading. Here you will find out specifically what fields will be tested.

2) Review your own background

Once you learn in general what the position is all about, and what you need to know to do the work, ask yourself which subjects you already know fairly well and which need improvement. You may wonder whether to concentrate on improving your strong areas or on building some background in your fields of weakness. When the announcement has specified "some knowledge" or "considerable knowledge," or has used adjectives like "beginning principles of..." or "advanced ... methods," you can get a clue as to the number and difficulty of questions to be asked in any given field. More questions, and hence broader coverage, would be included for those subjects which are more important in the work. Now weigh your strengths and weaknesses against the job requirements and prepare accordingly.

3) Determine the level of the position

Another way to tell how intensively you should prepare is to understand the level of the job for which you are applying. Is it the entering level? In other words, is this the position in which beginners in a field of work are hired? Or is it an intermediate or advanced level? Sometimes this is indicated by such words as "Junior" or "Senior" in the class title. Other jurisdictions use Roman numerals to designate the level – Clerk I, Clerk II, for example. The word "Supervisor" sometimes appears in the title. If the level is not indicated by the title, check the description of duties. Will you be working under very close supervision, or will you have responsibility for independent decisions in this work?

4) Choose appropriate study materials

Now that you know the subjects to be examined and the relative amount of each subject to be covered, you can choose suitable study materials. For beginning level jobs, or even advanced ones, if you have a pronounced weakness in some aspect of your training, read a modern, standard textbook in that field. Be sure it is up to date and has general coverage. Such books are normally available at your library, and the librarian will be glad to help you locate one. For entry-level positions, questions of appropriate difficulty are chosen – neither highly advanced questions, nor those too simple. Such questions require careful thought but not advanced training.

If the position for which you are applying is technical or advanced, you will read more advanced, specialized material. If you are already familiar with the basic principles of your field, elementary textbooks would waste your time. Concentrate on advanced textbooks and technical periodicals. Think through the concepts and review difficult problems in your field.

These are all general sources. You can get more ideas on your own initiative, following these leads. For example, training manuals and publications of the government agency which employs workers in your field can be useful, particularly for technical and professional positions. A letter or visit to the government department involved may result in more specific study suggestions, and certainly will provide you with a more definite idea of the exact nature of the position you are seeking.

III. KINDS OF TESTS

Tests are used for purposes other than measuring knowledge and ability to perform specified duties. For some positions, it is equally important to test ability to make adjustments to new situations or to profit from training. In others, basic mental abilities not dependent on information are essential. Questions which test these things may not appear as pertinent to the duties of the position as those which test for knowledge and information. Yet they are often highly important parts of a fair examination. For very general questions, it is almost impossible to help you direct your study efforts. What we can do is to point out some of the more common of these general abilities needed in public service positions and describe some typical questions.

1) General information

Broad, general information has been found useful for predicting job success in some kinds of work. This is tested in a variety of ways, from vocabulary lists to questions about current events. Basic background in some field of work, such as sociology or economics, may be sampled in a group of questions. Often these are principles which have become familiar to most persons through exposure rather than through formal training. It is difficult to advise you how to study for these questions; being alert to the world around you is our best suggestion.

2) Verbal ability

An example of an ability needed in many positions is verbal or language ability. Verbal ability is, in brief, the ability to use and understand words. Vocabulary and grammar tests are typical measures of this ability. Reading comprehension or paragraph interpretation questions are common in many kinds of civil service tests. You are given a paragraph of written material and asked to find its central meaning.

3) Numerical ability

Number skills can be tested by the familiar arithmetic problem, by checking paired lists of numbers to see which are alike and which are different, or by interpreting charts and graphs. In the latter test, a graph may be printed in the test booklet which you are asked to use as the basis for answering questions.

4) Observation

A popular test for law-enforcement positions is the observation test. A picture is shown to you for several minutes, then taken away. Questions about the picture test your ability to observe both details and larger elements.

5) Following directions

In many positions in the public service, the employee must be able to carry out written instructions dependably and accurately. You may be given a chart with several columns, each column listing a variety of information. The questions require you to carry out directions involving the information given in the chart.

6) Skills and aptitudes

Performance tests effectively measure some manual skills and aptitudes. When the skill is one in which you are trained, such as typing or shorthand, you can practice. These tests are often very much like those given in business school or high school courses. For many of the other skills and aptitudes, however, no short-time preparation can be made. Skills and abilities natural to you or that you have developed throughout your lifetime are being tested.

Many of the general questions just described provide all the data needed to answer the questions and ask you to use your reasoning ability to find the answers. Your best preparation for these tests, as well as for tests of facts and ideas, is to be at your physical and mental best. You, no doubt, have your own methods of getting into an exam-taking mood and keeping "in shape." The next section lists some ideas on this subject.

IV. KINDS OF QUESTIONS

Only rarely is the "essay" question, which you answer in narrative form, used in civil service tests. Civil service tests are usually of the short-answer type. Full instructions for answering these questions will be given to you at the examination. But in case this is your first experience with short-answer questions and separate answer sheets, here is what you need to know:

1) Multiple-choice Questions

Most popular of the short-answer questions is the "multiple choice" or "best answer" question. It can be used, for example, to test for factual knowledge, ability to solve problems or judgment in meeting situations found at work.

A multiple-choice question is normally one of three types—
- It can begin with an incomplete statement followed by several possible endings. You are to find the one ending which *best* completes the statement, although some of the others may not be entirely wrong.
- It can also be a complete statement in the form of a question which is answered by choosing one of the statements listed.

- It can be in the form of a problem – again you select the best answer.

Here is an example of a multiple-choice question with a discussion which should give you some clues as to the method for choosing the right answer:

When an employee has a complaint about his assignment, the action which will *best* help him overcome his difficulty is to
   A. discuss his difficulty with his coworkers
   B. take the problem to the head of the organization
   C. take the problem to the person who gave him the assignment
   D. say nothing to anyone about his complaint

In answering this question, you should study each of the choices to find which is best. Consider choice "A" – Certainly an employee may discuss his complaint with fellow employees, but no change or improvement can result, and the complaint remains unresolved. Choice "B" is a poor choice since the head of the organization probably does not know what assignment you have been given, and taking your problem to him is known as "going over the head" of the supervisor. The supervisor, or person who made the assignment, is the person who can clarify it or correct any injustice. Choice "C" is, therefore, correct. To say nothing, as in choice "D," is unwise. Supervisors have and interest in knowing the problems employees are facing, and the employee is seeking a solution to his problem.

2) True/False Questions

The "true/false" or "right/wrong" form of question is sometimes used. Here a complete statement is given. Your job is to decide whether the statement is right or wrong.

SAMPLE: A roaming cell-phone call to a nearby city costs less than a non-roaming call to a distant city.

This statement is wrong, or false, since roaming calls are more expensive.

This is not a complete list of all possible question forms, although most of the others are variations of these common types. You will always get complete directions for answering questions. Be sure you understand *how* to mark your answers – ask questions until you do.

V. RECORDING YOUR ANSWERS

Computer terminals are used more and more today for many different kinds of exams.

For an examination with very few applicants, you may be told to record your answers in the test booklet itself. Separate answer sheets are much more common. If this separate answer sheet is to be scored by machine – and this is often the case – it is highly important that you mark your answers correctly in order to get credit.

An electronic scoring machine is often used in civil service offices because of the speed with which papers can be scored. Machine-scored answer sheets must be marked with a pencil, which will be given to you. This pencil has a high graphite content which responds to the electronic scoring machine. As a matter of fact, stray dots may register as answers, so do not let your pencil rest on the answer sheet while you are pondering the correct answer. Also, if your pencil lead breaks or is otherwise defective, ask for another.

Since the answer sheet will be dropped in a slot in the scoring machine, be careful not to bend the corners or get the paper crumpled.

The answer sheet normally has five vertical columns of numbers, with 30 numbers to a column. These numbers correspond to the question numbers in your test booklet. After each number, going across the page are four or five pairs of dotted lines. These short dotted lines have small letters or numbers above them. The first two pairs may also have a "T" or "F" above the letters. This indicates that the first two pairs only are to be used if the questions are of the true-false type. If the questions are multiple choice, disregard the "T" and "F" and pay attention only to the small letters or numbers.

Answer your questions in the manner of the sample that follows:

32. The largest city in the United States is
    A. Washington, D.C.
    B. New York City
    C. Chicago
    D. Detroit
    E. San Francisco

1) Choose the answer you think is best. (New York City is the largest, so "B" is correct.)
2) Find the row of dotted lines numbered the same as the question you are answering. (Find row number 32)
3) Find the pair of dotted lines corresponding to the answer. (Find the pair of lines under the mark "B.")
4) Make a solid black mark between the dotted lines.

VI. BEFORE THE TEST

Common sense will help you find procedures to follow to get ready for an examination. Too many of us, however, overlook these sensible measures. Indeed, nervousness and fatigue have been found to be the most serious reasons why applicants fail to do their best on civil service tests. Here is a list of reminders:

- Begin your preparation early – Don't wait until the last minute to go scurrying around for books and materials or to find out what the position is all about.
- Prepare continuously – An hour a night for a week is better than an all-night cram session. This has been definitely established. What is more, a night a week for a month will return better dividends than crowding your study into a shorter period of time.
- Locate the place of the exam – You have been sent a notice telling you when and where to report for the examination. If the location is in a different town or otherwise unfamiliar to you, it would be well to inquire the best route and learn something about the building.
- Relax the night before the test – Allow your mind to rest. Do not study at all that night. Plan some mild recreation or diversion; then go to bed early and get a good night's sleep.
- Get up early enough to make a leisurely trip to the place for the test – This way unforeseen events, traffic snarls, unfamiliar buildings, etc. will not upset you.
- Dress comfortably – A written test is not a fashion show. You will be known by number and not by name, so wear something comfortable.

- Leave excess paraphernalia at home – Shopping bags and odd bundles will get in your way. You need bring only the items mentioned in the official notice you received; usually everything you need is provided. Do not bring reference books to the exam. They will only confuse those last minutes and be taken away from you when in the test room.
- Arrive somewhat ahead of time – If because of transportation schedules you must get there very early, bring a newspaper or magazine to take your mind off yourself while waiting.
- Locate the examination room – When you have found the proper room, you will be directed to the seat or part of the room where you will sit. Sometimes you are given a sheet of instructions to read while you are waiting. Do not fill out any forms until you are told to do so; just read them and be prepared.
- Relax and prepare to listen to the instructions
- If you have any physical problem that may keep you from doing your best, be sure to tell the test administrator. If you are sick or in poor health, you really cannot do your best on the exam. You can come back and take the test some other time.

VII. AT THE TEST

The day of the test is here and you have the test booklet in your hand. The temptation to get going is very strong. Caution! There is more to success than knowing the right answers. You must know how to identify your papers and understand variations in the type of short-answer question used in this particular examination. Follow these suggestions for maximum results from your efforts:

1) Cooperate with the monitor

The test administrator has a duty to create a situation in which you can be as much at ease as possible. He will give instructions, tell you when to begin, check to see that you are marking your answer sheet correctly, and so on. He is not there to guard you, although he will see that your competitors do not take unfair advantage. He wants to help you do your best.

2) Listen to all instructions

Don't jump the gun! Wait until you understand all directions. In most civil service tests you get more time than you need to answer the questions. So don't be in a hurry. Read each word of instructions until you clearly understand the meaning. Study the examples, listen to all announcements and follow directions. Ask questions if you do not understand what to do.

3) Identify your papers

Civil service exams are usually identified by number only. You will be assigned a number; you must not put your name on your test papers. Be sure to copy your number correctly. Since more than one exam may be given, copy your exact examination title.

4) Plan your time

Unless you are told that a test is a "speed" or "rate of work" test, speed itself is usually not important. Time enough to answer all the questions will be provided, but this does not mean that you have all day. An overall time limit has been set. Divide the total time (in minutes) by the number of questions to determine the approximate time you have for each question.

5) Do not linger over difficult questions

If you come across a difficult question, mark it with a paper clip (useful to have along) and come back to it when you have been through the booklet. One caution if you do this – be sure to skip a number on your answer sheet as well. Check often to be sure that you have not lost your place and that you are marking in the row numbered the same as the question you are answering.

6) Read the questions

Be sure you know what the question asks! Many capable people are unsuccessful because they failed to *read* the questions correctly.

7) Answer all questions

Unless you have been instructed that a penalty will be deducted for incorrect answers, it is better to guess than to omit a question.

8) Speed tests

It is often better NOT to guess on speed tests. It has been found that on timed tests people are tempted to spend the last few seconds before time is called in marking answers at random – without even reading them – in the hope of picking up a few extra points. To discourage this practice, the instructions may warn you that your score will be "corrected" for guessing. That is, a penalty will be applied. The incorrect answers will be deducted from the correct ones, or some other penalty formula will be used.

9) Review your answers

If you finish before time is called, go back to the questions you guessed or omitted to give them further thought. Review other answers if you have time.

10) Return your test materials

If you are ready to leave before others have finished or time is called, take ALL your materials to the monitor and leave quietly. Never take any test material with you. The monitor can discover whose papers are not complete, and taking a test booklet may be grounds for disqualification.

VIII. EXAMINATION TECHNIQUES

1) Read the general instructions carefully. These are usually printed on the first page of the exam booklet. As a rule, these instructions refer to the timing of the examination; the fact that you should not start work until the signal and must stop work at a signal, etc. If there are any *special* instructions, such as a choice of questions to be answered, make sure that you note this instruction carefully.

2) When you are ready to start work on the examination, that is as soon as the signal has been given, read the instructions to each question booklet, underline any key words or phrases, such as *least, best, outline, describe* and the like. In this way you will tend to answer as requested rather than discover on reviewing your paper that you *listed without describing*, that you selected the *worst* choice rather than the *best* choice, etc.

3) If the examination is of the objective or multiple-choice type – that is, each question will also give a series of possible answers: A, B, C or D, and you are called upon to select the best answer and write the letter next to that answer on your answer paper – it is advisable to start answering each question in turn. There may be anywhere from 50 to 100 such questions in the three or four hours allotted and you can see how much time would be taken if you read through all the questions before beginning to answer any. Furthermore, if you come across a question or group of questions which you know would be difficult to answer, it would undoubtedly affect your handling of all the other questions.

4) If the examination is of the essay type and contains but a few questions, it is a moot point as to whether you should read all the questions before starting to answer any one. Of course, if you are given a choice – say five out of seven and the like – then it is essential to read all the questions so you can eliminate the two that are most difficult. If, however, you are asked to answer all the questions, there may be danger in trying to answer the easiest one first because you may find that you will spend too much time on it. The best technique is to answer the first question, then proceed to the second, etc.

5) Time your answers. Before the exam begins, write down the time it started, then add the time allowed for the examination and write down the time it must be completed, then divide the time available somewhat as follows:
    - If 3-1/2 hours are allowed, that would be 210 minutes. If you have 80 objective-type questions, that would be an average of 2-1/2 minutes per question. Allow yourself no more than 2 minutes per question, or a total of 160 minutes, which will permit about 50 minutes to review.
    - If for the time allotment of 210 minutes there are 7 essay questions to answer, that would average about 30 minutes a question. Give yourself only 25 minutes per question so that you have about 35 minutes to review.

6) The most important instruction is to *read each question* and make sure you know what is wanted. The second most important instruction is to *time yourself properly* so that you answer every question. The third most important instruction is to *answer every question*. Guess if you have to but include something for each question. Remember that you will receive no credit for a blank and will probably receive some credit if you write something in answer to an essay question. If you guess a letter – say "B" for a multiple-choice question – you may have guessed right. If you leave a blank as an answer to a multiple-choice question, the examiners may respect your feelings but it will not add a point to your score. Some exams may penalize you for wrong answers, so in such cases *only*, you may not want to guess unless you have some basis for your answer.

7) Suggestions
    a. Objective-type questions
        1. Examine the question booklet for proper sequence of pages and questions
        2. Read all instructions carefully
        3. Skip any question which seems too difficult; return to it after all other questions have been answered
        4. Apportion your time properly; do not spend too much time on any single question or group of questions

5. Note and underline key words – *all, most, fewest, least, best, worst, same, opposite*, etc.
6. Pay particular attention to negatives
7. Note unusual option, e.g., unduly long, short, complex, different or similar in content to the body of the question
8. Observe the use of "hedging" words – *probably, may, most likely*, etc.
9. Make sure that your answer is put next to the same number as the question
10. Do not second-guess unless you have good reason to believe the second answer is definitely more correct
11. Cross out original answer if you decide another answer is more accurate; do not erase until you are ready to hand your paper in
12. Answer all questions; guess unless instructed otherwise
13. Leave time for review

b. Essay questions
1. Read each question carefully
2. Determine exactly what is wanted. Underline key words or phrases.
3. Decide on outline or paragraph answer
4. Include many different points and elements unless asked to develop any one or two points or elements
5. Show impartiality by giving pros and cons unless directed to select one side only
6. Make and write down any assumptions you find necessary to answer the questions
7. Watch your English, grammar, punctuation and choice of words
8. Time your answers; don't crowd material

8) Answering the essay question

Most essay questions can be answered by framing the specific response around several key words or ideas. Here are a few such key words or ideas:

M's: manpower, materials, methods, money, management
P's: purpose, program, policy, plan, procedure, practice, problems, pitfalls, personnel, public relations

a. Six basic steps in handling problems:
1. Preliminary plan and background development
2. Collect information, data and facts
3. Analyze and interpret information, data and facts
4. Analyze and develop solutions as well as make recommendations
5. Prepare report and sell recommendations
6. Install recommendations and follow up effectiveness

b. Pitfalls to avoid
1. *Taking things for granted* – A statement of the situation does not necessarily imply that each of the elements is necessarily true; for example, a complaint may be invalid and biased so that all that can be taken for granted is that a complaint has been registered

2. *Considering only one side of a situation* – Wherever possible, indicate several alternatives and then point out the reasons you selected the best one
3. *Failing to indicate follow up* – Whenever your answer indicates action on your part, make certain that you will take proper follow-up action to see how successful your recommendations, procedures or actions turn out to be
4. *Taking too long in answering any single question* – Remember to time your answers properly

IX. AFTER THE TEST

Scoring procedures differ in detail among civil service jurisdictions although the general principles are the same. Whether the papers are hand-scored or graded by machine we have described, they are nearly always graded by number. That is, the person who marks the paper knows only the number – never the name – of the applicant. Not until all the papers have been graded will they be matched with names. If other tests, such as training and experience or oral interview ratings have been given, scores will be combined. Different parts of the examination usually have different weights. For example, the written test might count 60 percent of the final grade, and a rating of training and experience 40 percent. In many jurisdictions, veterans will have a certain number of points added to their grades.

After the final grade has been determined, the names are placed in grade order and an eligible list is established. There are various methods for resolving ties between those who get the same final grade – probably the most common is to place first the name of the person whose application was received first. Job offers are made from the eligible list in the order the names appear on it. You will be notified of your grade and your rank as soon as all these computations have been made. This will be done as rapidly as possible.

People who are found to meet the requirements in the announcement are called "eligibles." Their names are put on a list of eligible candidates. An eligible's chances of getting a job depend on how high he stands on this list and how fast agencies are filling jobs from the list.

When a job is to be filled from a list of eligibles, the agency asks for the names of people on the list of eligibles for that job. When the civil service commission receives this request, it sends to the agency the names of the three people highest on this list. Or, if the job to be filled has specialized requirements, the office sends the agency the names of the top three persons who meet these requirements from the general list.

The appointing officer makes a choice from among the three people whose names were sent to him. If the selected person accepts the appointment, the names of the others are put back on the list to be considered for future openings.

That is the rule in hiring from all kinds of eligible lists, whether they are for typist, carpenter, chemist, or something else. For every vacancy, the appointing officer has his choice of any one of the top three eligibles on the list. This explains why the person whose name is on top of the list sometimes does not get an appointment when some of the persons lower on the list do. If the appointing officer chooses the second or third eligible, the No. 1 eligible does not get a job at once, but stays on the list until he is appointed or the list is terminated.

X. HOW TO PASS THE INTERVIEW TEST

The examination for which you applied requires an oral interview test. You have already taken the written test and you are now being called for the interview test – the final part of the formal examination.

You may think that it is not possible to prepare for an interview test and that there are no procedures to follow during an interview. Our purpose is to point out some things you can do in advance that will help you and some good rules to follow and pitfalls to avoid while you are being interviewed.

What is an interview supposed to test?

The written examination is designed to test the technical knowledge and competence of the candidate; the oral is designed to evaluate intangible qualities, not readily measured otherwise, and to establish a list showing the relative fitness of each candidate – as measured against his competitors – for the position sought. Scoring is not on the basis of "right" and "wrong," but on a sliding scale of values ranging from "not passable" to "outstanding." As a matter of fact, it is possible to achieve a relatively low score without a single "incorrect" answer because of evident weakness in the qualities being measured.

Occasionally, an examination may consist entirely of an oral test – either an individual or a group oral. In such cases, information is sought concerning the technical knowledges and abilities of the candidate, since there has been no written examination for this purpose. More commonly, however, an oral test is used to supplement a written examination.

Who conducts interviews?

The composition of oral boards varies among different jurisdictions. In nearly all, a representative of the personnel department serves as chairman. One of the members of the board may be a representative of the department in which the candidate would work. In some cases, "outside experts" are used, and, frequently, a businessman or some other representative of the general public is asked to serve. Labor and management or other special groups may be represented. The aim is to secure the services of experts in the appropriate field.

However the board is composed, it is a good idea (and not at all improper or unethical) to ascertain in advance of the interview who the members are and what groups they represent. When you are introduced to them, you will have some idea of their backgrounds and interests, and at least you will not stutter and stammer over their names.

What should be done before the interview?

While knowledge about the board members is useful and takes some of the surprise element out of the interview, there is other preparation which is more substantive. It *is* possible to prepare for an oral interview – in several ways:

1) Keep a copy of your application and review it carefully before the interview

This may be the only document before the oral board, and the starting point of the interview. Know what education and experience you have listed there, and the sequence and dates of all of it. Sometimes the board will ask you to review the highlights of your experience for them; you should not have to hem and haw doing it.

2) Study the class specification and the examination announcement

Usually, the oral board has one or both of these to guide them. The qualities, characteristics or knowledges required by the position sought are stated in these documents. They offer valuable clues as to the nature of the oral interview. For example, if the job involves supervisory responsibilities, the announcement will usually indicate that knowledge of modern supervisory methods and the qualifications of the candidate as a supervisor will be tested. If so, you can expect such questions, frequently in the form of a hypothetical situation which you are expected to solve. NEVER go into an oral without knowledge of the duties and responsibilities of the job you seek.

3) Think through each qualification required

Try to visualize the kind of questions you would ask if you were a board member. How well could you answer them? Try especially to appraise your own knowledge and background in each area, *measured against the job sought*, and identify any areas in which you are weak. Be critical and realistic – do not flatter yourself.

4) Do some general reading in areas in which you feel you may be weak

For example, if the job involves supervision and your past experience has NOT, some general reading in supervisory methods and practices, particularly in the field of human relations, might be useful. Do NOT study agency procedures or detailed manuals. The oral board will be testing your understanding and capacity, not your memory.

5) Get a good night's sleep and watch your general health and mental attitude

You will want a clear head at the interview. Take care of a cold or any other minor ailment, and of course, no hangovers.

What should be done on the day of the interview?

Now comes the day of the interview itself. Give yourself plenty of time to get there. Plan to arrive somewhat ahead of the scheduled time, particularly if your appointment is in the fore part of the day. If a previous candidate fails to appear, the board might be ready for you a bit early. By early afternoon an oral board is almost invariably behind schedule if there are many candidates, and you may have to wait. Take along a book or magazine to read, or your application to review, but leave any extraneous material in the waiting room when you go in for your interview. In any event, relax and compose yourself.

The matter of dress is important. The board is forming impressions about you – from your experience, your manners, your attitude, and your appearance. Give your personal appearance careful attention. Dress your best, but not your flashiest. Choose conservative, appropriate clothing, and be sure it is immaculate. This is a business interview, and your appearance should indicate that you regard it as such. Besides, being well groomed and properly dressed will help boost your confidence.

Sooner or later, someone will call your name and escort you into the interview room. *This is it.* From here on you are on your own. It is too late for any more preparation. But remember, you asked for this opportunity to prove your fitness, and you are here because your request was granted.

What happens when you go in?

The usual sequence of events will be as follows: The clerk (who is often the board stenographer) will introduce you to the chairman of the oral board, who will introduce you to the other members of the board. Acknowledge the introductions before you sit down. Do not be surprised if you find a microphone facing you or a stenotypist sitting by. Oral interviews are usually recorded in the event of an appeal or other review.

Usually the chairman of the board will open the interview by reviewing the highlights of your education and work experience from your application – primarily for the benefit of the other members of the board, as well as to get the material into the record. Do not interrupt or comment unless there is an error or significant misinterpretation; if that is the case, do not hesitate. But do not quibble about insignificant matters. Also, he will usually ask you some question about your education, experience or your present job – partly to get you to start talking and to establish the interviewing "rapport." He may start the actual questioning, or turn it over to one of the other members. Frequently, each member undertakes the questioning on a particular area, one in which he is perhaps most competent, so you can expect each member to participate in the examination. Because time is limited, you may also expect some rather abrupt switches in the direction the questioning takes, so do not be upset by it. Normally, a board member will not pursue a single line of questioning unless he discovers a particular strength or weakness.

After each member has participated, the chairman will usually ask whether any member has any further questions, then will ask you if you have anything you wish to add. Unless you are expecting this question, it may floor you. Worse, it may start you off on an extended, extemporaneous speech. The board is not usually seeking more information. The question is principally to offer you a last opportunity to present further qualifications or to indicate that you have nothing to add. So, if you feel that a significant qualification or characteristic has been overlooked, it is proper to point it out in a sentence or so. Do not compliment the board on the thoroughness of their examination – they have been sketchy, and you know it. If you wish, merely say, "No thank you, I have nothing further to add." This is a point where you can "talk yourself out" of a good impression or fail to present an important bit of information. Remember, *you close the interview yourself*.

The chairman will then say, "That is all, Mr. _____, thank you." Do not be startled; the interview is over, and quicker than you think. Thank him, gather your belongings and take your leave. Save your sigh of relief for the other side of the door.

How to put your best foot forward
Throughout this entire process, you may feel that the board individually and collectively is trying to pierce your defenses, seek out your hidden weaknesses and embarrass and confuse you. Actually, this is not true. They are obliged to make an appraisal of your qualifications for the job you are seeking, and they want to see you in your best light. Remember, they must interview all candidates and a non-cooperative candidate may become a failure in spite of their best efforts to bring out his qualifications. Here are 15 suggestions that will help you:

1) Be natural – Keep your attitude confident, not cocky
If you are not confident that you can do the job, do not expect the board to be. Do not apologize for your weaknesses, try to bring out your strong points. The board is interested in a positive, not negative, presentation. Cockiness will antagonize any board member and make him wonder if you are covering up a weakness by a false show of strength.

2) Get comfortable, but don't lounge or sprawl
Sit erectly but not stiffly. A careless posture may lead the board to conclude that you are careless in other things, or at least that you are not impressed by the importance of the occasion. Either conclusion is natural, even if incorrect. Do not fuss with your clothing, a pencil or an ashtray. Your hands may occasionally be useful to emphasize a point; do not let them become a point of distraction.

3) Do not wisecrack or make small talk
This is a serious situation, and your attitude should show that you consider it as such. Further, the time of the board is limited – they do not want to waste it, and neither should you.

4) Do not exaggerate your experience or abilities

In the first place, from information in the application or other interviews and sources, the board may know more about you than you think. Secondly, you probably will not get away with it. An experienced board is rather adept at spotting such a situation, so do not take the chance.

5) If you know a board member, do not make a point of it, yet do not hide it

Certainly you are not fooling him, and probably not the other members of the board. Do not try to take advantage of your acquaintanceship – it will probably do you little good.

6) Do not dominate the interview

Let the board do that. They will give you the clues – do not assume that you have to do all the talking. Realize that the board has a number of questions to ask you, and do not try to take up all the interview time by showing off your extensive knowledge of the answer to the first one.

7) Be attentive

You only have 20 minutes or so, and you should keep your attention at its sharpest throughout. When a member is addressing a problem or question to you, give him your undivided attention. Address your reply principally to him, but do not exclude the other board members.

8) Do not interrupt

A board member may be stating a problem for you to analyze. He will ask you a question when the time comes. Let him state the problem, and wait for the question.

9) Make sure you understand the question

Do not try to answer until you are sure what the question is. If it is not clear, restate it in your own words or ask the board member to clarify it for you. However, do not haggle about minor elements.

10) Reply promptly but not hastily

A common entry on oral board rating sheets is "candidate responded readily," or "candidate hesitated in replies." Respond as promptly and quickly as you can, but do not jump to a hasty, ill-considered answer.

11) Do not be peremptory in your answers

A brief answer is proper – but do not fire your answer back. That is a losing game from your point of view. The board member can probably ask questions much faster than you can answer them.

12) Do not try to create the answer you think the board member wants

He is interested in what kind of mind you have and how it works – not in playing games. Furthermore, he can usually spot this practice and will actually grade you down on it.

13) Do not switch sides in your reply merely to agree with a board member

Frequently, a member will take a contrary position merely to draw you out and to see if you are willing and able to defend your point of view. Do not start a debate, yet do not surrender a good position. If a position is worth taking, it is worth defending.

14) Do not be afraid to admit an error in judgment if you are shown to be wrong

The board knows that you are forced to reply without any opportunity for careful consideration. Your answer may be demonstrably wrong. If so, admit it and get on with the interview.

15) Do not dwell at length on your present job

The opening question may relate to your present assignment. Answer the question but do not go into an extended discussion. You are being examined for a *new* job, not your present one. As a matter of fact, try to phrase ALL your answers in terms of the job for which you are being examined.

Basis of Rating

Probably you will forget most of these "do's" and "don'ts" when you walk into the oral interview room. Even remembering them all will not ensure you a passing grade. Perhaps you did not have the qualifications in the first place. But remembering them will help you to put your best foot forward, without treading on the toes of the board members.

Rumor and popular opinion to the contrary notwithstanding, an oral board wants you to make the best appearance possible. They know you are under pressure – but they also want to see how you respond to it as a guide to what your reaction would be under the pressures of the job you seek. They will be influenced by the degree of poise you display, the personal traits you show and the manner in which you respond.

ABOUT THIS BOOK

This book contains tests divided into Examination Sections. Go through each test, answering every question in the margin. We have also attached a sample answer sheet at the back of the book that can be removed and used. At the end of each test look at the answer key and check your answers. On the ones you got wrong, look at the right answer choice and learn. Do not fill in the answers first. Do not memorize the questions and answers, but understand the answer and principles involved. On your test, the questions will likely be different from the samples. Questions are changed and new ones added. If you understand these past questions you should have success with any changes that arise. Tests may consist of several types of questions. We have additional books on each subject should more study be advisable or necessary for you. Finally, the more you study, the better prepared you will be. This book is intended to be the last thing you study before you walk into the examination room. Prior study of relevant texts is also recommended. NLC publishes some of these in our Fundamental Series. Knowledge and good sense are important factors in passing your exam. Good luck also helps. So now study this Passbook, absorb the material contained within and take that knowledge into the examination. Then do your best to pass that exam.

EXAMINATION SECTION

EXAMINATION SECTION
TEST 1

DIRECTIONS: Each question or incomplete statement is followed by several suggested answers or completions. Select the one that BEST answers the question or completes the statement. *PRINT THE LETTER OF THE CORRECT ANSWER IN THE SPACE AT THE RIGHT.*

1. The dial of a water meter shall be a MAXIMUM height above the floor of _____ ft.

   A. 1   B. 2   C. 3   D. 4

2. A stop-and-waste cock is GENERALLY used on

   A. soil lines
   B. gas supply lines
   C. water supply lines subjected to low temperatures
   D. refrigerant lines connected to compressors

3. Assume that your superior has directed you to make certain changes in your established inspection procedure. After using this modified procedure on several inspections, you find that the original procedure was distinctly superior and you wish to return to it.
   You should

   A. let your superior find this out for himself
   B. simply change back to the original procedure
   C. compile definite data and information to prove your case to your superior
   D. persuade one of the more experienced inspectors to take this matter up with your superior

4. When automatic sprinklers are attached to a piping system containing air under pressure, the sprinkler system is called a _____ system.

   A. wet-pipe   B. dry-pipe
   C. deluge   D. compressed air

5. When making an inspection of one of the buildings under your supervision, the BEST procedure to follow in making a record of the inspection is to

   A. return immediately to the office and write a report from memory
   B. write down all the important facts during or as soon as you complete the inspection
   C. fix in your mind all important facts so that you can repeat them from memory if necessary
   D. fix in your mind all important facts so that you can make out your report at the end of the day

6. The MAIN reason for pitching a steam pipe in a heating system is to

   A. reduce friction in the pipe
   B. prevent the formation of scale
   C. facilitate repairs
   D. prevent accumulation of condensate

7. Nozzles on 2 1/2" diameter hose for standpipe systems must GENERALLY have a minimum length of _____ inches.

   A. 3 B. 6 C. 10 D. 15

8. An inspector visited a large building under construction. He inspected the soil lines at 9 A.M., water lines at 10 A.M., fixtures at 11 A.M., and did his office work in the afternoon. He followed the same pattern daily for weeks.
   This procedure was

   A. *good*, because it was methodical and he did not miss anything
   B. *good*, because it gave equal time to all phases of the plumbing
   C. *bad*, because not enough time was devoted to fixtures
   D. *bad*, because the tradesmen knew when the inspection would occur

9. When an unusually long run of supply pipe for sprinklers is needed, an increase in pipe size over that called for in the schedules may be required to

   A. compensate for increased friction
   B. provide enough water if the pipe diameter decreases due to corrosion deposits
   C. adequately protect areas which are separated by fire walls
   D. provide enough water in case more than one fire occurs at the same time

10. Roof drainage downspouts or leaders should be sized according to the

    A. type of sewer connection
    B. type of building occupancy
    C. size of cold water risers
    D. area of the roof to be drained

11. The type of pipe which is GENERALLY advantageous to use where corrosion is severe is

    A. cast iron   B. wrought iron
    C. steel   D. galvanized iron

12. A contractor has made an unjustified complaint against an inspector to the inspector's superior.
    In future contacts with this contractor, the inspector should be

    A. very careful in what he says
    B. courteous and fair in enforcing the law
    C. cool and distant to avoid more trouble
    D. exceptionally friendly in order to ease matters

13. A tank is filled with fresh water to a height of 20 ft. The pressure at the bottom of the tank is _____ pounds per square foot.

    A. 1168 B. 1248 C. 1322 D. 1404

14. The one of the following terms which is NOT used to classify buildings for purposes of sprinkler installations is _____ hazard.

    A. light B. ordinary C. regular D. extra

15. The PROPER type of fitting to use in a horizontal hot water heating main, when changing pipe size, is a(n)

    A. concentric reducer B. eccentric reducer
    C. hexagon bushing D. face bushing

16. Fire pumps shall be tested after installation to ascertain that the pump is supplying its rated capacity at

    A. the lowest required hose outlet
    B. the highest required hose outlet
    C. every hose outlet in the building
    D. one hose outlet which has been selected for testing

17. A pipe chase is a

    A. wire brush for cleaning the inside of pipes
    B. wire brush used for cleaning the outside of pipes
    C. continuous space in a building through which pipes run
    D. thimble through a wall to allow a pipe to pierce the wall

18. The utility line that USUALLY enters or leaves the building at the lowest elevation is the

    A. water inlet B. gas line
    C. electric supply D. building drain

19. The standpipe system shall be zoned by use of gravity tanks, automatic fire pumps, pressure tanks, and street pressure so that the MAXIMUM pressure at the inlet of any hose valve in the zone is _____ psig.

    A. 40 B. 60 C. 80 D. 100

20. Yard hydrant systems which are connected to city water mains shall be provided with post indicator valves located in an accessible position.
    Such post indicator valves shall be locked _____ and painted _____ .

    A. shut; green B. shut; red
    C. open; green D. open; red

21. A practice which is likely to cause some confusion when dealing with contractors is for an inspector to

    A. issue detailed instruction only in writing
    B. relay instructions to the contractor through one or two of the contractor's men
    C. transmit simple instructions orally
    D. follow up all his instructions after issuing them

22. Small commercial sizes of steel pipe are GENERALLY designated by their _____ diameter.

    A. exact inside B. exact outside
    C. nominal inside D. nominal outside

23. A head of water of 50 feet is equivalent to a pressure of MOST NEARLY _____ psi.

    A. 16 B. 22 C. 28 D. 34

24. A contractor demands to see your supervisor after accusing you of being prejudiced against him.
    The BEST course of action for you to follow is to

    A. convince him that you are not prejudiced
    B. remind him that you can make trouble for him if he fails to show you proper respect
    C. take him to your superior as he requests
    D. do nothing if you feel that you are not prejudiced

25. The water supply pipe which extends from the street main to the house control valve is GENERALLY called the _____ pipe.

    A. main   B. intake   C. service   D. gooseneck

26. The number of threads per inch on standard steel pipe threads GENERALLY

    A. decreases as the diameter of the pipe increases
    B. increases as the diameter of the pipe increases
    C. does not vary with the diameter of the pipe
    D. depends solely on the pressure the pipe must withstand

27. A specification requires that sewer pipe be laid with a smooth and uniform invert.
    The term *invert* refers to the _____ of the pipe, _____.

    A. inside; all around   B. outside; all around
    C. inside; at the bottom   D. outside; at the bottom

Questions 28-40.

DIRECTIONS: Questions 28 through 40 refer to the Riser Diagram shown below.

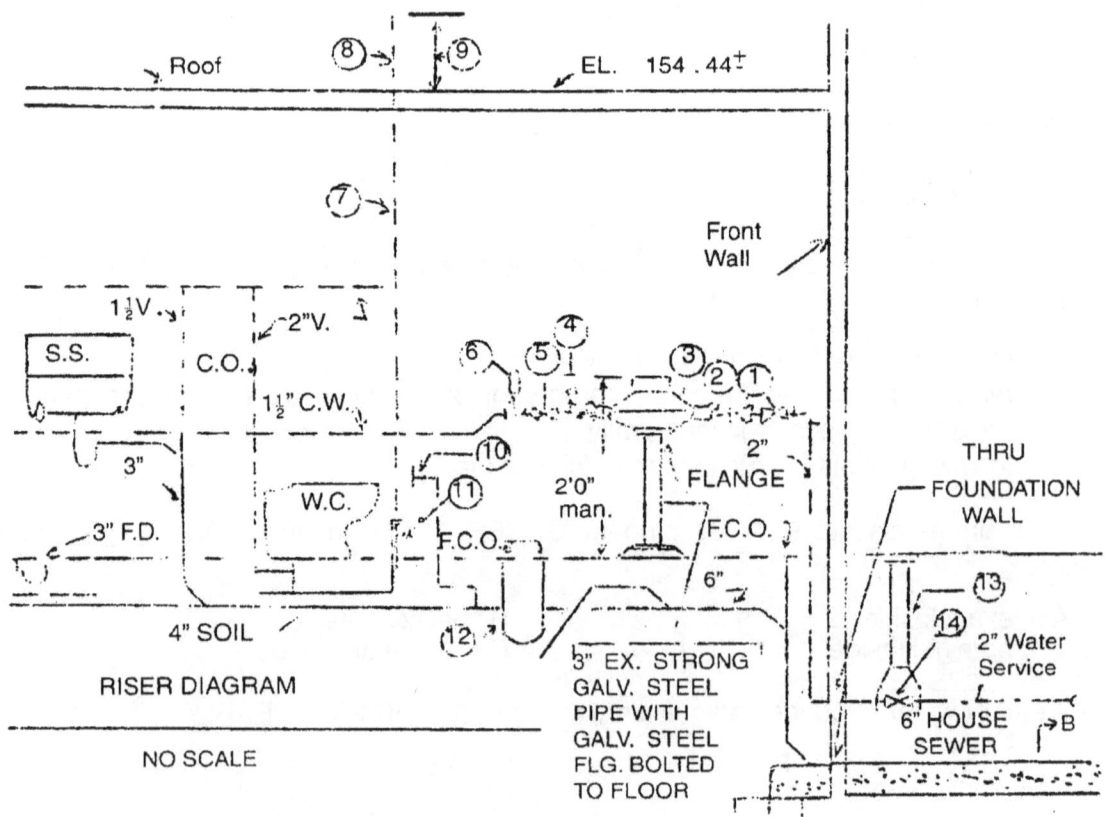

RISER DIAGRAM

NO SCALE

28. Item *1* is a _____ valve.   28._____

    A. check   B. globe   C. gate   D. pressure

29. Item *2* is a   29._____

    A. valve   B. union   C. reducer   D. flange

30. Item *3* is a   30._____

    A. meter   B. sink
    C. water fountain   D. reducing valve

31. Item *4* is a   31._____

    A. pressure valve   B. test connection
    C. relief fitting   D. supply valve

32. Item *6* is   32._____

    A. meter   B. pressure gauge
    C. water indicator   D. shock absorber

33. Item *7* is a   33._____

    A. soil line   B. vent line
    C. water supply line   D. heater exhaust

34. Item *8* should have a minimum diameter of _____ inches.   34._____

    A. 2   B. 3   C. 4   D. 6

35. Distance *9* should be a minimum of _____ ft.   35._____

    A. 1   B. 2   C. 4   D. 6

36. Item *10* is a   36._____

    A. sprinkler connection   B. clean-out plug
    C. fresh air inlet   D. floor drain

37. Item *11* is a   37._____

    A. hot water connection   B. clean-out plug
    C. flushometer fitting   D. floor drain

38. Item *12* is a   38._____

    A. trap   B. running trap
    C. floor drain   D. return bend

39. Item *13* is a   39._____

    A. curb box   B. sewer access
    C. metering point   D. pressure gage location

40. Item *14* has the main purpose of 40._____
    A. permitting water supply to be turned off
    B. reducing water supply pressure
    C. checking backflow
    D. permitting a pressure check

KEY (CORRECT ANSWERS)

1.	C	11.	A	21.	B	31.	B
2.	C	12.	B	22.	C	32.	D
3.	C	13.	B	23.	B	33.	B
4.	B	14.	C	24.	C	34.	C
5.	B	15.	B	25.	C	35.	B
6.	D	16.	B	26.	A	36.	C
7.	D	17.	C	27.	C	37.	B
8.	D	18.	D	28.	C	38.	B
9.	A	19.	B	29.	C	39.	A
10.	D	20.	D	30.	A	40.	A

TEST 2

DIRECTIONS: Each question or incomplete statement is followed by several suggested answers or completions. Select the one that BEST answers the question or completes the statement. *PRINT THE LETTER OF THE CORRECT ANSWER IN THE SPACE AT THE RIGHT.*

1. Two full lengths of black standard steel gas pipe in a continuous run should be connected together by a   1.____

    A. running thread coupling
    B. right and left coupling
    C. gasketed union
    D. tee with side outlet plugged

2. The factor which is NOT generally considered to be a major cause of accidents is   2.____

    A. failure to use personal protective devices
    B. working at a very rapid speed
    C. using inoperative safety devices
    D. lack of familiarity with a particular job

3. Underground mains and lead-in connections to system risers shall be flushed thoroughly before any connection is made to sprinkler piping in order to   3.____

    A. make sure that there are no leaks in the mains
    B. check that the pressure meets building code requirements
    C. make sure that the proper number of gpm can flow through the pipes
    D. remove foreign materials which may have entered during the course of installation

4. A plumbing specification states: *Each pipe shall have clearly impressed on its outer surface the name of the manufacturer and of the factory in which it was made.* The BEST reason for this requirement is that this   4.____

    A. identifies the grade of the pipe
    B. helps locate the pipe in the field
    C. insures that approved material is used
    D. shows who is responsible for defective material

5. A plumbing system should be tested at a water pressure which is determined by multiplying the working pressure of the system by a factor of   5.____

    A. 1.0   B. 1.25   C. 1.5   D. 2.0

6. A *by-pass loop* in a piping system   6.____

    A. tends to eliminate pulsations of fluid flow
    B. provides a method for increasing the capacity of the piping system
    C. prevents excessive piping stresses by providing for expansion and contraction
    D. provides emergency routing of flow if the primary system is shut down

7. In an accident report, the information which may be MOST useful in decreasing the recurrence of similar type accidents is the

   A. time the accident happened
   B. cause of the accident
   C. extent of injuries sustained
   D. number of people involved

8. Joints in glass pipe used for chemical waste should NOT be made by use of

   A. compression couplings   B. adapter couplings
   C. caulking   D. adjustable joints

9. Assume that 90 gallons per minute flow through a certain 3-inch pipe which is tapped into a street main.
   The amount of water which would flow through a 1-inch pipe tapped into the same street main is MOST NEARLY _____ gpm

   A. 90   B. 45   C. 30   D. 10

10. Accessible cleanouts in drainage piping shall be installed at each change of direction GREATER than _____ °.

    A. 20   B. 45   C. 90   D. 135

11. The kitchen sink in a dwelling may be used to receive the discharge of an indirect waste pipe from a

    A. clothes washer   B. dishwasher
    C. refrigerator   D. drinking fountain

12. The material which should NOT generally be used for roof drains is

    A. wrought iron   B. lead
    C. stainless steel D. copper

13. The time required to pump 2500 gallons of water out of a sump at the rate of 12 1/2 gallons per minute would be _____ hour(s), _____ minutes.

    A. 1; 40   B. 2; 30   C. 3; 20   D. 6; 40

14. Copper tubing which has an inside diameter of 1 1/16 inches and a wall thickness of .095 inches has an outside diameter which is MOST NEARLY _____ inches.

    A. 1 5/32   B. 1 3/16   C. 1 7/32   D. 1 1/4

15. Valves used to control a standpipe system shall have the name of the manufacturer

    A. on a tag which is permanently attached to each valve by means of a chain
    B. cast on or in each valve
    C. on a tag which is welded to each valve
    D. readily available in the records kept by the building custodian

16. The PREFERRED type of feed to sprinklers, especially where there are over six sprinklers on a branch line is _____ feed.

    A. center central   B. central end
    C. side end   D. cross main

17. A *branch interval* is defined as

    A. the length along the center line of pipe and fittings both horizontal and vertical
    B. a distance along a soil or waste stack corresponding in general to a story height, but in no case less than 8 feet, within which the horizontal branches from one floor or story of a building are connected to the stack
    C. a vent connecting one or more individual vents with a vent stack or stack vent
    D. that part of a piping system other than a main riser or stack that extends to fixtures on two or less consecutive floors

18. The distance which is measured along the center line of pipes and fittings is called the _____ length.

    A. system
    B. effective
    C. equivalent
    D. developed

19. The HEAVIEST commercially obtainable steel and wrought iron pipe is called

    A. extra strong
    B. double extra strong
    C. heavy duty
    D. high strength

20. Pressure tanks for sprinkler systems should be located

    A. in the basement of the building
    B. at or above the top level of sprinklers
    C. at any convenient location in the building
    D. on any floor where they will be easily accessible

21. Fire pumps in standpipe systems should be

    A. in sump pits below the pump room floor level
    B. mounted directly on the pump room floor
    C. on concrete foundations at least 1 foot above the pump room floor level
    D. on concrete platforms at least 3 feet above the pump room floor level

22. A *street ell* is a fitting which has

    A. threads on the inside of one end and on the outside of the other end
    B. threads on the inside of both ends
    C. threads on the outside of both ends
    D. non-tapered threads on both ends

23. The MAIN difference between schedule-80 pipe and schedule-40 pipe is that schedule-80 pipe

    A. weighs more per foot
    B. has a smaller wall thickness
    C. has a larger inside diameter
    D. has more threads per inch.

24. If a 4-inch pipe is directly coupled to a 2-inch pipe and 16 gallons per minute are flowing through the 4-inch pipe, then the flow through the 2-inch pipe will be _____ gallons per minute.

    A. 4
    B. 8
    C. 16
    D. 32

25. A contractor is always complaining that he is being treated too harshly by an inspector. The BEST action for the inspector to take is to

   A. consider the complaints on their merit
   B. tell the contractor that he will not listen to any of his complaints
   C. *ride* the contractor until he stops complaining
   D. ignore the contractor's complaints

26. Each standpipe system control valve shall have a metal disk at least 3 inches in diameter securely attached to the valve.
The disk shall have white markings with a red background and should ALWAYS indicate

   A. the number assigned to it on the riser diagram for the standpipe system
   B. the direction to turn the valve to open and shut
   C. whether the water is good for drinking
   D. whether the valve is in the open or closed position

27. Riser control valves for standpipe systems shall, where practicable, be located

   A. outside the building in an easily accessible location
   B. as near as possible to the main control valves in the basement
   C. in the lobby of the building
   D. within a required stair enclosure serving the entrance floor

28. The BEST method to use to determine whether a large cast iron fitting is cracked is to

   A. visually examine the fitting for cracks
   B. put a water test on the fitting
   C. bang the fitting on concrete to see if it breaks
   D. *ring* the fitting with a hammer

29. Hydrostatic pressure tests for standpipe systems shall NORMALLY be performed for a period of at least

   A. 15 minutes   B. 1 hour
   C. 12 hours   D. 24 hours

30. The weight of a 6 foot length of 8-inch pipe which weighs 24.70 pounds per foot is _____ lbs.

   A. 148.2   B. 176.8   C. 197.6   D. 212.4

31. A *dresser* is MOST frequently used on _____ pipe.

   A. chrome-plated   B. brass
   C. lead   D. wrought iron

32. The cast iron fitting which is called a l/8th bend changes the direction of flow by an angle of

   A. 12 1/2°   B. 22 1/2°   C. 45°   D. 30°

33. Each service directly supplying a standpipe system or a fire pump shall be equipped with a control valve located

    A. in an exposed location within 1 ft. above the sidewalk
    B. in an exposed location within 2 ft. above the sidewalk
    C. under the sidewalk in a flush sidewalk box located within 1 ft. of the street line
    D. under the sidewalk in a flush sidewalk box located within 2 ft. of the street line

34. The MOST important requirement of a well-written report is that it should

    A. be very long and detailed
    B. have a proper heading
    C. be clear and brief
    D. have good punctuation

35. Gas service connections which supply gas to small residential buildings shall be provided with a regulator that will reduce the pressure of the gas to _____ psi.

    A. 4   B. 1   C. 2   D. 3

36. Each fixture trap in a building shall have a liquid seal of AT LEAST _____ inch(es).

    A. 4   B. 3   C. 2   D. 1

37. A pneumatic water supply system supplies water to the fixtures by means of _____ pressure.

    A. street   B. air   C. pump   D. steam

38. The opening pressure of the pressure relief valve on a boiler should be AT LEAST _____ pounds above the _____.

    A. 10; rated pressure of the boiler
    B. 25; rated pressure of the boiler
    C. 10; normal working pressure
    D. 25; normal working pressure

39. The plumbing term *pot piece* is GENERALLY used in connection with work involving the

    A. installation of water closets
    B. soldering of a lead cap
    C. caulking of a cast iron joint
    D. storing of fixtures and trim

40. The one of the following which is MOST likely to influence the minimum required size of a soil or waste stack is the

    A. number of offsets needed in the stack
    B. slope of the house drain
    C. height of the stack
    D. number and type of fixtures serviced by the stack

KEY (CORRECT ANSWERS)

1.	B	11.	B	21.	C	31.	C
2.	D	12.	A	22.	A	32.	C
3.	D	13.	C	23.	A	33.	D
4.	C	14.	D	24.	C	34.	C
5.	B	15.	B	25.	A	35.	A
6.	D	16.	A	26.	A	36.	C
7.	B	17.	B	27.	D	37.	B
8.	C	18.	D	28.	D	38.	D
9.	D	19.	B	29.	B	39.	C
10.	B	20.	B	30.	A	40.	D

EXAMINATION SECTION
TEST 1

DIRECTIONS: Each question or incomplete statement is followed by several suggested answers or completions. Select the one that BEST answers the question or completes the statement. *PRINT THE LETTER OF THE CORRECT ANSWER IN THE SPACE AT THE RIGHT.*

1. A pipe which is properly connected on the fixture side of a fixture trap through which pipe vapors or foul air is removed is COMMONLY known as a   1.____

   A. circuit vent pipe
   B. local ventilating pipe
   C. back vent pipe to relieve back pressure
   D. independent revent pipe

2. In order that a branch may be correctly termed a *dead end,* it shall be terminated by a fitting not used to admit liquids to the pipe and at a developed length NOT GREATER THAN _____ feet.   2.____

   A. 5   B. 4   C. 3   D. 2

3. You are assigned to the inspection of a 10-story apartment house. On your first inspection, you note that a particular waste pipe is run from a main stack to receive flow only from a group of fixtures on the second and fourth floors, respectively.
   As the inspector, you shall   3.____

   A. rightly call this pipe a branch
   B. require the contractor to pipe it as a separate waste stack
   C. allow the contractor to install the uppermost fixture on this pipe without a vent
   D. allow the contractor to use yoke venting for the two groups of fixtures

4. The *size* of copper tubing of other than iron pipe size relates to the   4.____

   A. inside diameter
   B. outside diameter
   C. inside diameter plus wall thickness at any end
   D. inside diameter plus the average wall thickness of any length

5. With respect to a fixture trap, the trap seal is the vertical distance measured from the   5.____

   A. center line of the outlet to the dip of the trap
   B. center line of the inlet to the dip of the trap
   C. crown weir to the dip of the trap
   D. center line of the inlet to the center line of the outlet

6. Which one of the following statements is CORRECT?   6.____

   A. Any line of storm water piping is known as a *leader.*
   B. A local ventilating pipe is commonly used to prevent back siphonage in a drainage system in a building.
   C. A sub-house drainage system is one which is used only to receive flow from basement fixtures.
   D. The waste from a sink (which does not receive fecal matter) may be tied into a soil line.

7. In an office building under construction, each of the men's toilets are made up of six w.c.'s and three urinals. The floor area of each of these rooms is two hundred square feet (200 sq.ft.). The effective area of the windows (on a yard) in each of these toilet rooms is thirty square feet.
In accordance with the code, EACH of these toilet rooms

   A. must be provided with a vent flue at least three square feet in section
   B. may be considered adequately ventilated
   C. must be provided with mechanical ventilation having a capacity of 250 cfm
   D. must be provided with mechanical ventilation having a capacity of 340 cfm

8. Plans are submitted for the construction of an office building. These plans show a stack of slop sinks arranged alongside an elevator shaft, which is designated as only for the use of a penthouse office leasee. Due to space limitations, the architect and the master plumber request permission to install the vent stack for these fixtures in the elevator shaft.
Relative to this request, you, as an inspector of plumbing, should recommend that

   A. permission should not be granted as this would be a violation of the code
   B. the request be directed to the superintendent or the commissioner
   C. permission be granted as it would reduce the contract cost
   D. permission be granted as it would greatly simplify the vent piping

9. A fixture trap shall be so constructed as not to affect the flow of sewage or waste water and yet PREVENT the passage of

   A. air or foul gas through the fixture
   B. silver eels through the fixture
   C. sewage or waste water into the water supply system
   D. sewage or waste water from one fixture into an adjacent fixture

10. Adequate drainage is to be provided for a ramp leading to a garage.
If no storm or combined public sewer is available for the disposal of such drainage water, then this water shall be disposed of in

    A. a sub-surface drainage field made up of perforated fibre pipe with broken joints
    B. adequate dry wells
    C. a diffusion well driven to a depth of 60 feet in shale or porous rock
    D. an injection well of the jet type

11. A provision of the plumbing code states that W.I. pipe shall conform to the standard specifications for welded W.I. pipe of the A.S.T.M., D., A72-33, and shall be galvanized. If you wish to secure a copy of this specification, you should write to the

    A. Association of Standard Testing Methods
    B. Association for Standards, Tests, and Modifications
    C. American Society for Testing Materials
    D. American Society for Test Methods

12. A part of a house drain is made up of 8 lengths of 6" C.I. (XH) soil pipe (unit weight is 95 lbs.). The total weight of this run, including minimum caulking lead for 7 joints, is *most nearly* _____ lbs.

    A. 600   B. 750   C. 800   D. 850

13. An article of the plumbing code, in addition to other specifications, states that cast iron soil pipe shall be *uncoated*.
An IMPORTANT reason for this specification is that

    A. the soil pipe will better withstand the corrosive action of a cinder bed and backfill
    B. the soil pipe will better withstand galvanic action
    C. other adjacent metals will ultimately plate onto the cast iron and protect it
    D. casting defects in the pipe can more easily be seen

13.____

14. Cesspools, privy vaults, and septic tanks, when use thereof is permitted, shall be located on the same lot as the structure which they are to serve.
A *further* restriction on the location of these units is that their distance from any structure must be AT LEAST _____ feet.

    A. 10   B. 15   C. 7.5   D. 5.0

14.____

15. Throughout the plumbing code, frequent reference is made to *the superintendent*.
The reference is to *the superintendent*

    A. department of water supply, gas and electricity
    B. board of standards and appeals
    C. department of public works
    D. department of housing and buildings

15.____

16. A plumbing system has been lawfully installed in a residential building. Presently, an alteration job is being planned for this building.
This entire plumbing system shall be made to comply with the present code if the planned alterations involve fixture units and piping used in connection therewith in the system in excess of AT LEAST _____ thereof.

    A. 25.0%   B. 37.5%   C. 50.0%   D. 62.5%

16.____

17. Sheet lead is being used to make a shower safe on an alteration job. As an inspector, you question the weight of the sheet lead being used. The safe is 48" x 42" x 4" when made up ready for installation (2'" drain hole not cut).
In order to meet the requirements of the code, this shower safe should weigh *most nearly* _____ lbs.

    A. 40   B. 80   C. 120   D. 55

17.____

18. The code fixes the minimum weight in lbs-oz per line of a foot of drainage lead pipe based upon the internal diameter.
A study of this table in the code would show that _____ pipe should have a minimum weight of ____ lbs. per foot.

    A. 3"; 4.5   B. 4"; 8   C. 2"; 5   D. 1 1/2"; 2

18.____

19. The code states that lead water supply pipes shall be of the quality and weight known commercially as grade AA for pressures less than eighty pounds.
    The code also states that, where lead pipe is used for a service in which the pressure is 70 pounds per square inch or more, such lead shall be in conformity with specifications for AAA lead pipe.
    With regard to these two statements, it can be said that

    A. they apply to the same thing and are not, therefore, in conflict
    B. the first statement does not apply when the water pressure exceeds 80 pounds
    C. the second statement does not apply when the water pressure exceeds 80 pounds per square inch
    D. they apply to different parts of a water piping system and are, therefore, not in conflict

20. During an inspection of an alteration job in a two-family residence, you note that lead waste pipe has been installed to receive the waste from a double laundry tub in the basement.
    In keeping with the requirements of the building laws, the MAXIMUM developed length to which this lead waste pipe may be used with this fixture is _____ feet.

    A. 3 B. 4 C. 5 D. 6

KEY (CORRECT ANSWERS)

1.	B	11.	C
2.	D	12.	C
3.	B	13.	D
4.	B	14.	B
5.	C	15.	A
6.	D	16.	C
7.	B	17.	B
8.	A	18.	B
9.	A	19.	D
10.	B	20.	C

TEST 2

DIRECTIONS: Each question or incomplete statement is followed by several suggested answers or completions. Select the one that BEST answers the question or completes the statement. *PRINT THE LETTER OF THE CORRECT ANSWER IN THE SPACE AT THE RIGHT.*

1. For a commercial building which is under construction, a registered Master Plumber proposed the use of a new type of combined flushometer valve and vacuum breaker for half of the w.c.'s and urinals.
   This equipment may be used PROVIDED it has been approved by the

   A. U.S. Testing Laboratory
   B. National Underwriters Laboratory
   C. Dept. of Water Supply, Gas and Electricity
   D. Board of Standards and Appeals

   1.____

2. A two-story residence is under construction, and outside copper leaders are specified for the job. The layout is such that these leaders must be run underground for a distance before tying into the house drain through a running trap.
   The kind of pipe which should be used for this underground run is

   A. galvanized steel   B. wrought iron
   C. extra-heavy cast iron   D. Orangeburg Fibre

   2.____

3. Back-water valves shall have all bearing parts made of corrosion-resisting metals and other materials.
   The word *corrosion*, as used above, means *most nearly*

   A. to wear away slowly
   B. to build up in thickness due to chemical plating action
   C. to burn away rapidly
   D. non-rusting

   3.____

4. The MINIMUM seal of an improved house trap is

   A. 2"   B. 2 1/2"   C. 3"   D. 3 1/2"

   4.____

Questions 5-7.

DIRECTIONS: Questions 5 through 7, inclusive, are related to the statement below.

In structures exceeding 250 feet in height, adequate means shall be provided for taking care of the expansion and contraction of all vertical lines of pipe. In addition, adequate means shall be provided to properly support all vertical lines of pipe.

5. The word *adequate*, as used above, means *most nearly*

   A. liquid devices
   B. properly designed and sufficient
   C. strong and thick-walled
   D. in very great numbers

   5.____

17

6. The word *expansion,* as used above, means *most nearly* a(n)

   A. bulbous swelling
   B. transverse projection
   C. large increase in diameter
   D. increase in length

7. The word *contraction*, as used above, means *most nearly*

   A. contract to install the vertical line
   B. reduction in length
   C. to group all vertical lines together
   D. to decrease the equivalent length

8. The type of fitting which may NOT be used on the stacks of a plumbing system for a five-story residence is

   A. double hubs   B. inverted Y
   C. *Tee Y's*   D. test tees

9. In the course of making a water test on the roughing for a five-story apartment house, you note that the wiped joints of several lead bends are very close but not quite two inches long.
   In keeping with the building laws, these are

   A. too long but may be accepted, depending upon a ruling from the superintendent
   B. not long enough
   C. all right
   D. not long enough but within the acceptable tolerance

10. The word *impervious* is used in several places in the building laws.
    Its meaning, with respect to plumbing systems and fixtures, is *most nearly*

    A. fast moving   B. gas or moisture proof
    C. non-siphoning   D. siphoning

11. Which one of the following statements is CORRECT?

    A. A battery of 2 or 3 laundry trays, one sink and 2 laundry trays may connect with a single trap when the outlets of such types of fixtures are 1 1/2 inches or less.
    B. Fixture traps shall have a water seal of at least 2 1/2".
    C. The minimum diameter of traps for water closets shall be two and a half inches.
    D. Two compartment sinks may connect with a single trap when the outlets of such types of fixtures are 1 1/2" or less.

12. Traps for bathtubs, lavatories, sinks, and other similar fixtures and which are not integral with the fixture shall NOT be made of

    A. cast iron
    B. steel
    C. galvanized malleable iron
    D. brass

13. Along with several other types of traps, the code prohibits the use of bell traps. However, an EXCEPTION is made relative to the use of bell traps on

    A. refrigerator safes
    B. basement floor drains
    C. bidets
    D. prefabricated shower safes

14. An 8" house drain which receives flow from w.c.'s has a total horizontal run of approximately 75' before connecting to the house trap.
    The MINIMUM number and MINIMUM size of cleanouts which shall be provided in this run of the house drain

    A. is one cleanout, 4" in size
    B. are two cleanouts, 8" in size
    C. is one cleanout, 6" in size
    D. are two cleanouts, 4" in size

15.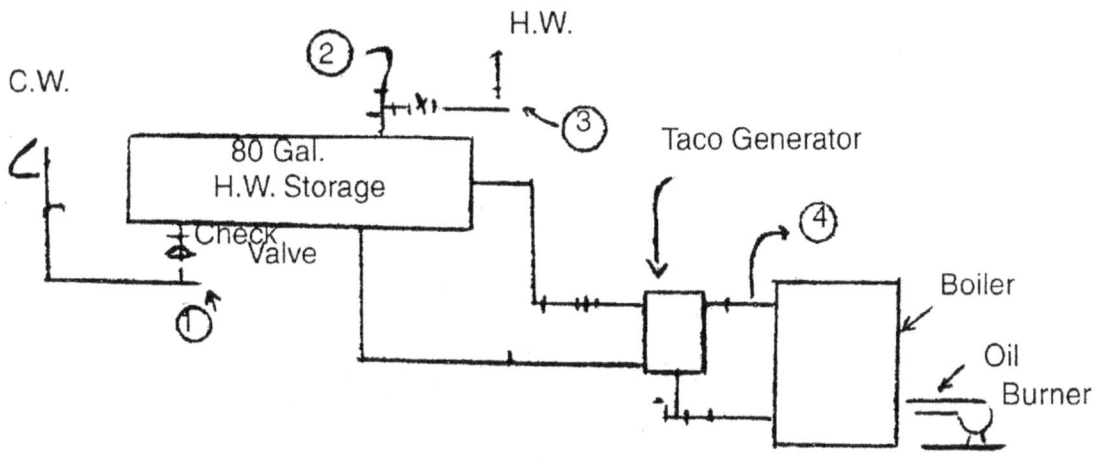

    The domestic hot water supply for an alteration job is piped up as shown in the typical sketch above. The PROPER numbered location for a pressure-temperature relief valve is

    A. 2   B. 1   C. 4   D. 3

16. Which one of the following is generally considered a clean-out equivalent?
    A wall-hung

    A. urinal   B. sterilizer
    C. lavatory   D. water closet

17. A horizontal house drain is to be run for its entire length above the cellar floor. This house drain measures 75'6" in length.
    The MINIMUM number of properly designed supports for this run of house drain is

    A. 7   B. 8   C. 9   D. 10

4 (#2)

18. In all buildings which are equipped with a domestic hot water supply, a return circulation system shall be installed if the buildings are MORE THAN _____ stories high.   18.____

    A. 4   B. 3   C. 5   D. 2

19. Which one of the following statements is CORRECT?   19.____

    A. The minimum diameter of all water supply riser lines shall be 3/4" without exception.
    B. The minimum size of water supply branches shall be 1/2" without exception.
    C. Water closets equipped with approved flush valves and vacuum breakers shall be supplied from risers and branches from which other supply branches may be taken.
    D. A separate stopcock or valve shall be placed upon the service pipe inside the front wall and within five feet of the point of entrance of such service pipe.

20. In a given residential area, the water pressure in the street main varies from 60#/sq. in. to 40#/sq. in. daily.   20.____
    If a new apartment house were to be built in this area (with flush valves requiring 12#/sq. in. at the valve), then theoretically the height of the upper floor should not exceed (assume water main 4' below grade) _____ feet above grade.

    A. 40   B. 90   C. 148   D. 60

KEY (CORRECT ANSWERS)

1.	D	11.	C
2.	C	12.	B
3.	A	13.	A
4.	C	14.	D
5.	B	15.	A
6.	D	16.	D
7.	B	17.	C
8.	A	18.	A
9.	C	19.	C
10.	B	20.	D

EXAMINATION SECTION
TEST 1

DIRECTIONS: Each question or incomplete statement is followed by several suggested answers or completions. Select the one that BEST answers the question or completes the statement. *PRINT THE LETTER OF THE CORRECT ANSWER IN THE SPACE AT THE RIGHT.*

1. A new apartment house is constructed and equipped with a roof house tank. This tank has a net capacity of 6500 gal.
   Then, the MINIMUM diameter of the emptying pipe for this tank shall be

   A. 2 1/2" B. 3" C. 4" D. 2"

2. The water supply system of a particular building is equipped with self-closing devices and such other conditions exist which require the installation of air chambers.
   These air chambers should be of such size and design as to comply with the rules of the

   A. department of health
   B. department of housing and buildings
   C. department of water supply, gas, and electricity
   D. board of standards and appeals

3. The plumbing code requires that water closets shall be provided with properly designed and constructed integral flushing rims so constructed as to

   A. deliver flush water at a minimum velocity of 30 ft. per sec.
   B. flush the entire interior of the bowl
   C. flush the front and rear surfaces of the bowl with high velocity streams
   D. prevent siphoning of water closet trap

4. The type of water closet which may be used with the consent of the superintendent is the _____ type.

   A. pan   B. offset washout
   C. washout   D. long hopper

5. Which one of the following statements is CORRECT?

   A. An anti-siphon device is most commonly used to prevent the complete loss of the seal of a fixture trap.
   B. An anti-siphon device is commonly called a vacuum breaker when it is made a part of the water supply system to a plumbing fixture.
   C. An anti-siphon device must be located at the overflow level of the fixture which it serves.
   D. Plumbing fixtures with submerged inlets need not be equipped with an anti-siphon device on the water supply thereto.

6. Water closets with low tanks are being installed in a housing project in which space is limited. As a result of space limitations, special tanks have been built for use in this project.
   A check of the inside dimensions of these tanks should show that the volume available for the storage of flush water shall be NOT LESS THAN _____ cu.ft.

   A. 1350   B. 0.75   C. 0.90   D. 1250

7. A private swimming pool is to be constructed as part of an elaborate home. The pool will have a capacity of 7500 gallons to the high water line.
   The MINIMUM size of the drain line with which this pool shall be installed is

   A. 3"   B. 4"   C. 2"   D. 2 1/2"

8. This private pool is to be equipped with a recirculating system for the filtering and sterilizing of the recirculated water. The pool has sufficient surface to accommodate 15 bathers in any one hour.
   The capacity of the recirculating pump, in gallons per minute, shall be AT LEAST

   A. 5   B. 10   C. 15   D. 20

9. A large industrial building is to be constructed within the city limits. It is estimated that approximately 200 people (equally divided between each sex) will be employed on each floor. Toilet facilities are to be provided on alternate floors for each sex.
   The MINIMUM number of water closets which shall be provided in any one of the ladies toilet rooms is

   A. 8   B. 7   C. 6   D. 5

10. Sanitary plans for an apartment house refer all elevations to the first floor as the 0.00 datum. These plans call for the installation of a main house drain which has a developed length of 1200". This house drain is to be installed at the minimum uniform grade permitted in the code.
    If the center-line elevation of the farthest end of this house drain is -10.08, then the center-line elevation at the house trap end is MOST NEARLY

    A. -8.83   B. -12.58   C. -7.58   D. -11.33

11. A particular waste stack is to receive flow from a considerable number of fixtures having a total F.U. of 110. The total developed length is less than 300. There are no water closets connected to the stack.
    Therefore, the MINIMUM diameter of this stack may be

    A. 3"   B. 4"   C. 2"   D. 2 1/2"

12. MINIMUM size of any house drain receiving discharge from a water closet is

    A. 2 1/2"   B. 3"   C. 4"   D. 5"

13. Every oil separator shall have an individual vent extending from the top of such separator to the outer air. The size of, and the terminal point above street level, of such individual vent shall be, respectively,

    A. 3" and 06"   B. 3" and 10"
    C. 4" and 06"   D. 3" and 120"

14. The plumbing code permits the use of many different types of fittings in a plumbing system without exception to the manner of use thereof.
However, the short turn tee wye may be used only on

    A. a horizontal branch vent
    B. any vertical stack
    C. the horizontal run of the fresh air inlet
    D. a horizontal water supply branch to a flush valve

14.____

15. As an inspector, you are conducting a water test on the roughing for a 6-story apartment house. In the course of your inspection, you notice that a 3" F.A.I. pipe has been installed just ahead of the house trap on a 6" house drain. This F.A.I. pipe extends to the outside air and terminates 18" above grade.
In keeping with requirements of the code, you should require

    A. that this line be changed to 4" and terminated 6" above grade
    B. that this line be changed to 4"
    C. no change in present installation
    D. that this line be changed to 5" and terminated 6" above grade

15.____

16. A new apartment house is to be constructed. The approved sanitary plans show that there are to be 60 family units, each of which contains a combination kitchen sink, and one bathroom group made up of a W.C., lavatory, and a bathtub with a shower therein.
The MINIMUM number of F.U.'s for which this house drain should be sized is MOST NEARLY

    A. 540   B. 600   C. 720   D. 1080

16.____

17. In the sanitary system for a school building, the piping layout calls for a branch soil line to pick up 14 W.C.s, 6 urinals, and 6 lavatories.
The MINIMUM size of soil stack which is required to receive the flow from these fixtures plus the flow from 8 drinking fountains is MOST NEARLY

    A. 8"   B. 6"   C. 4"   D. 5"

17.____

18. The superintendent may permit the discharge, in the regular plumbing system, of chemically neutralized acid waste or other liquids which would otherwise be injurious to the system, if, in his opinion, the treatment of these liquids renders them no more harmful than regular waste and drainage. A neutralizing tank is specified for use in the treatment of the chemical waste from a school chemistry laboratory.
The neutralizing material which is COMMONLY used in the treatment of this waste is

    A. water   B. limestone
    C. oil of vitriol   D. Nesslers Solution

18.____

19. A sanitary and drainage system has been laid out for a particular building.
With regard to the method which should be used to size the combined storm and sanitary house sewer, which one of the following statements is CORRECT? The allowance in

    A. sq.ft. for the first 30 F.U.'s is 490
    B. F.U.'s for the first 64 sq.ft. is 30

19.____

C. sq.ft. for all F.U.'s in excess of 3000 is 4
D. F.U.'s for all sq.ft. in excess of 3000 is 4

20. For a large industrial building, the total number of roof and yard storm water drain lines is 6. The number of roof drain lines is 4. All of these lines finally combine and tee into the house drain resulting in a combined storm and sanitary sewer.
The MINIMUM number of leader traps which may be used to serve these roof and yard storm water drain lines is(are)

   A. 2 B. 6 C. 5 D. 1

KEY (CORRECT ANSWERS)

1.	B	11.	A
2.	C	12.	C
3.	B	13.	D
4.	D	14.	B
5.	B	15.	C
6.	C	16.	A
7.	A	17.	D
8.	A	18.	B
9.	A	19.	A
10.	D	20.	D

TEST 2

DIRECTIONS: Each question or incomplete statement is followed by several suggested answers or completions. Select the one that BEST answers the question or completes the statement. *PRINT THE LETTER OF THE CORRECT ANSWER IN THE SPACE AT THE RIGHT.*

1. Basically, the plumbing code requires that all fixture traps shall be individually vented with several specific exceptions. One of these exceptions relates to the topmost fixture on a stack.
   This topmost fixture may be without an individual vent if the distance from the stack to the fixture does NOT exceed

   A. 3'6" B. 2'0" C. 2'6" D. 5'0"

   1.____

2. In schools, traps of sinks in chemical laboratories which receive acid waste may be installed without vents provided that the traps are of the

   A. drum type with 2" seals
   B. bottle type with 2" seals
   C. D-type
   D. deep seal type

   2.____

3. With respect to fixture traps which are individually vented, it can be said that these individual vents protect the seal of the fixture trap *against*

   A. capillary attraction and evaporation
   B. momentum and evaporation
   C. siphonage and back pressure
   D. back siphonage and back pressure

   3.____

4. When inspecting the vent piping for all the fixtures on a given stack, one should note carefully that the branch vent pipes are so graded as to drip back by gravity to

   A. a soil or waste pipe
   B. a local vent pipe
   C. the vent stack
   D. the inlet of the farthest fixture trap

   4.____

5. A basin is to be installed in the center of a room. The individual vent first rises above the flood rim level of the fixture, drops down through the floor, crosses to a partition wall, rises therein, and finally ties into a vent stack three feet above the floor immediately above. At the low point of this branch vent, the plumbing contractor MUST

   A. set a drain cock of the plug type
   B. provide a gravity drip connection to soil or waste pipe
   C. provide an approved air eliminator
   D. provide a high level float trap to rid this branch vent of any condensate

   5.____

6. In your inspection of a given sanitary system, you find that the plumbing contractor has connected the vent stack to the soil stack at a point five feet below the lowest vent branch being served by these stacks.
   You may advise the plumbing contractor that the relative elevations at which these stacks are connected is

   A. not in exact accordance with the code
   B. not in exact accordance with the code but need not be changed as it is not a major violation
   C. acceptable
   D. not good plumbing practice although it is in keeping with the general purpose of the code

7. All other things being in accordance with the code, the diameter of a vent stack shall be AT LEAST

   A. one-half the diameter of the soil stack served
   B. 3" when serving 40 F.U. with a developed length of 60 ft.
   C. 2" in diameter
   D. 4" when serving 115 F.U. with a developed length of 115 ft.

8. Four 2" main stacks are grouped together at the top of a structure into one pipe. This one pipe then extends through the roof.
   The MINIMUM size of this one pipe shall be

   A. 3" B. 6" C. 4" D. 8"

9. The roof terminal of a vent pipe is 8 ft. from a window on an adjacent building. The top of this window is 5 ft. above the elevation of the considered roof.
   Under these conditions, the MINIMUM extension of this vent pipe above the roof shall be (the roof is used for weather protection only and is flat)

   A. 4'0" B. 8'0" C. 5'0" D. 1'0"

10. The plans for a 2-family residential structure show that the roof is of peak design and the maximum angle or pitch of any part of this roof is 25 to the horizontal. This roof is intended for weather protection only.
    Other conditions permitting, the MINIMUM roof extension of any soil, waste or vent pipe shall be _____ above the roof.

    A. 4'0" B. 5'0" C. 10'0" D. 1'0"

11. Which one of the following statements is CORRECT?

    A. Bar sinks, soda fountains, and drinking fountains shall be installed with indirect wastes.
    B. Where refrigerators, ice boxes or receptacles wherein food is stored, are not water supplied, drips therefrom may be installed with indirect wastes.
    C. Indirect wastes which receive the discharge from fixtures on more than two floors or which exceed 100 ft. in length shall be extended through the roof.
    D. Fixtures connected to indirect wastes shall be trapped, but it shall be unnecessary to vent such fixtures.

3 (#2)

12. A sub-house drainage system is of the atmosphere type and receives flow from fixtures other than floor drains and drips from machinery.
    With respect to the above system, which one of the following statements is CORRECT?

    A. Receiving tank shall be airtight and vented, and shall be provided with a 3" vent pipe which may be connected to a 3" or larger gravity vent system.
    B. The inlet to such receiving tank may be provided with a house trap and F.A.I.
    C. The vents of the sub-house drainage system shall be run independently of the vents of the gravity system.
    D. Receiving tank shall be airtight and vented, and shall be provided with a 2" vent pipe run independent of the gravity vent system.

12.____

13. The sanitary system for a large apartment house is to be given a final smoke test. This system has been designed and installed with 5 stacks and has 5 roof extensions. The PROPER procedure to be followed is, *briefly*:
    Plug

    A. 4 of the stack openings on roof, then apply smoke, and, when smoke appears at 5th stack opening on roof, plug that one
    B. 3 of the stack openings on roof, then apply smoke, and, when smoke appears at each of the other two stack openings on roof, plug them
    C. 2 of the stack openings on roof and, when smoke appears at each of the other 3 stack openings on roof, plug them
    D. none of stack openings on roof; as smoke appears at each of stack openings on roof, plug them

13.____

14. A sanitary and storm water drainage system is to be water tested in sections.
    When testing the uppermost section, the upper footage of the next lower section which is to be retested is MOST NEARLY

    A. 10'   B. 5'   C. 2.32'   D. 4'

14.____

15. Express permission is obtained from the superintendent to use an air test in place of a water test for the sanitary system of an apartment house (under construction).
    The pressure, in lbs. per sq.in., to which all parts of this system shall be tested is MOST NEARLY

    A. 3   B. 5   C. 4   D. 2

15.____

16. A contracting master plumber has properly followed the department procedure and has made an appointment for a test of gas piping. Upon the inspectors arrival on the job site, he finds all the piping installed (exposed), connections properly made to the gas ranges, an approved pressure imposing device, and a mercury gage.
    The inspector should

    A. go ahead with the air pressure test and make sure that a pressure equal to a column of mercury 6" high is held for 15 minutes
    B. go ahead with the air pressure test and make sure that a pressure equal to a column of mercury 12" high is held for 10 minutes

16.____

C. go ahead with the air pressure test and make sure that a pressure equal to a column of mercury 6" high is held for 10 minutes
D. advise the contracting master plumber that he has not complied with the conditions of the code titled *Test of Gas Piping* and suggest that he make the necessary changes before requesting another test

17. In the inspection of gas distribution piping, the inspector should note that all pipes should be run straight without sag or traps and shall be so pitched as to drain

    A. to gas ranges or gas fixtures
    B. to a drip pocket at the base of riser
    C. back to riser and from riser to meter
    D. to a drip pocket at farthest end (from the meter) of the gas main in the basement

18. The code permits the use of steel, wrought iron, cast iron, copper, and brass pipe, respectively, for use in gas piping systems.
    However, in a gas piping system, cast iron pipe is restricted for use ONLY

    A. for risers
    B. underground or outside of buildings
    C. for long horizontal runs or runouts to risers
    D. in fabrication of drip pockets

19. Arrangements have been made to conduct a final smoke test on a sanitary system of a given building.
    The EQUIVALENT pressure, in inches of water, which should be applied to the system before an inspection is made, is NOT LESS THAN

    A. 1   B. 2   C. 3   D. 6

20. A cooking gas distribution system has been installed in an apartment house. As the inspector, you are making a preliminary inspection of this piping system.
    The type of pipe fitting which should NOT be used in this system is a

    A. malleable elbow   B. brass elbow
    C. malleable tee   D. malleable union

KEY (CORRECT ANSWERS)

1. B
2. D
3. C
4. A
5. B
6. C
7. A
8. C
9. B
10. A
11. D
12. A
13. D
14. A
15. B
16. D
17. C
18. B
19. A
20. D

EXAMINATION SECTION
TEST 1

DIRECTIONS: Each question or incomplete statement is followed by several suggested answers or completions. Select the one that BEST answers the question or completes the statement. *PRINT THE LETTER OF THE CORRECT ANSWER IN THE SPACE AT THE RIGHT.*

1. It is usually necessary to insulate the hot water riser from the cold water riser when the distance between the two risers is

    A. 4"   B. 7"   C. 9"   D. 11"

    1._____

2. The number of threads per inch of 3/4" pipe, as compared with the number of threads per inch of 1/4" pipe, is that the

    A. 3/4" pipe has less threads per inch than 1 1/4" pipe
    B. 3/4" pipe and 1 1/4" pipe have the same number of threads per inch
    C. 1 1/4" pipe has less threads per inch than the 3/4" pipe
    D. 1 1/4" pipe has more threads per inch than 3/4" pipe.

    2._____

3. In comparing the volume of water flowing through 1/2" I.D. tubing line and a 1" I.D. tubing line with the same pressure in each line, the volume through the

    A. 1/2" tubing and the 1" tubing will be the same
    B. 1" tubing will be double the volume of the 1/2" tubing
    C. 1" tubing will be three times the volume of the 1/2" tubing
    D. 1" tubing will be four times the volume of the 1/2" tubing

    3._____

4. Pressure relief valves must be installed on hot water heaters. The reason for this is

    A. to drain water from the tank for repair
    B. that when pressure becomes excessive, the relief valve will open and reduce the pressure
    C. that water will be released when tank is full
    D. to prevent air pockets from forming at the bottom of the tank

    4._____

5. The plumbing code requires that water service piping be buried at least four feet below outside ground level. The reason for this is to

    A. prevent the water in the pipe from freezing during the winter season
    B. permit gas service lines to be installed two feet below outside ground level
    C. permit the use of larger diameter pipes
    D. keep the water cool the year round

    5._____

6. A building drain which is buried under ground may NOT be made of

    A. extra heavy cast iron   B. brass
    C. galvanized steel   D. lead

    6._____

7. Brass is an alloy of

    A. lead and copper   B. tin and copper
    C. lead and tin   D. zinc and copper

    7._____

31

8. The MAIN reason for providing a trap for a plumbing fixture is to 8.____
   A. permit cleaning of the fixture when clogged
   B. equalize the pressure in the system
   C. prevent the passage of gases in a reverse direction
   D. catch foreign objects such as jewelry, hair pins, etc.

9. The pipe which delivers water under pressure from a street main to a building is called 9.____
   the _____ pipe.
   A. service   B. interceptor
   C. distribution   D. fixture

10. The MAIN reason that a trap must be properly ventilated is to 10.____
    A. vary the pressure in the waste line
    B. provide an overflow for the fixture
    C. drain the waste water when the trap is closed
    D. maintain the water seal in the trap

11. The valve which offers the LEAST resistance to water flow in a plumbing system is a(n) 11.____
    _____ valve.
    A. angle   B. gate   C. check   D. globe

12. Outlets for gas ranges must have a MINIMUM standard pipe size of 12.____
    A. 1/4"   B. 3/8"   C. 3/4"   D. 1"

13. The oakum for a caulked joint is packed into place by ramming it down with a 13.____
    A. yarning iron   B. jointer
    C. caulking tool   D. cold chisel

14. The ESSENTIAL difference in making up vertical and horizontal caulked joints in cast 14.____
    iron pipe is that horizontal caulked joints require the use of
    A. less lead   B. less oakum
    C. a pouring rope   D. a special caulking tool

15. Galvanized pipe has a coating of 15.____
    A. tin   B. zinc   C. lead   D. aluminum

16. A fixture unit has a discharge rate of one cubic foot of water per minute. 16.____
    This discharge rate, expressed in gallons per minute, is equal to
    A. 4.5   B. 5   C. 7.5   D. 9.5

17. Sweating or condensation of moisture on the outside of a pipe is MOST likely to occur on 17.____
    _____ pipe.
    A. live steam   B. compressed air
    C. hot water   D. cold water

18. Extra strong pipe, as compared to standard pipe of the same nominal size, has _____ diameter.

    A. *the same* outside diameter but a smaller inside
    B. *a larger* outside diameter and a smaller inside
    C. *the same* inside diameter but a larger outside
    D. *a larger* inside and outside diameter

19. You observe a plumber use a hammer to strike the hub and spigot ends of each piece of cast iron pipe before installing it in a soil line.
    This practice is

    A. *poor* because it may nick and weaken the pipe
    B. *poor* because it may break the brittle cast iron
    C. *good* because it loosens any rust which may have gathered
    D. *good* because it enables the plumber to tell if the pipe is sound

20. If a drain line pitches one foot in a length of 48 feet, the pitch of the line is MOST NEARLY _____ per foot.

    A. 1/4"   B. 3/8"   C. 1/2"   D. 3/4"

21. A plumbing sketch is drawn to a scale of eighth-size.
    A line measuring 3" on the sketch would be equivalent to _____ feet.

    A. 2   B. 6   C. 12   D. 24

22. Plumbing riser diagrams are GENERALLY drawn to _____ scale.

    A. no   B. 1/8" = 1'0"
    C. 1/4" = 1'0"   D. 1/2" = 1'0"

23. A building has a color marked dual water distribution system, one potable water and the other non-potable. The color used to identify the potable water system is

    A. yellow   B. orange   C. green   D. blue

24. Of the following potable water supply systems, the one which is NOT considered to be an auxiliary potable water supply system is a

    A. street main water supply system
    B. elevated gravity water supply system
    C. hydropneumatic pressure booster
    D. water pressure pump system

25. A pit and cover and/or manhole with cover is required for a building (house) trap when the distance from the center-line of the drain to the floor exceeds

    A. 12"   B. 16"   C. 18"   D. 24"

26. The MINIMUM rinse water temperature that can be used in a commercial type dishwasher is _____ °F.

    A. 140   B. 160   C. 180   D. 200

27. Assume that the flow rate through a grease interceptor is 60 g.p.m. Under this flow rate, the grease interceptor should have a minimum *grease retention capacity* of _____ pounds.

    A. 6 B. 30 C. 60 D. 120

28. The MAIN purpose for increasing the diameter of a vent stack from 2" to 4" when going through a roof is to

    A. provide sufficient area for proper flashing
    B. minimize clogging by hoarfrost
    C. increase the stability of the stack
    D. facilitate testing procedures

29. A pot of wiping solder is overheated.
    If this wiping soldier is used, the appearance of the wiped joint would MOST likely be

    A. flaky
    B. spotted with bright specks
    C. frosty
    D. coarse and grainy

30. Assume that the end of a piece of pipe has been threaded with a well-constructed threading pipe die.
    The number of imperfect threads that would be formed due to the chamfer on the die would be MOST NEARLY

    A. zero B. 2 1/2 C. 3 1/2 D. 4 1/2

31. A pipe threading die with four chasers is used to thread the end of a length of pipe. The resultant threads are rough and torn.
    This condition is MOST probably caused by

    A. an improper lip angle
    B. too little clearance between the heel of the chaser and the work
    C. insufficient chip space
    D. not using a cutting oil

32. A deep seal trap has a minimum liquid seal of

    A. 2" B. 3" C. 4" D. 5"

33. Of the following installations, the one which does NOT conform to the plumbing code (i.e., illegal) is the installation of a

    A. water closet with a 4" x 3" closet bend
    B. shower receptor with a 3" drain outlet
    C. washdown urinal with an integral strainer
    D. ball cock in a flush tank 1" above the floor rim of the bowl and provided with a vacuum breaker

34. A *dual vent* is commonly known as a _____ vent.

    A. crown B. common C. side D. yoke

35. Of the following piping materials, the one which is NOT used for potable water service is

    A. copper pipe
    B. type *L* tubing
    C. type *K* tubing
    D. type *TP* tubing

36. The discharge rate for an ejector pump is 100 g.p.m. The *fixture unit value* for this pump is

    A. 10 B. 50 C. 75 D. 100

37. The flood level rim of a fixture is defined as

    A. the invert or bottom of the overflow
    B. the inside top of the overflow pipe
    C. 1" above the top of the overflow pipe
    D. the top edge or rim of the fixture

38. Of the following statements, the one which BEST defines the plumbing term *cross-connection* is the connection between

    A. the domestic hot water and potable cold water
    B. steam and a potable water supply
    C. potable water at 40 psig and potable water at 90 psig
    D. two different potable water distribution pipes

39. Of the following types of water closets, the one which shall be used for public use is the _____ type.

    A. elongated bowl   B. pan
    C. washout   D. offset

40. The MAXIMUM interval between hangers for supporting horizontal 1 1/2" diameter threaded pipe is _____ feet.

    A. 6 B. 8 C. 10 D. 12

KEY (CORRECT ANSWERS)

1. A	11. B	21. A	31. A
2. C	12. C	22. A	32. B
3. D	13. A	23. C	33. C
4. B	14. C	24. A	34. B
5. A	15. B	25. C	35. B
6. C	16. C	26. C	36. D
7. D	17. D	27. D	37. D
8. C	18. A	28. B	38. B
9. A	19. D	29. D	39. A
10. D	20. A	30. C	40. D

TEST 2

DIRECTIONS: Each question or incomplete statement is followed by several suggested answers or completions. Select the one that BEST answers the question or completes the statement. *PRINT THE LETTER OF THE CORRECT ANSWER IN THE SPACE AT THE RIGHT.*

1. The pipe fitting which should be used to connect a 1" pipe to a 1 1/2" valve is a   1._____

    A. reducing elbow
    B. bushing
    C. reducing coupling
    D. street ell

2. A 2 percent pitch in a pipe line is MOST NEARLY equal to a slope of _____ to the foot.   2._____

    A. 1/16"   B. 1/8"   C. 1/4"   D. 1/2"

3. The MAIN function of a standpipe system in a building is to   3._____

    A. supply water for the roof tank
    B. keep the hot water circulating in order to maintain a constant temperature
    C. provide water for use in case of fire
    D. increase the pressure in the water supply piping

4. The one of the following valves which offers the LEAST resistance to the flow of water is a(n) _____ valve.   4._____

    A. check   B. gate   C. globe   D. angle

5. The cast iron drainage fitting that is called a Tucker connection has   5._____

    A. male threads on one end and female threads on the other end
    B. one end in the form of a hub and female threads on the other end
    C. one end in the form of a hub and male threads on the other end
    D. each end in the form of a hub

6. When bending copper tubing in the field, special equipment is required _____ -temper tubing.   6._____

    A. only for hard
    B. only for soft
    C. for both soft-temper and hard
    D. for neither soft-temper nor hard.

7. If the diameter of the vertical stack in a building is smaller than the diameter of the house drain which connects to it, then the bend which joins them should be   7._____

    A. *at least* one size smaller than the stack
    B. *at least* one size larger than the stack
    C. *at least* one size larger than the drain
    D. *larger* than both the stack and the drain

8. If water is flowing into the top of a tank at the rate of 150 gallons per hour and flowing out at the rate of 3/4 of a gallon every 20 seconds, then the amount of water in the tank is _____ gallon per minute.   8._____

    A. *increasing* by 1/4
    B. *increasing* by 3/4
    C. *decreasing* by 1/4
    D. *decreasing* by 3/4

9. A flexible coupling between a pump shaft and a motor shaft is GENERALLY provided in order to

    A. reduce the load on the pump
    B. permit excess heat to escape
    C. permit minor misalignment between the shafts
    D. increase the power of the motor

10. The BEST way to prevent a water pocket from forming when two horizontal steam pipes of different diameter are joined is to

    A. use an eccentric fitting
    B. use a long fitting so that the slope between the pipes is very gradual
    C. provide a drain cock
    D. slope the pipe so that the smaller pipe is lower

11. The BEST way to make a temporary repair in a water line with a small leak is by

    A. wrapping a rag around it
    B. welding or brazing
    C. using a clamped patch
    D. drilling, tapping, and inserting a plug

12. Brass is an alloy of

    A. lead and copper
    B. lead and tin
    C. tin and copper
    D. zinc and copper

13. The information that a plumber would NOT normally expect to find on each section of cast iron pipe delivered from the factory is the

    A. manufacturer's name
    B. weight category
    C. diameter
    D. length

14. Steel pipe is GENERALLY connected to copper tubing by

    A. brazing
    B. soldering
    C. wiping
    D. special fittings

15. Pipe is galvanized by coating it with

    A. chrome   B. tin   C. aluminum   D. zinc

16. A return bend in a pipe line changes the direction of flow by

    A. 45°   B. 90°   C. 135°   D. 180°

17. When lagging is used on steam pipes, its MAIN function is to

    A. compensate for expansion
    B. prevent corrosion
    C. reduce radiation heat loss
    D. reduce steam leaks

18. If the drawing of a piping layout is made to a scale of 1/4" equals one foot, then a 7'9" length of piping would be represented by a scaled length on the drawing of APPROXIMATELY _____ inches.

    A. 2 B. 7 3/4 C. 23 1/4 D. 31

19. A pipe reducing coupling normally has _____ thread(s).

    A. two female
    B. two male
    C. one continuous female
    D. one male and one female

20. All bullhead tees have run openings which are

    A. smaller than the outlet
    B. larger than the outlet
    C. of the same size
    D. of different sizes

21. A close nipple

    A. has a short section with no threads
    B. is always less than 3/4" long
    C. has ends of different diameters
    D. has threads over its entire length

22. A reducing tee ALWAYS has

    A. one opening which is larger than the other two
    B. openings of three different sizes
    C. a branch opening which is smaller than the run
    D. a branch which is at an angle of 45 degrees to the run

23. In addition to acting as a filler between threads, pipe joint compound ALSO acts as a

    A. lubricant
    B. hardener
    C. coolant
    D. permanent bond

24. The valve which is used to permit flow of water in one direction only is called a _____ valve.

    A. check B. globe C. gate D. angle

25. A method which should be used to free a pipe die from chips while threading a pipe is to

    A. use as little lubricating oil as possible
    B. set the die loosely on the pipe stock
    C. clean the chips off the pipe after each thread is cut
    D. partially back off the die at intervals during the turning process

26. The MAIN difference between making up horizontal and vertical caulked joints in cast iron pipe is that, when making up a vertical caulked joint, you should NOT use a

    A. smaller amount of lead
    B. smaller amount of oakum
    C. pouring rope
    D. special caulking tool

27. Assume that a 2" pipe is connected to a 3" pipe by means of a coupling. If the velocity of flow in the 2" pipe is 36 feet per second, then the velocity of flow in the 3" pipe is APPROXIMATELY _____ feet per second.

    A. 16 B. 24 C. 54 D. 81

28. When ordering a cross which is to have two outlet openings which are 1" in diameter and two run openings which are 1 1/2" in diameter, a plumber should specify a _____ cross.

    A. 1" x 1 1/2" x 1" x 1 1/2"
    B. 1 1/2" x 1" x 1 1/2" x 1"
    C. 1" x 1 1/2"
    D. 1 1/2" x 1"

29. The LEAST likely cause of a leak in a threaded pipe joint is that

    A. not enough pipe joint compound was used
    B. the threads are not smooth
    C. the number of threads is not sufficient
    D. too much pipe joint compound has been used

30. The BEST way to assemble a line of piping between a waste stack and a trapped fixture is to

    A. start at the fixture and work toward the waste stack
    B. start at the waste stack and work toward the fixture
    C. let the order of assembly be determined by the details of the proposed installation
    D. work from the most accessible location

31. When referring to a building drainage system, the term *waste pipe* should NORMALLY be applied to

    A. piping which does not receive human waste
    B. piping which drains water closets
    C. any pipe which carries water-borne wastes
    D. any pipe which connects to the building drain

32. The one of the following which has the SMALLEST *fixture unit rating* is a

    A. drinking fountain
    B. wash basin
    C. slop sink
    D. shower head

33. Pipe joint compound should be applied on

    A. the threads of male fittings only
    B. the threads of female fittings only
    C. the threads of both male and female fittings
    D. either male or female threads, depending on the type of fitting

34. If a pipe with an outside diameter of 7" is to be fastened against the ceiling with a U-strap, the distance from the ceiling around the pipe and back to the ceiling should be APPROXIMATELY _____ inches.

    A. 14   B. 16   C. 18   D. 20

35. The MAIN reason cast iron pipe is particularly suitable for underground service is that it

    A. resists corrosion very well
    B. has a low initial cost
    C. is easy to handle and join
    D. can withstand high pressures

36. The BEST procedure to follow in most cases when a pipe does not screw into a fitting easily is to

    A. use a heavier pipe wrench
    B. cut the threads off the end of the pipe and rethread
    C. attempt to true up defective threads with a die or a tap
    D. heat the fitting with a torch

37. If the hand-operated shut-off valve in a water line is turned to the fully closed position, and water continues to flow through the valve, the MOST likely defect a plumber would expect to find is

    A. a loose gland
    B. excessive packing
    C. improper seating of the valve disc
    D. a loose stuffing nut

38. The MAIN function of a trap in a drainage system is to

    A. prevent freezing of the pipes
    B. block off sewer gases
    C. prevent loss of water pressure
    D. catch rings and other objects

39. A combustible gas which may be present in sewer air and which is explosive in the presence of oxygen is

    A. carbon dioxide   B. freon
    C. hydrogen sulfide   D. nitrogen

40. The MAIN function of a back-pressure valve which is sometimes found in the connection between a water drain pipe and the sewer system is to

    A. equalize the pressure between the drain pipe and the sewer
    B. prevent sewer water from flowing into the drain pipe
    C. provide pressure to enable waste to reach the sewer
    D. make sure that there is not too much water pressure in the sewer line

KEY (CORRECT ANSWERS)

1. B	11. C	21. D	31. A
2. C	12. D	22. C	32. A
3. C	13. D	23. A	33. A
4. B	14. D	24. A	34. C
5. B	15. D	25. D	35. A
6. A	16. D	26. C	36. C
7. B	17. C	27. A	37. C
8. A	18. A	28. D	38. B
9. C	19. A	29. D	39. C
10. A	20. A	30. B	40. B

TEST 3

DIRECTIONS: Each question or incomplete statement is followed by several suggested answers or completions. Select the one that BEST answers the question or completes the statement. *PRINT THE LETTER OF THE CORRECT ANSWER IN THE SPACE AT THE RIGHT.*

1. The piping of a newly installed drainage system shall be tested upon completion of the rough plumbing with a head of water of NOT LESS THAN _____ feet. 1._____
   A. 10   B. 15   C. 20   D. 25

2. The one of the following which should NOT be considered as a *water conserving device* is a(n) 2._____
   A. evaporative condenser
   B. water cooling tower
   C. spray pond
   D. water closet

3. In high pressure steam heating systems, the steam pressure is GREATER than _____ psig. 3._____
   A. 15   B. 20   C. 25   D. 30

4. Type *K* water service pipe is made of 4._____
   A. cast iron
   B. copper
   C. lead
   D. galvanized steel

5. All water services shall be installed below the finished ground surface at a distance of AT LEAST _____ feet. 5._____
   A. 2   B. 4   C. 6   D. 8

6. The piping in all buildings having dual water distribution systems shall be identified by a color coding of _____ for potable water lines and _____ for non-potable water lines. 6._____
   A. green; red
   B. green; yellow
   C. yellow; green
   D. yellow; red

7. In buildings over four stories high, approved plastic pipe may be used for 7._____
   A. water service pipe only
   B. all water distribution system piping
   C. all drainage system piping
   D. chemical waste drainage systems only

8. The minimum required diameter of any soil stack extension which passes through the roof is _____ inches. 8._____
   A. 3   B. 4   C. 5   D. 6

9. A device used to prevent backflow by siphonic action is called a 9._____
   A. relief valve
   B. sewage ejector
   C. foot valve
   D. vacuum breaker

10. The MAXIMUM distance permitted between cleanouts in horizontal drainage lines is _____ feet.

    A. 10   B. 30   C. 50   D. 70

11. A horizontal drainage pipe must have a minimum slope of 1/4" per foot if the pipe diameter measures _____ inches.

    A. 2   B. 4   C. 6   D. 8

12. Curb valves should be installed on all domestic service pipes with a diameter larger than _____ inch(es).

    A. 1   B. 1 1/2   C. 2   D. 2 1/2

13. A public water supply system shall be deemed available to a two-family dwelling if a property line of such dwelling is within a distance from the public water supply which is NO GREATER THAN _____ feet.

    A. 50   B. 100   C. 150   D. 200

14. The minimum pressure available near a faucet or water outlet with the water outlet wide open shall be _____ psi.

    A. 2   B. 4   C. 6   D. 8

15. When it is necessary to open a sidewalk in order to do plumbing work, a permit shall be obtained from the department of

    A. water resources
    B. public works
    C. buildings
    D. highways

16. The MINIMUM number of fixture units allowed for a bathroom group containing one lavatory, one bathtub, and one water closet (flush tank) is

    A. 4   B. 6   C. 8   D. 10

17. The MINIMUM number of plumbing fixtures required for a particular type of building occupancy depends MAINLY on

    A. the number of persons expected to use the building
    B. whether the building is publicly or privately owned
    C. the load factor numbers
    D. the age group of the occupants

18. The waste water which would be MOST likely to corrode a cast iron pipe would have a pH value of

    A. 3.0   B. 5.0   C. 7.0   D. 9.0

19. The MAIN factor to consider in determining whether permission from a city department is required before connecting automatic power pumps directly to the street main is the

    A. total water storage capacity in the building
    B. total automatic pump capacity
    C. number of persons expected to occupy the building
    D. number of fixture units in the building

20. In locations where tags are used to designate certain water lines, non-potable water lines should be identified by _____ tags which say _____.

    A. round; WATER UNSAFE
    B. triangular; WATER UNSAFE
    C. round; UNSAFE FOR DRINKING
    D. triangular; UNSAFE FOR DRINKING

21. Trap seals should be vented so that they are at no time subjected to a pressure differential of MORE THAN

    A. 1 inch of water
    B. 2 inches of water
    C. .1 pound per square inch
    D. .2 pound per square inch

22. One trap may serve more than one drain if none of the drains are at a greater distance from the trap than _____ feet.

    A. 5   B. 10   C. 15   D. 20

23. With the exception of commercial dishwashers or laundries, hot water may NOT be discharged into any part of a drainage system at a temperature above

    A. 150°   B. 160°   C. 170°   D. 180°

24. A type of hospital equipment which does NOT require an air gap on the water supply is a(n)

    A. operating table   B. aspirator
    C. toilet   D. sterilizer

25. The percentage of the total connected fixture unit flow rate is likely to occur at any point in the drainage system is called the

    A. discharge coefficient   B. velocity coefficient
    C. load factor   D. hydraulic factor

26. The top edge over which water in a receptacle can overflow is called the

    A. inlet rim   B. air-gap level
    C. drain level   D. flood-level rim

27. A device designed to separate and retain undesirable matter from normal wastes and permit normal sewage to discharge into the disposal terminal is called a(n)

    A. catch basin   B. dead end
    C. seepage pit   D. interceptor

28. Paint is NOT permitted on the jointing material at a joint in cast iron pipe

    A. at any time
    B. until two days after construction of the joint
    C. until the entire plumbing installation is complete
    D. until after the joint has been tested and accepted

29. Wall-hung trough urinals are permitted in

   A. public bath houses
   B. only in temporary locations
   C. where a limited number of people are expected to use them
   D. under no circumstances

30. Drainage pipe cleanouts are required

   A. to be not more than 80 feet apart in a horizontal direction
   B. to extend horizontally from an underground drain
   C. at each change of direction greater than 45°
   D. to be 3/4 of the nominal size of pipe for diameters up to 4 inches

31. All water used in the construction of a building shall be metered if the building is higher than _____ stories.

   A. 3   B. 4   C. 5   D. 6

32. Gas piping should be tested under a pressure of NO LESS THAN _____ psig.

   A. 3   B. 5   C. 7   D. 9

33. When installing gas lines in a building, it is permissible to

   A. reuse gas pipe which has been removed from an existing installation
   B. use gas piping for an electrical ground
   C. use malleable iron fittings
   D. use gasket unions.

34. If the water pressure in the street main is 100 psi,

   A. a gravity tank shall be installed on the roof
   B. the pressure at the closed fixtures shall be reduced to 85 psi
   C. a stop-and-waste valve shall be installed underground
   D. a booster pump shall be connected to the main

35. When modernizing a multiple dwelling, a plumbing permit is required if

   A. several broken toilets are to be replaced by new fixtures
   B. an additional washing machine and standpipe are to be installed in the laundry room
   C. gas stoves in all apartments are to be replaced by a newer model
   D. the hot water storage tank is to be replaced

36. When an adjoining building is erected next to an existing building which is higher, all waste stacks of the new building shall be located a distance from the common lot line of AT LEAST _____ feet.

   A. 5   B. 10   C. 15   D. 20

37. A type of trap which is prohibited is the _____ trap.

   A. S   B. 1/2S   C. bottle   D. running

38. Air chambers installed at individual fixtures   38.____

    A. need not be accessible
    B. shall be accessible
    C. are required for loads of less than 5 fixture units
    D. are required for loads of more than 5 fixture units

39. In the installation of a hot water storage tank, it is PROHIBITED to install a   39.____

    A. combination pressure and temperature relief valve
    B. separate pressure relief valve and separate temperature relief valve
    C. pressure relief valve whose opening pressure is greater than 25 lbs. above normal system working pressure
    D. check valve between the relief valve and the storage tank

40. Sanitary drainage piping must be sloped so that the minimum velocity of flow is _____   40.____
    ft. per second.

KEY (CORRECT ANSWERS)

1.	A	11.	A	21.	A	31.	D
2.	D	12.	C	22.	C	32.	A
3.	A	13.	B	23.	A	33.	C
4.	B	14.	D	24.	C	34.	B
5.	B	15.	D	25.	C	35.	B
6.	B	16.	B	26.	D	36.	B
7.	D	17.	A	27.	D	37.	C
8.	B	18.	A	28.	D	38.	A
9.	D	19.	B	29.	B	39.	D
10.	C	20.	B	30.	C	40.	C

EXAMINATION SECTION
TEST 1

DIRECTIONS: Each question or incomplete statement is followed by several suggested answers or completions. Select the one that BEST answers the question or completes the statement. *PRINT THE LETTER OF THE CORRECT ANSWER IN THE SPACE AT THE RIGHT.*

1. Leaks from the stem of a faucet can GENERALLY be stopped by replacing the   1.____
   - A. bibb washer
   - B. seat
   - C. packing
   - D. gasket

2. Of the following, the BEST procedure to follow with a frozen water pipe is to   2.____
   - A. allow the pipe to thaw out by itself as the weather gets warmer
   - B. put anti-freeze into the pipe above the section that is frozen
   - C. turn on the hot water heater
   - D. open the faucet closest to the frozen pipe and warm the pipe with a blow torch, starting at this point

3. Rubber will deteriorate FASTEST when it is constantly in contact with   3.____
   - A. air
   - B. water
   - C. oil
   - D. soapsuds

4. Stoppage of water flow is often caused by dirt accumulating in an elbow.   4.____
   As used in the above sentence, the word *accumulating* means MOST NEARLY
   - A. clogging
   - B. collecting
   - C. rusting
   - D. confined

5. The symbol shown at the right on a plumbing plan MOST likely represents a   5.____
   - A. check valve
   - B. vent
   - C. sump
   - D. trap

6. Of the following outside lines entering a building, the one for which grades must be MOST carefully controlled is the   6.____
   - A. sewer line
   - B. water line
   - C. gas line
   - D. electric cable

7. Threads are cut on the ends of a length of steel pipe by the use of a   7.____
   - A. brace and bit
   - B. counterbore
   - C. stock and die
   - D. doweling jig

8. When installing a catch basin, the outlet should be located   8.____
   - A. at the same level as the inlet
   - B. above the inlet
   - C. below the inlet
   - D. at the invert

47

9. The copper float in a low down water tank is perforated so that water enters the ball. As a result, the tank will

   A. flush once, and then will not operate again
   B. not flush at all
   C. not flush completely
   D. continue to flush, but water will be wasted

10. If water leaks from the stem of a faucet when the faucet is opened, the _____ should be _____.

    A. faucet; replaced
    B. cap nut; rethreaded
    C. seat; reground
    D. packing; replaced

11. Which of the following would ordinarily occur FIRST in a toilet tank after the handle is pushed down to flush the toilet?

    A. Float ball drops with water level, opening the ball-cock assembly through which fresh water flows into the tank.
    B. Tank ball sinks slowly into place.
    C. Rising water pushes the float ball up until it closes the ballcock assembly, shutting off the supply of fresh water when the tank is full.
    D. The tank ball lifts, opening the outlet so water can flow from tank to bowl.

12. When repairing a hole in a leaking pipe, which of the following should be done FIRST?

    A. Wrap tape around the hole
    B. Turn off the water supply
    C. Tighten a clamp around the hole
    D. Seal the hole with epoxy

13. If water is leaking from the top part of a bibcock, the part that should be replaced is MOST likely the

    A. bibb washer
    B. packing
    C. seat
    D. bibb screw

14. The pipe fitting that would be used to connect a 2" pipe at a 45° angle to another 2" pipe is called a(n)

    A. tee
    B. orifice flange
    C. reducer
    D. elbow

15. An order of 600 feet of 1-inch pipe is shipped in 24-foot lengths. The number of 7-foot pieces that can be cut from this shipment is

    A. 25   B. 72   C. 75   D. 85

16. The tool shown at the right is a
    A. countersink
    B. counterbore
    C. star drill
    D. burring reamer

17. The temperature of a domestic hot water system is MOST often controlled by a(n)

   A. relief valve B. aquastat
   C. barometer D. thermostat

18. Insulation of steam pipes was MOST often done with

   A. asbestos B. celotex C. alundum D. sheathing

19. The BEST tool to use to remove the burr and sharp edge resulting from cutting tubing with a tube cutter is a

   A. file B. scraper C. reamer D. knife

20. Gaskets are seldom made of

   A. rubber B. lead C. asbestos D. vinyl

21. The composition of plumber's solder for wiping is APPROXIMATELY (ratio of tin to lead)

   A. 40-60 B. 50-50 C. 60-40 D. 70-30

22. A device used to lift sewage to the level of a sewer from a floor below the sewer grade is known as a(n)

   A. elevator B. ejector C. sump D. conveyer

23. A check valve in a piping system will

   A. permit excessive pressures in a boiler
   B. eliminate water hammer
   C. permit water to flow in only one direction
   D. control the rate of flow of water

24. The chemical MOST frequently used to clean drains clogged with grease is

   A. muriatic acid B. soda ash
   C. ammonia D. caustic soda

25. A full thread cutting set would have both taps and

   A. cutters B. bushings C. dies D. plugs

KEY (CORRECT ANSWERS)

1.	C	11.	D
2.	D	12.	B
3.	C	13.	B
4.	B	14.	D
5.	D	15.	C
6.	A	16.	D
7.	C	17.	B
8.	C	18.	A
9.	D	19.	C
10.	D	20.	D

21. A
22. B
23. C
24. D
25. C

TEST 2

DIRECTIONS: Each question or incomplete statement is followed by several suggested answers or completions. Select the one that BEST answers the question or completes the statement. *PRINT THE LETTER OF THE CORRECT ANSWER IN THE SPACE AT THE RIGHT.*

1. To test for leaks in a newly installed C.I. waste stack,   1.____

    A. oil of peppermint is poured into the top of the stack
    B. smoke under pressure is pumped into the stack
    C. a water meter is used to measure the water flow
    D. dye is placed in the system at the top of the stack

2.   2.____

    The wrench whose PRINCIPAL purpose is to hold taps for threading is numbered

    A. 1   B. 2   C. 3   D. 4

3. An alloy used where resistance to corrosion is important is   3.____

    A. tungsten   B. mild steel
    C. monel   D. tin

4. The size of iron pipe is given in terms of its nominal   4.____

    A. weight   B. inside diameter
    C. outside diameter   D. wall thickness

5. When preparing surfaces to be soldered, the FIRST step is   5.____

    A. tinning   B. sweating   C. heating   D. cleaning

6. To test for leaks in an acetylene torch, it is BEST that one use   6.____

    A. soapy water
    B. a match
    C. a gas with a strong odor
    D. a pressure gauge

51

7. To close off one opening in a pipe tee when the line connecting into it is to be temporarily removed, it is necessary to use a

    A. pipe cap   B. pipe plug   C. nipple   D. bushing

8. A 1-inch pipe is to span exactly 12 inches between the faces of two fittings. If a pipe thread table shows that 1-inch pipe has good threads extending for a distance of 11/16 inch at each end, then the necessary piece of 1-inch pipe must be cut to a total length of

    A. 12 11/32"   B. 12 11/16"   C. 13 1/32"   D. 13 3/8"

9. The letters W.C. on a building plan indicate

    A. water closet   B. wet concrete
    C. wire coil   D. workman's cloakroom

10. The letters D.S. on a building plan indicate a

    A. door saddle   B. down spout
    C. dumbwaiter shaft   D. dead space

11. From a length of pipe 6'9" long, you are asked to cut a piece 4'5" long. The length of the remainder, in inches, should be

    A. 24   B. 26   C. 28   D. 53

12. The fitting which usually is easiest to disconnect FIRST when disassembling a piping run is a(n)

    A. cross   B. union
    C. return bend   D. elbow

13. For convenience in case of future repairs to a long pipe line, it is DESIRABLE to fit the pipe together with several

    A. street ells   B. elbows
    C. return bends   D. unions

14. If four pipes are to be connected to each other at a common point, it would be NECESSARY to use a(n)

    A. tee fitting   B. street ell
    C. cross   D. offset

15. Rubber gaskets are frequently placed between the faces of the flanges when making up a flanged joint in a pipe line in order to

    A. prevent corrosion of the machined faces
    B. permit full tightening of the flange bolts without danger of thread stripping
    C. eliminate the necessity for accurate alignment of the pipe
    D. make a tight joint

16. The percentage of the tank shown at the right that is filled with water is MOST NEARLY
    A. 33
    B. 35
    C. 37
    D. 39

17. Of the following statements, the one that MOST closely identifies the term *house sewer* is: The house sewer is
    A. located outside the building area and connects to the public sewer in the street
    B. located inside the building area and ends at the outside of the front wall of the building
    C. the pipe which carries the discharge from the plumbing fixtures to the house drain
    D. the house drain

18. Of the following, the BEST tool to use to remove a chrome-plated bonnet from a faucet is a(n)
    A. vise-grip plier
    B. open end wrench
    C. stillson wrench
    D. chisel

19. The BEST flux to use for soldering galvanized iron is
    A. resin
    B. sal ammoniac
    C. borax
    D. muriatic acid

20. The one of the following that is NOT a common type of oilstone is
    A. silicon carbide
    B. aluminum oxide
    C. hard Arkansas
    D. pumice

21. A method of joining metals using temperatures intermediate between soldering and welding is
    A. corbelling
    B. brazing
    C. annealing
    D. lapping

22. The specifications of piping require the use of graphite on cleanout plugs. Of the following, the BEST reason for the use of graphite is to
    A. facilitate installing the plug
    B. facilitate removing the plug
    C. make the plug watertight
    D. give the plug a dark color for identification purposes

23. Practically all valves used in plumbing work are made so that the handwheel is turned clockwise instead of counterclockwise to close the valve.
The PROBABLE reason is that

    A. it is easier to remember since screws and nuts move inward when turned clockwise
    B. the handwheel is less likely to loosen
    C. greater force can be exerted
    D. most people are right-handed

23.____

24. Specifications may state that a standpipe system will be provided in each building.
The MAIN purpose of a standpipe system is to

    A. supply the roof water tank
    B. provide water for firefighting
    C. circulate water for the heating system
    D. provide adequate pressure for the water supply

24.____

25. A cast iron soil pipe-bend having an angle of 45 is COMMONLY called a _____ bend.

    A. 1/16   B. 1/8   C. 1/4   D. return

25.____

KEY (CORRECT ANSWERS)

1. B		11. C	
2. A		12. B	
3. C		13. D	
4. B		14. C	
5. D		15. D	
6. A		16. D	
7. B		17. A	
8. D		18. B	
9. A		19. D	
10. B		20. D	

21. B
22. B
23. A
24. B
25. B

TEST 3

DIRECTIONS: Each question or incomplete statement is followed by several suggested answers or completions. Select the one that BEST answers the question or completes the statement. *PRINT THE LETTER OF THE CORRECT ANSWER IN THE SPACE AT THE RIGHT.*

1. Faucet leakage in a large building is BEST controlled by periodic

    A. faucet replacement
    B. addition of a sealing compound to the water supply
    C. packing replacement
    D. faucet inspection and repair

    1.____

2. The one of the following that is the MOST practical method to use in making a temporary repair in a straight portion of a water pipe which has a small leak is to

    A. attach a clamped patch over the leak
    B. weld or braze the pipe, depending on the material
    C. drill and tap the pipe, then insert a plug
    D. fill the hole with an epoxy sealer

    2.____

3. When constructing a tall reinforced concrete building, the pipeline system that should be built FIRST is the

    A. drainage plumbing   B. standpipe system
    C. hot water system   D. cold water system

    3.____

4. The coefficient of expansion for brass pipe is 0.00001 inch per º F.
   When the temperature of the water in a 110-foot length of brass pipe increases from 40º to 140º F, the increase in the length of the pipe is _____ inches.

    A. 0.32   B. 1.32   C. 2.31   D. 21.2

    4.____

5. The pipe taking water from a roof supply tank should extend at least six inches above the bottom of the tank PRIMARILY in order to

    A. allow some water to remain in the tank at all times
    B. prevent sediment from being carried into the plumbing
    C. provide sufficient pressure to the top floors of the building
    D. avoid corrosion of the bottom of the tank

    5.____

6. The PROPER wrench to use in installing or tightening brass or chrome plated fittings is a(n)

    A. alligator   B. stillson   C. S   D. strap

    6.____

7. Which one of the wrenches pictured below is designed to grip round pipes in making plumbing repairs?

    7.____

55

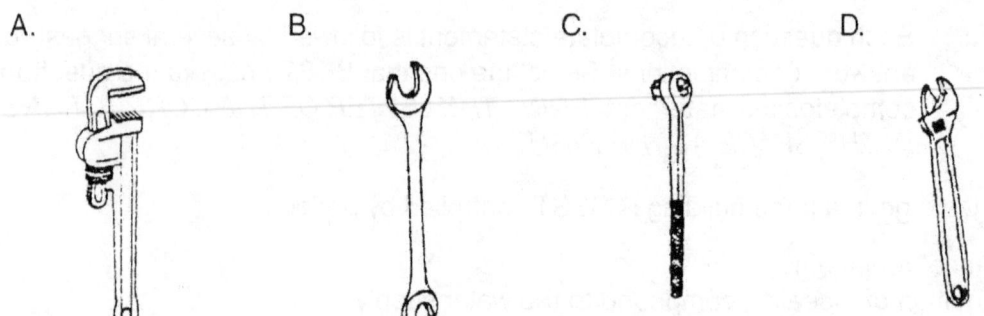

A.   B.   C.   D.

8. A fresh air inlet for a house drainage system would be connected to the system   8._____

   A. just ahead of the house trap
   B. at each horizontal branch line
   C. at the top of the stack through the roof
   D. at the trap of each water closet

9. If combination faucet is in off position and water leaks from swivel, you should   9._____

   A. replace faucet washers
   B. repack swivel gland
   C. replace both washers and tighten swivel gland
   D. replace the faucet

10. The MAXIMUM number of gaskets shown which can be cut from the gasket material as shown is   10._____
    A. 19
    B. 60
    C. 135
    D. 270

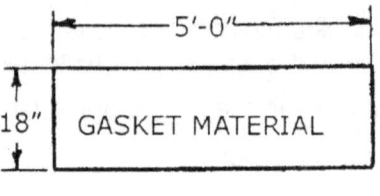
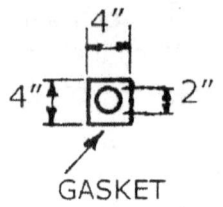

11. To bring the level of the water in the two open-top tanks down to a height of 6 inches, the quantity of water to be removed by opening the valve is _____ gallons.   11._____
    A. 10 1/2
    B. 9
    C. 7 1/2
    D. 6

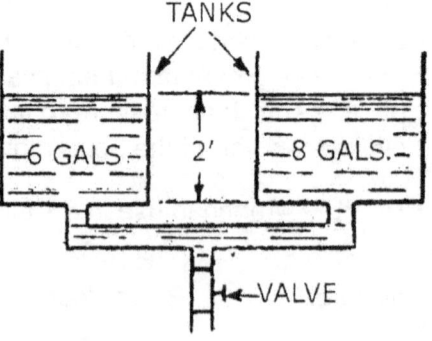

12. A neoprene gasket would normally be used in a pipeline carrying   12._____

    A. steam   B. compressed air
    C. carbon dioxide   D. light oil

13. A mixing valve for domestic water blends   13._____

    A. cold water with hot boiler water
    B. hot and cold water

C. cold water and hot water from coil submerged in boiler water
D. hot and cold water from cooling coil

14. In accordance with the uniform method of identifying piping in public buildings, pipes carrying materials classified as being dangerous are colored

    A. blue
    B. red
    C. orange and yellow
    D. green and white

15. The MAIN reason for preventing sewer gas from entering buildings through the plumbing system is because the gas

    A. is highly inflammable and explosive in nature and could result in a fire hazard
    B. has an eroding effect on plumbing fixtures and pipe lines
    C. is highly infectious and contagious in nature
    D. has a nuisance effect on occupants

16. In a multi-story building, standpipes are installed FIRST by the plumber for

    A. water supply
    B. sanitary facilities
    C. fire protection
    D. steam supply

17. A plumber's friend operates by

    A. oscillation of water and air in the pipe
    B. density of water and pressure
    C. snake action
    D. water pressure *only*

18. Compound is applied to pipe thread.
    When threading pipe, where would you apply compound?

    A. Male and female thread
    B. Female *only*
    C. Male *only*
    D. At the end of the male connection *only*

19. In reference to domestic gas piping,

    A. couplings with running threads are used to join pipes
    B. risers must have a drip leg and cap at bottom
    C. gasketed unions may be used in joining pipe
    D. composition disc globe valves are used to throttle the gas

20. In the sketch at the right, the measurement of the inside diameter is MOST NEARLY _____ inches.

    A. 2 1/2
    B. 3
    C. 3 1/2
    D. 4

21. The FIRST item which should be checked when a sump pit overflows because the automatic electric sump pump is not operating properly is the

    A. feedwater pressure
    B. ficat switch mechanism
    C. stat switch
    D. discharge line check valve

22. The plumbing fixture that contains a ball cock is the

    A. trap
    B. water closet
    C. sprinkler
    D. dishwasher

23. A plumbing sketch is drawn to a scale of 1/8" = 1 foot. A horizontal water line measuring 6 3/4 inches on the sketch would be equivalent to _____ feet of water pipe.

    A. 27   B. 41   C. 54   D. 64

24. The tool that holds the die when threading a 2" pipe is called a

    A. yoke   B. punch   C. vise   D. stock

25. The type of valve that permits fluid to flow in one direction ONLY in a pipe run is a _____ valve.

    A. check   B. gate   C. globe   D. cross

KEY (CORRECT ANSWERS)

1. C		11. A	
2. A		12. D	
3. B		13. B	
4. B		14. C	
5. B		15. D	
6. D		16. C	
7. A		17. A	
8. A		18. C	
9. A		19. B	
10. B		20. B	

21. B
22. B
23. C
24. D
25. A

EXAMINATION SECTION
TEST 1

DIRECTIONS: Each question or incomplete statement is followed by several suggested answers or completions. Select the one that BEST answers the question or completes the statement. *PRINT THE LETTER OF THE CORRECT ANSWER IN THE SPACE AT THE RIGHT.*

1. The combustion efficiency of a boiler can be determined with a CO_2 indicator and the   1.____

    A. under fire draft
    B. boiler room humidity
    C. flue gas temperature
    D. outside air temperature

2. A quick, practical method of determining if the cast-iron waste pipe delivered to a job has been damaged in transit is to   2.____

    A. hydraulically test it
    B. "ring" each length with a hammer
    C. drop each length to see whether it breaks
    D. visually examine the pipe for cracks

3. An electrostatic precipitator is used to   3.____

    A. filter the air supply
    B. remove sludge from the fuel oil
    C. remove particles from the fuel gas
    D. supply samples for an Orsat analysis

4. The PRIMARY cause of cracking and spalling of refractory lining in the furnace of a steam generator is *most likely* due to   4.____

    A. continuous over-firing of boiler
    B. slag accumulation on furnace walls
    C. change in fuel from solid to liquid
    D. uneven heating and cooling within the refractory brick

5. The term "effective temperature" in air conditioning means   5.____

    A. the dry bulb temperature
    B. the average of the wet and dry bulb temperatures
    C. the square root of the product of wet and dry bulb temperatures
    D. an arbitrary index combining the effects of temperature, humidity, and movement

6. The piping in all buildings having dual water distribution systems should be identified by a color coding of _____ for potable water lines and _____ for non-potable water lines.   6.____

    A. green; red
    B. green; yellow
    C. yellow; green
    D. yellow; red

7. The breaking of a component of a machine subjected to excessive vibration is called   7.____

    A. tensile failure
    B. fatigue failure
    C. caustic embrittlement
    D. amplitude failure

8. The TWO MOST important factors to be considered in selecting fans for ventilating systems are

   A. noise and efficiency
   B. space available and weight
   C. first cost and dimensional bulk
   D. construction and arrangement of drive

9. In the modern power plant deaerator, air is removed from water to

   A. reduce heat losses in the heaters
   B. reduce corrosion of boiler steel due to the air
   C. reduce the load of the main condenser air pumps
   D. prevent pumps from becoming vapor bound

10. The abbreviations BOD, COD, and DO are associated with

    A. flue gas analysis
    B. air pollution control
    C. boiler water treatment
    D. water pollution control

11. The piping of a newly installed drainage system should be tested upon completion of the rough plumbing with a head of water of NOT LESS THAN _____ feet.

    A. 10   B. 15   C. 20   D. 25

12. Of the following statements concerning aquastats, the one which is CORRECT is:

    A. Aquastats may be obtained with either a narrow or wide range of settings
    B. Aquastats have a mercury tube switch which is controlled by the stack switch
    C. An aquastat is a device used to shut down the burner in the event of low water in the boiler
    D. An aquastat should be located about 4 inches above the normal water line of the boiler

13. The SAFEST way to protect the domestic water supply from contamination by sewage or non-potable water is to insert

    A. air gaps
    B. swing connections
    C. double check valves
    D. tanks with overhead discharge

14. The MAIN function of a back-pressure valve which is sometimes found in the connection between a water drain pipe and the sewer system is to

    A. equalize the pressure between the drain pipe and the sewer
    B. prevent sewer water from flowing into the drain pipe
    C. provide pressure to enable waste to reach the sewer
    D. make sure that there is not too much water pressure in the sewer line

15. Boiler water is neutral if its pH value is

    A. 0   B. 1   C. 7   D. 14

16. A domestic hot water mixing or tempering valve should be preceded in the hot water line by a

    A. strainer
    B. foot valve
    C. check valve
    D. steam trap

16._____

17. Between a steam boiler and its safety valve there should be

    A. no valve of any type
    B. a gate valve of the same size as the safety valve
    C. a swing check valve of at least the same size as the safety valve
    D. a cock having a clear opening equal in area to the pipe connecting the boiler and safety valve

17._____

18. A diagram of horizontal plumbing drainage lines should have cleanouts shown

    A. at least every 25 feet
    B. at least every 100 feet
    C. wherever a basin is located
    D. wherever a change in direction occurs

18._____

19. When a Bourdon gauge is used to measure steam pressures, some form of siphon or water seal must be maintained.
The reason for this is to

    A. obtain "absolute" pressure readings
    B. prevent steam from entering the gage
    C. prevent condensate from entering the gage
    D. obtain readings below atmospheric pressure

19._____

20. In a closed heat exchanger, oil is cooled by condensate which is to be returned to a boiler. In order to avoid the possibility of contaminating the condensate with oil should a tube fail in the oil cooler, it would be good practice to

    A. cool the oil by air instead of water
    B. treat the condensate with an oil solvent
    C. keep the oil pressure in the exchanger higher than the water pressure
    D. keep the water pressure in the exchanger higher than the oil pressure

20._____

21. A radiator thermostatic trap is used on a vacuum return type of heating system to

    A. release the pocketed air only
    B. reduce the amount of condensate
    C. maintain a predetermined radiator water level
    D. prevent the return of live steam to the return line

21._____

22. According to the color coding of piping, fire protection piping should be painted

    A. green   B. yellow   C. purple   D. red

22._____

23. The MAIN purpose of a standpipe system is to

    A. supply the roof water tank
    B. provide water for firefighting

23._____

C. circulate water for the heating system
D. provide adequate pressure for the water supply

24. The name "Saybolt" is associated with the measurement of

    A. viscosity   B. Btu content
    C. octane rating   D. temperature

25. Recirculation of conditioned air in an air-conditioned building is done MAINLY to

    A. reduce refrigeration tonnage required
    B. increase room entrophy
    C. increase air specific humidity
    D. reduce room temperature below the dewpoint

26. In a plumbing installation, vent pipes are GENERALLY used to

    A. prevent the loss of water seal from traps by evaporation
    B. prevent the loss of water seal due to several causes other than evaporation
    C. act as an additional path for liquids to flow through during normal use of a plumbing fixture
    D. prevent the backflow of water in a cross-connection between a drinking water line and a sewage line

27. The designation "150 W" cast on the bonnet of a gate valve is an indication of the

    A. water working temperature
    B. water working pressure
    C. area of the opening in square inches
    D. weight of the valve in pounds

28. In the city, the size soil pipe necessary in a sewage drainage system is determined by the

    A. legal occupancy of the building
    B. vertical height of the soil line
    C. number of restrooms connected to the soil line
    D. number of "fixture units" connected to the soil line

29. Fins or other extended surfaces are used on heat exchanger tubes when

    A. the exchanger is a water-to-water exchanger
    B. water is on one side of the tube and condensing steam on the other side
    C. the surface coefficient of heat transfer on both sides of the tube is high
    D. the surface coefficient of heat transfer on one side of the tube is low compared to the coefficient on the other side of the tube

30. A fusible plug may be put in a fire tube boiler as an emergency device to indicate low water level. The fusible plug is installed so that under normal operating conditions,

    A. both sides are exposed to steam
    B. one side is exposed to water and the other side to steam
    C. one side is exposed to steam and the other side to hot gases
    D. one side is exposed to the water and the other side to hot gases

31. Extra strong wrought-iron pipe, as compared to standard wrought-iron pipe of the same nominal size, has

    A. the same outside diameter but a smaller inside diameter
    B. the same inside diameter but a larger outside diameter
    C. a larger outside diameter and a smaller inside diameter
    D. larger inside and outside diameters

32. Fans may be rated on a dynamic or a static efficiency basis. The dynamic efficiency would *probably* be

    A. lower in value because of the energy absorbed by the air velocity
    B. the same as the static in the case of centrifugal blowers running at various speeds
    C. the same as the static in the case of axial flow blowers running at various speeds
    D. higher in value than the static

33. The function of the stack relay in an oil burner installation is to

    A. regulate the draft over the fire
    B. regulate the flow of fuel oil to the burner
    C. stop the motor if the oil has not ignited
    D. stop the motor if the water or steam pressure is too high

34. The type of centrifugal pump which is inherently balanced for hydraulic thrust is the

    A. double suction impeller type
    B. single suction impeller type
    C. single stage type
    D. multistage type

35. The specifications for a job using sheet lead calls for "4-lb. sheet lead." This means that each sheet should weigh

    A. 4 lbs.
    B. 4 lbs. per square
    C. 4 lbs. per square foot
    D. 4 lbs. per cubic inch

36. The total cooling load design conditions for a building are divided for convenience into two components.
    These are:

    A. infiltration and radiation
    B. sensible heat and latent heat
    C. wet and dry bulb temperatures
    D. solar heat gain and moisture transfer

37. The function of a Hartford loop used on some steam boilers is to

    A. limit boiler steam pressure
    B. limit temperature of the steam
    C. prevent high water levels in the boiler
    D. prevent back flow of water from the boiler into the return main

38. Vibration from a ventilating blower can be prevented from being transmitted to the duct work by

   A. installing straighteners in the duct
   B. throttling the air supply to the blower
   C. bolting the blower tightly to the duct
   D. installing a canvas sleeve at the blower outlet

39. A specification states that access panels to suspended ceiling will be of metal. The MAIN reason for providing access panels is to

   A. improve the insulation of the ceiling
   B. improve the appearance of the ceiling
   C. make it easier to construct the building
   D. make it easier to maintain the building

40. A plumber on a job reports that the steamfitter has installed a 3" steam line in a location at which the plans show the house trap. On inspecting the job, you should

   A. tell the steamfitter to remove the steam line
   B. study the condition to see if the house trap can be relocated
   C. tell the plumber and steamfitter to work it out between themselves and then report to you
   D. tell the plumber to find another location for the trap because the steamfitter has already completed his work

41. In the installation of any heating system, the MOST important consideration is that

   A. all elements be made of a good grade of cast iron
   B. all radiators and connectors be mounted horizontally
   C. the smallest velocity of flow of heating medium be used
   D. there be proper clearance between hot surfaces and surrounding combustible material

42. Which one of the following is the PRIMARY object in drawing up a set of specifications for materials to be purchased?

   A. Control of quality
   B. Outline of intended use
   C. Establishment of standard sizes
   D. Location and method of inspection.

43. The drawing which should be used as a LEGAL reference when checking completed construction work is the _____ drawing.

   A. contract
   B. assembly
   C. working or shop
   D. preliminary

Questions 44-50.

DIRECTIONS: Questions 44 through 50 refer to the plumbing drawing shown below.

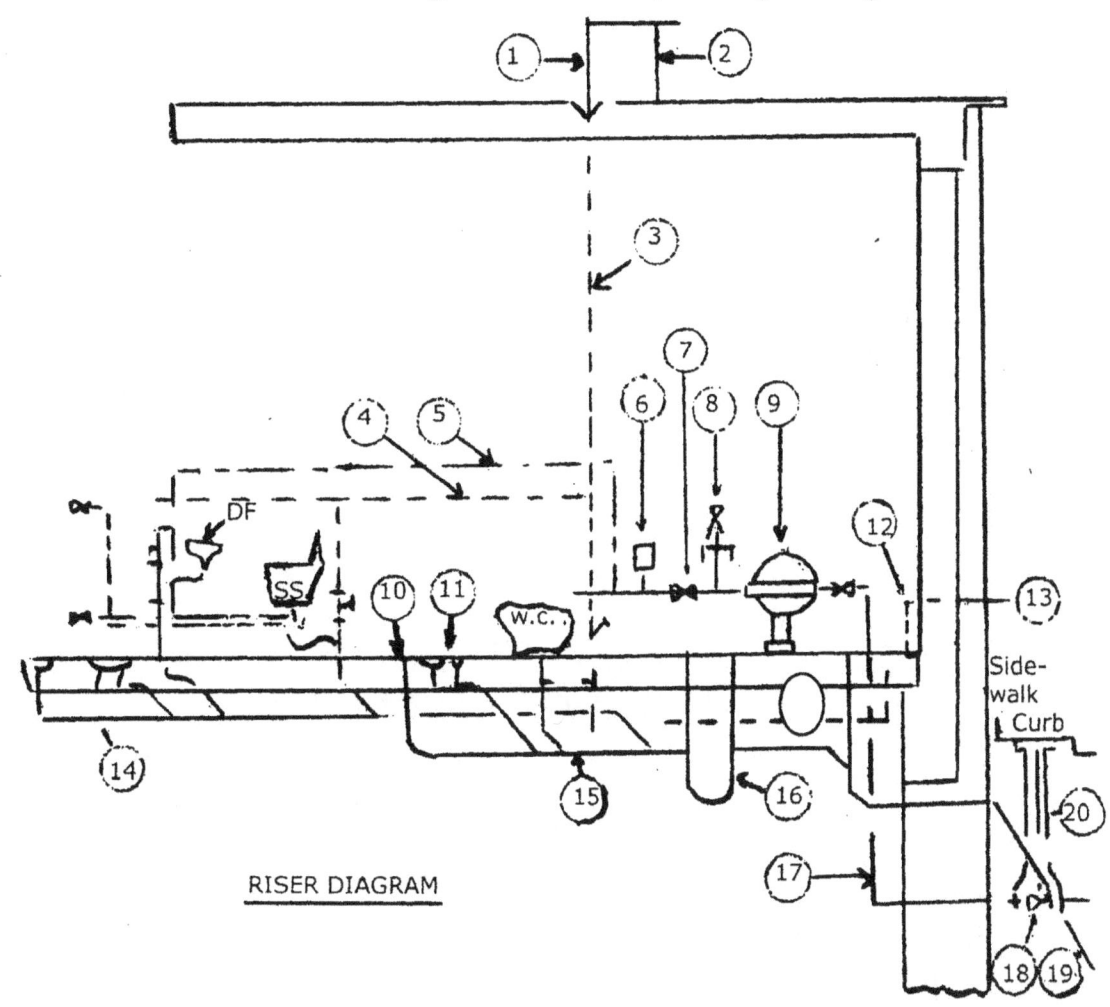

RISER DIAGRAM

44. According to the building code, the MINIMUM diameter of No. 1 and its minimum height, No. 2 respectively, are

    A. 2" and 12"   B. 3" and 18"
    C. 4" and 24"   D. 6" and 36"

44.____

45. No 6 is a

    A. relief valve   B. shock absorber
    C. testing connection   D. drain

45.____

46. No. 9 is a

    A. strainer   B. float valve
    C. meter   D. pedestal

46.____

47. No. 11 is a

    A. floor drain   B. cleanout
    C. trap   D. vent connection

47.____

48. No. 13 is a

    A. standpipe   B. air inlet
    C. sprinkler head   D. cleanout

49. The size of No. 16 is

    A. 2" x 2"   B. 2" x 3"
    C. 3" x 3"   D. 4" x 4"

50. No. 18 is a

    A. pressure reducing valve
    B. butterfly valve
    C. curb cock
    D. sprinkler head

KEY (CORRECT ANSWERS)

1. C	11. A	21. D	31. A	41. D
2. B	12. C	22. D	32. D	42. A
3. C	13. A	23. B	33. C	43. A
4. D	14. B	24. A	34. A	44. C
5. D	15. C	25. A	35. C	45. B
6. B	16. A	26. B	36. B	46. C
7. B	17. A	27. B	37. D	47. A
8. A	18. D	28. D	38. D	48. B
9. B	19. B	29. D	39. D	49. D
10. D	20. D	30. D	40. B	50. C

READING COMPREHENSION
UNDERSTANDING AND INTERPRETING WRITTEN MATERIAL
EXAMINATION SECTION
TEST 1

DIRECTIONS: Each question or incomplete statement is followed by several suggested answers or completions. Select the one that BEST answers the question or completes the statement. *PRINT THE LETTER OF THE CORRECT ANSWER IN THE SPACE AT THE RIGHT.*

Questions 1-5.

DIRECTIONS: Questions 1 through 5 are to be answered SOLELY on the basis of the following paragraph.

The strength of the seal of a trap is closely proportional to the depth of the seal, regardless of the size of the trap. Unfortunately, an increase in the depth of the seal also increases the probability of solids being retained in the trap, and a limit of about a 4" depth of seal for traps that must pass solids has been imposed by some plumbing codes. The depth of seal most commonly found in simple traps is between $1\frac{1}{2}$" and 2". The Hoover Report recommends a minimum depth of 2" as a safeguard against seal rupture and a maximum depth of 4" to avoid clogging, fungus growths, and similar difficulties. Traps in rain-water leaders and other pipes carrying clear-water wastes only, and which are infrequently used, should have seal depths equal to or greater than 4". The increase in the volume of water retained in the trap helps very little in increasing the strength of the seal, but it does materially reduce the velocity of flow through the trap so as to increase the probability of the sedimentation of solids therein.

1. In accordance with the above, it may be said that traps carrying rain-water should have a seal of   1._____

   A. 5"   B. $3\frac{1}{2}$"   C. 2"   D. $1\frac{1}{2}$"

2. In accordance with the preceding paragraph, which one of the following statements is MOST NEARLY correct?   2._____

   A. Simple traps have a depth of seal between $1\frac{1}{2}$" to 4".
   B. A minimum depth of 4" is recommended to avoid seal rupture.
   C. The strength of the seal is proportional to the size of the trap.
   D. The higher the depth of seal, the more chance of collecting solids.

3. In accordance with the above, it may be said that increasing the volume of water retained in a trap may

   A. *greatly* increase the velocity of flow
   B. *slightly* increase the velocity of flow
   C. *greatly* increase the trap seal
   D. *slightly* increase the trap seal

4. Of the following, the title which BEST explains the main idea of this paragraph is

   A. TRAP SEAL DEPTHS
   B. THE EFFECTS OF SEDIMENTATION ON TRAP SEALS
   C. COMMON TRAP SIZES
   D. TRAP SIZES AND VELOCITY OF FLOW

5. Assume that the strength of a trap seal is indicated by 8 units when the trap depth is 2". In accordance with the above paragraph, increasing the depth of seal to 4" will cause the strength of the trap seal to be MOST NEARLY _____ units.

   A. 2   B. 4   C. 8   D. 16

Questions 6-10.

DIRECTIONS: Questions 6 through 10 are to be answered SOLELY on the basis of the following paragraph.

The thickness of insulation necessary for the most economical results varies with the steam temperature. The standard covering consists of 85 percent magnesia with 10 percent of long-fibre asbestos as a binder. Both magnesia and laminated asbestos—felt and other forms of mineral wool including glass wool—are also used for heat insulation. The magnesia and laminated asbestos coverings may be safely used at temperatures up to 600° F. Pipe insulation is applied in molded sections 3 feet long. The sections are attached to the pipe by means of galvanized iron wire or netting. Flanges and fittings can be insulated by direct application of magnesia cement to the metal without reinforcement. Insulation should always be maintained in good condition because it saves fuel. Routine maintenance of warm-pipe insulation should include prompt repair of damaged surfaces. Steam and hot water leaks concealed by insulation will be difficult to detect. Underground steam or hotwater pipes are best insulated using a concrete trench with removable cover.

6. The word *reinforcement*, as used above, means MOST NEARLY

   A. resistance   B. strengthening
   C. regulation   D. removal

7. According to the above paragraph, magnesia and laminated-asbestos coverings may be safely used at temperatures up to

   A. 800° F   B. 720° F   C. 675° F   D. 600° F

8. According to the above paragraph, insulation should ALWAYS be maintained in good condition because it

   A. is laminated   B. saves fuel
   C. is attached to the pipe D. prevents leaks

9. According to the above paragraph, pipe insulation sections are attached to the pipe by means of

   A. binders
   B. mineral wool
   C. netting
   D. staples

10. According to the above paragraph, a leak in a hot-water pipe may be difficult to detect because when insulation is used, the leak is

    A. underground
    B. hidden
    C. routine
    D. cemented

Questions 11-15.

DIRECTIONS: Questions 11 through 15 are to be answered SOLELY on the basis of the following paragraph.

Reductions in pipe size of a building heating system are made with eccentric fittings and are pitched downward. The ends of mains with gravity return shall be at least 18" above the water line of the boiler. As condensate flows opposite to the stream, runouts are one size larger than the vertical pipe and are pitched upward. In a one-pipe system, an automatic air vent must be provided at each main to relieve air pressure and to let steam enter the radiator. As steam enters the radiator, a thermal device causes the vent to close, thereby holding the steam. Steam mains should not be less than two inches in diameter. The end of the steam main should have a minimum size of one-half of its greatest diameter. Small steam systems should be sized for a 2 oz. pressure drop. Large steam systems should be sized for a 4 oz. pressure drop.

11. The word *thermal,* as used in the above paragraph, means MOST NEARLY

    A. convector   B. heat   C. instrument   D. current

12. According to the above paragraph, the one of the following that is one size larger than the vertical pipe is the

    A. steam main
    B. valve
    C. water line
    D. runout

13. According to the above paragraph, small steam systems should be sized for a pressure drop of _____ ounces.

    A. 2   B. 3   C. 4   D. 5

14. According to the above paragraph, ends of mains with gravity return shall be AT LEAST

    A. 18" above the water line of the boiler
    B. one-quarter of the greatest diameter of the main
    C. twice the size of the vertical pipe in the main
    D. 18" above the steam line of the boiler

15. According to the above paragraph, the one of the following that is provided at each main to relieve air pressure is a(n)

    A. gravity return
    B. convector
    C. eccentric
    D. vent

Questions 16-17.

DIRECTIONS: Questions 16 and 17 are to be answered SOLELY on the basis of the following paragraph.

In determining the size of a storm drain, a number of factors must be taken into consideration. One factor which makes sizing the storm drain difficult is the matter of predicting rainfall over a given period. Using a maximum estimate of about 1 inch of rain in a 10-minute interval, the approximate volume of water that will fall on a roof or surface in one minute's time can be determined readily. Another factor is the pitch and material of a roof or surface upon which the rain falls. A surface that has a pitch and smooth surface would increase the flow of water into a drain pipe.

16. According to the above paragraph, the statement which includes all factors needed to determine the size of a drain pipe is the

    A. maximum rainfall on a surface
    B. pitch and surface of the area
    C. amount of water to be piped in a definite time interval
    D. area of the surface

17. A roof that has a 45° pitch would PROBABLY have a drain pipe size

    A. smaller than a roof with no pitch
    B. larger than a roof with no pitch
    C. equal to that of a flat roof
    D. equal to the amount of water falling in ten minutes

Questions 18-19.

DIRECTIONS: Questions 18 and 19 are to be answered SOLELY on the basis of the following paragraph.

Because of the large capacity of unit heaters, care should be taken to see that the steam piping leading to them is of sufficient size. Unit heaters should not be used on one-pipe systems. If the heating system contains direct radiators operated with steam under vacuum, it is best to have the unit heaters served by a separate main so that steam above atmospheric pressure can be supplied to the units, if desired, without interfering with the operation of the direct radiators.

18. According to the above paragraph, unit heaters are supplied with

    A. steam under vacuum
    B. steam from direct radiators
    C. separate steam lines
    D. steam preferably from a one-pipe system

19. According to the above paragraph, it may be said that unit heaters work BEST with

    A. steam above atmospheric pressure   B. direct radiators
    C. one-pipe system   D. vacuum systems

Questions 20-21.

DIRECTIONS: Questions 20 and 21 are to be answered SOLELY on the basis of the following paragraph.

Most heating units emit heat by radiation and convection. An exposed radiator emits approximately half of its heat by radiation, the amount depending upon the size and number of sections. In general, a thin radiator, such as a wall radiator, emits a larger proportion of its heat by radiation than does a thick radiator. When a radiator is enclosed or shielded, the proportion of heat emitted by radiation is reduced. The balance of the emission occurs by conduction to the air in contact with the heating surface, and this heated air rises by circulation due to convection and transmits this warm air to the space which is to be heated.

20. According to the above paragraph, when a radiator is enclosed, a GREATER portion of the heat is emitted to the room by

 A. convection
 B. radiation
 C. conduction
 D. transmission

21. According to the above paragraph, the amount of heat that a radiator emits is

 A. approximately half of its heat by radiation
 B. determined by the thickness of the radiator
 C. dependent upon whether it is exposed or enclosed
 D. dependent upon the size and number of sections of the radiator

Questions 22-25.

DIRECTIONS: Questions 22 through 25 are to be answered SOLELY on the basis of the following paragraph.

Safety valves are required to operate without chattering and to be set to close after blowing down not more than 4% of the set pressure, but not less than 2 lbs. in any case. For pressure between 100 and 300 lbs., inclusive, the blow down is required to be not less than 2% of the set pressure. The blow down adjustment is made and sealed by the manufacturer. The popping-point tolerance plus or minus is required not to exceed 2 lbs. for pressure up to and including 70 lbs., 3 lbs. for pressure 71 to 300 lbs., and 10 lbs. for pressure over 300 lbs.

22. A boiler is being installed to operate at a maximum allowable pressure of 10 lb., and the safety valve has been set to blow at this pressure.
 This valve should close after the boiler blows down to NOT MORE THAN _____ lb.

 A. 9.6　　B. 4.0　　C. 9.8　　D. 8.0

23. A boiler is being installed to operate at a maximum allowable working pressure of 300 lb., and the safety valve is set to blow at this pressure. This valve should close after the boiler blows down to NOT MORE THAN _____ lb.

 A. 204　　B. 298　　C. 12　　D. 6

6 (#1)

24. A sealed safety valve is to be installed on a superheater header in a power steam generating plant. The marking on this valve shows that it is set to pop at 425 lb.
This valve would operate satisfactorily if it popped at EITHER _____ or _____ lb.

    A. 425; 445   B. 415; 435
    C. 372.5; 467.5   D. 412.25; 437.75

25. A sealed safety valve is to be installed on a boiler in a high pressure steam generating station. The marking on the valve shows that it is set to pop at 300 lb.
This valve would operate satisfactorily if it popped at EITHER _____ or _____ lb.

    A. 290; 310   B. 297; 303
    C. 291; 309   D. 288; 312

KEY (CORRECT ANSWERS)

1.	A	11.	B
2.	D	12.	D
3.	D	13.	A
4.	A	14.	A
5.	D	15.	D
6.	B	16.	C
7.	D	17.	B
8.	B	18.	C
9.	C	19.	A
10.	B	20.	A

21. D
22. D
23. A
24. B
25. B

TEST 2

DIRECTIONS: Each question or incomplete statement is followed by several suggested answers or completions. Select the one that BEST answers the question or completes the statement. *PRINT THE LETTER OF THE CORRECT ANSWER IN THE SPACE AT THE RIGHT.*

Questions 1-6.

DIRECTIONS: Questions 1 through 6 are to be answered SOLELY on the basis of the following paragraph.

FIRST AID INSTRUCTIONS

The main purpose of first aid is to put the injured person in the best possible position until medical help arrives. This includes the performance of emergency treatment for the purpose of saving a life if a doctor is not present. When a person is hurt, a crowd usually gathers around the victim. If nobody uses his head, the injured person fails to get the care he needs. You must stay calm and, most important, it is your duty to take charge at an accident. The first thing for you to do is to see, as best you can, what is wrong with the injured person. Leave the victim where he is until the nature and extent of his injury are determined. If he is unconscious, he should not be moved, except to lay him flat on his back if he is in some other position. Loosen the clothing of any seriously hurt person, and make him as comfortable as possible. Medical help should be called as soon as possible. You should remain with the injured person and send someone else to call the doctor. You should try to make sure that the one who calls for a doctor is able to give correct information as to the location of the injured person. In order to help the physician to know what equipment may be needed in each particular case, the person making the call should give the doctor as much information about the injury as possible.

1. If nobody uses his head at the scene of an accident, there is danger that   1._____

    A. no one will get the names of all the witnesses
    B. a large crowd will gather
    C. the victim will not get the care he needs
    D. the victim will blame the city for negligence

2. When an accident occurs, the FIRST thing you should do is   2._____

    A. call a doctor
    B. loosen the clothing of the injured person
    C. notify the victim's family
    D. try to find out what is wrong with the injured person

3. If you do NOT know the extent and nature of the victim's injuries, you should   3._____

    A. let the injured person lie where he is
    B. immediately take the victim to a hospital yourself
    C. help the injured person to his feet to see if he can walk
    D. have the injured person sit up on the ground while you examine him

4. If the injured person is breathing and unconscious, you should　　　　　　　　　　　　　　　　　　　　　4.___

   A. get some hot liquid such as coffee or tea into him
   B. give him artificial respiration
   C. lift up his head to try to stimulate blood circulation
   D. see that he lies flat on his back

5. If it is necessary to call a doctor, you should　　　　　　　　　　　　　　　　　　　　　　　　　　　　5.___

   A. go and make the call yourself since you have all the information
   B. find out who the victim's family doctor is before making the call
   C. have someone else make the call who know the location of the victim
   D. find out which doctor the victim can afford

6. It is important for the caller to give the doctor as much information as is available regard-　　　6.___
   ing the injury so that the doctor

   A. can bring the necessary equipment
   B. can make out an accident report
   C. will be responsible for any malpractice resulting from the first aid treatment
   D. can inform his nurse on how long he will be in the field

Questions 7-8.

DIRECTIONS:　　Questions 7 and 8 are to be answered SOLELY on the basis of the following paragraph.

PRECIPITATION AND RUNOFF

In the United States, the average annual precipitation is about 30 inches, of which about 21 inches is lost to the atmosphere by evaporation and transpiration. The remaining 9 inches becomes runoff into rivers and lakes. Both the precipitation and runoff vary greatly with geography and season. Annual precipitation varies from more than 100 inches in parts of the northwest to only 2 or 3 inches in parts of the southwest. In the northeastern part of the country, including New York State, the annual average precipitation is about 45 inches, of which about 22 inches becomes runoff. Even in New York State, there is some variation from place to place and considerable variation from time to time. During extremely dry years, the precipitation may be as low as 30 inches and the runoff below 10 inches. In general, there are greater variations in runoff rates from smaller watersheds. A critical water supply situation occurs when there are three or four abnormally dry years in succession.

Precipitation over the state is measured and recorded by a network of stations operated by the U.S. Weather Bureau. All of the precipitation records and other data such as temperature, humidity, and evaporation rates are published monthly by the Weather Bureau in *Climatological Data*. Runoff rates at more than 200 stream-gauging stations in the state are measured and recorded by the U.S. Geological Survey in cooperation with various state agencies. Records of the daily average flows are published annually by the U.S. Geological Survey in *Surface Water Records of New York*. Copies may be obtained by writing to the Water Resources Division, United States Geological Survey, Albany, New York 23301.

7. From the above paragraphs, it is APPROPRIATE to conclude that

   A. critical supply situations do not occur
   B. the greater the rainfall, the greater the runoff
   C. there are greater variations in runoff from larger watersheds
   D. the rainfall in the southwest is greater than the average in the country

8. From the above paragraphs, it is APPROPRIATE to conclude that

   A. an annual rainfall of about 50 inches does not occur in New York State
   B. the U.S. Weather Bureau is only interested in rainfall
   C. runoff is equal to rainfall less losses to the atmosphere
   D. information about rainfall and runoff in New York State is unavailable to the public

Questions 9-10.

DIRECTIONS: Questions 9 through 10 are to be answered SOLELY on the basis of the following paragraph.

NATURAL LAKES

Large lakes may yield water of exceptionally fine quality except near the shore line and in the vicinity of sewer outlets or near outlets of large streams. Therefore, minimum treatment is required. The availability of practically unlimited quantities of water is also a decided advantage. Unfortunately, however, the sewage from a city is often discharged into the same lake from which the water supply is taken. Great care must be taken in locating both the water intake and the sewer outlet so that the pollution handled by the water treatment plant is a minimum.

Sometimes the distance from the shore where dependable, satisfactory water can be found is so great that the cost of water intake facilities is prohibitive for a small municipality. In such cases, another supply must be found, or water must be obtained from a neigh-boring large city. Lake water is usually uniform in quality from day to day and does not vary in temperature as much as water from a river or small impounding reservoir.

9. A DISADVANTAGE of drawing a water supply from a large lake is that

   A. expensive treatment is required
   B. a limited quantity of water is available
   C. nearby cities may dump sewage into the lake
   D. the water is too cold

10. An ADVANTAGE of drawing a water supply from a large lake is that the

    A. water is uniform in quality
    B. water varies in temperature
    C. intake is distant from the shore
    D. intake may be near a sewer outlet

Questions 11-13.

DIRECTIONS: Questions 11 through 13 are to be answered SOLELY on the basis of the following paragraph.

Excavation of trench—The trench shall be excavated as directed; one side of the street or avenue shall be left open for traffic at all times. In paved streets, the length of trench that may be opened between the point where the backfilling has been completed and the point where the pavement is being removed shall not exceed fifteen hundred feet for pipes 24 inches or less in diameter. For pipes larger than 24-inch, the length of open trenches shall not exceed one thousand feet. The completion of the backfilling shall be interpreted to mean the backfilling of the trench and the consolidation of the backfill so that vehicular traffic can be resumed over the backfill, and also the placing of any temporary pavement that may be required.

11. According to the above paragraph, the street

    A. can be closed to traffic in emergencies
    B. can be closed to traffic only when laying more than 1500 feet of pipe
    C. is closed to traffic as directed
    D. shall be left open for traffic at all times

12. According to the above paragraph, the MAXIMUM length of open trench permitted in paved streets depends on the

    A. traffic on the street
    B. type of ground that is being excavated
    C. water conditions met with in excavation
    D. diameter of the pipe being laid

13. According to the above paragraph, the one of the following items that is included in the *completion of the backfilling* is

    A. sheeting and bracing   B. cradle
    C. temporary pavement   D. bridging

Questions 14-16.

DIRECTIONS: Questions 14 through 16 are to be answered SOLELY on the basis of the following paragraph.

The Contractor shall notify the Engineer by noon of the day immediately preceding the date when he wishes to shut down any main; and if the time set be approved, the Contractor shall provide the men necessary to shut down the main at the time stipulated, and to previously notify all consumers whose supply may be affected. These men shall be under the direction of the Department employees, who will superintend all operations of valves and hydrants. Shutdowns for making connections will not be made unless and until the Contractor has everything on the ground in readiness for the work.

14. According to the above paragraph, before a contractor can make a shut-down, he MUST notify the

    A. police department   B. District Foreman
    C. Engineer   D. Highway Department

15. According to the above paragraph, the operation of the valves will be supervised by the   15._____

    A. Department employees
    B. Contractor's men
    C. Contractor's superintendent
    D. Engineer

16. According to the above paragraph, shut-downs for connections are made   16._____

    A. the day before the connection is to be made
    B. first and then consumers are notified
    C. at any time convenient to the Contractor
    D. when the Contractor has everything on the ground in readiness for the work

Questions 17-22.

DIRECTIONS: Questions 17 through 22 are to be answered SOLELY on the basis of the following paragraphs.

HOT WATER GENERATION

The hot water that comes from a faucet is called Domestic Hot Water. It is heated by a steam coil that runs through a storage tank full of water in the basement of each building.

As the tenants take the hot water, fresh cold water enters the tank and is heated. The temperature of this water is automatically kept at approximately 140° F.

The device which controls the temperature is called a temperature regulator valve. It is operated by a bellows, capillary tube, and thermo bulb which connects between the valve and the hot water being stored in the tank. This bulb, tube, and bellows contains a liquid which expands and contracts with changes in temperatures.

As the water in the tank reaches 140° F, the liquid in the thermo bulb expands and causes pressure to travel along the capillary tube and into the bellows. The expanded liquid forces the bellows to push the Temperature Regulator Valve Stem down, closing the valve. No more steam can enter the coil in the tank, and the water will get no hotter.

As the hot water is used by the tenants, cold water enters the tank and pulls the temperature down. This causes the liquid in the thermo bulb to cool and contract (shrink). The pressure is no longer in the bellows, and a spring pushes it up, allowing the valve to open and allowing steam to again enter the heating coil in the storage tank, raising the temperature of the Domestic Hot Water to 140° F.

17. Domestic hot water is heated by   17._____

    A. coal   B. electricity
    C. hot water   D. steam

18. The temperature of domestic hot water is MOST NEARLY   18._____

    A. 75° F   B. 100° F   C. 140° F   D. 212° F

19. The temperature of the hot water is controlled by a

    A. thermometer
    B. temperature regulator valve
    C. pressuretrol
    D. pressure gauge

20. The temperature regulator valve is operated by a combination of a

    A. thermometer and a thermo bulb
    B. thermometer and a pyrometer
    C. bellows, capillary tube, and a thermometer
    D. bellows, capillary tube, and a thermo bulb

21. Closing of the temperature regulator valve prevents _____ from entering the heating coil in the tank.

    A. water
    B. steam
    C. electricity
    D. air

22. As hot water is used by the tenants, the temperature of the water in the tank

    A. increases
    B. decreases
    C. remains the same
    D. approaches 212° F

Question 23.

DIRECTIONS: Question 23 is to be answered SOLELY on the basis of the following paragraph.

Lack of service meters has a definite effect on water consumption. Metering of all services of a city should reduce consumption to about 50 percent of the consumption without meters. Although metering reduces water consumption, there is a tendency for consumption to increase gradually after all services are metered.

23. According to the above paragraph, the one of the following statements that is CORRECT is:

    A. Consumption of water is cut approximately in half by metering, but once all services are metered, the consumption then increases gradually
    B. After all services are metered, water consumption continues to decrease steadily
    C. Metering of all services reduces the consumption of water by much more than half
    D. Water consumption is not affected by metering of all services

Question 24.

DIRECTIONS: Questions 24 is to be answered SOLELY on the basis of the following paragraph.

A venturi meter operates without moving parts and hence is the simplest type of meter in use so far as its construction is concerned. It is a velocity meter, and it is suitable for measuring only high rates of flow. Rates of flow below its capacity limit are not accurately measured. It is, therefore, not suitable for use in measuring the low intermittent demand of most consumers.

24. According to the above paragraph, the flow in a pipe which would MOST accurately be measured by a venturi meter is

    A. an intermittent flow below the meter's capacity
    B. a steady flow below the meter's capacity
    C. a steady flow at the meter's capacity
    D. intermittent flows above or below capacity of the meter

Question 25.

DIRECTIONS: Question 25 is to be answered SOLELY on the basis of the following paragraph.

A house service water supply connection may be taken from the sprinkler water supply connection to the public main if the diameter of the house service water supply connection is not greater than onehalf the diameter of the sprinkler water supply connection. No shutoff valve shall be placed on the sprinkler supply line other than the main shut-off valve for the building on the street side of the house service water supply connection. If such a connection is made and if a tap also exists for the house service water supply, the tap shall be plugged.

25. According to the above paragraph, the one of the following statements that is CORRECT is:

    A. A sprinkler water supply connection should be at least twice the diameter of any house service water supply connection taken from it
    B. A shut-off valve, in addition to the main shut-off valve, is required on sprinkler supply lines on the street side of the house service water supply connection
    C. Where a house service water supply is connected to the sprinkler water supply and there is a tap for the house service water supply, the tap may remain in service
    D. A house service water supply connection may be taken off each side of the main shut-off valve of the sprinkler water supply

KEY (CORRECT ANSWERS)

1. C		11. D	
2. D		12. D	
3. A		13. C	
4. D		14. C	
5. C		15. A	
6. A		16. D	
7. B		17. D	
8. C		18. C	
9. C		19. B	
10. A		20. D	

21. B
22. B
23. A
24. C
25. A

TEST 3

DIRECTIONS: Each question or incomplete statement is followed by several suggested answers or completions. Select the one that BEST answers the question or completes the statement. *PRINT THE LETTER OF THE CORRECT ANSWER IN THE SPACE AT THE RIGHT.*

Questions 1-4.

DIRECTIONS: Questions 1 through 4 are to be answered SOLELY on the basis of the following paragraph.

    Welds in sheet metal up to 1/16 inch in thickness can be made satisfactorily by flanging the edges of the joint. The edges are prepared by turning up a very thin lip or flange along the line of the joint. The height of this flange should be equal to the thickness of the sheet being welded. The edges should be aligned so that the flanges stand up, and the joint should be tack-welded every 5 or 6 inches. Heavy angles or bars should be clamped on each side of the joint to prevent distortion or buckling. No filler metal is required for making this joint. The raised edges are quickly melted by the heat of the welding flame so as to produce an even weld bead which is nearly flush with the original sheet metal surface. By controlling the speed of welding and the motion of the flame, good fusion to the under side of the sheets can be obtained without burning through.

1. According to the above paragraph, satisfactory welds may be made in sheet metal by flanging the edges.
   The MAXIMUM thickness of metal recommended is

   A. 20 gauge   B. 18 gauge
   C. 1/16"   D. 5/64"

   1.____

2. According to the above paragraph, good fusion may be obtained without burning through of the metal by controlling the motion of the flame and the

   A. size of tip   B. speed of welding
   C. oxygen flow   D. acetylene flow

   2.____

3. According to the above paragraph, if the thickness of the metal is 1/32", then the flange height should be

   A. 1/64"   B. 1/32"   C. 1/16"   D. 1/8"

   3.____

4. According to the above paragraph, distortion in the welding of sheet metal may be prevented by

   A. controlling the speed of welding
   B. use of a flange of correct height
   C. use of proper filler metal
   D. clamping angles on each side of the joint

   4.____

Questions 5-12.

DIRECTIONS: Questions 5 through 12 are to be answered SOLELY on the basis of the Edison storage battery maintenance procedure below.

EDISON STORAGE BATTERY MAINTENANCE PROCEDURE

Take a voltage reading of each cell in the battery with a voltmeter. Any battery with two or more dead or reverse cells is to be removed and sent to the shop. All cell caps are to be opened, and the water level brought up to 2 3/4" above the plates. Any battery requiring a considerable amount of water must be called to the foreman's attention. All cell caps must be brushed clean and Edison battery oil applied to them. No batteries are to remain in service with cell caps broken or missing. The normal specific gravity reading of the solution must not be above 1.230 nor below 1.160. This reading is to be taken only on batteries which are found to be weak. Batteries with specific gravity lower than 1.160 must be sent to the shop. Be careful when disconnecting leads from the battery since a slight turn of the connecting post will result in a dead cell due to the cell plates becoming short-circuited. When disconnecting leads, use a standard Edison terminal puller. When recording defective cells, give the battery number, the car number, and the position of the cell in the battery. No. 1 cell is the cell to which the positive battery lead is connected and so on up to the last cell, No. 26, to which the negative lead is connected.

5. A normal specific gravity reading would be

   A. 1.450   B. 1.294   C. 1.200   D. 1.180

6. Batteries with below normal specific gravity reading MUST

   A. always have water added
   B. be called to the foreman's attention
   C. not be given a voltmeter test
   D. be sent to the shop

7. The battery leads are disconnected by using

   A. gas pliers
   B. Edison battery oil to free them
   C. a screwdriver to pry them off
   D. a standard Edison terminal puller

8. To completely record a defective cell, _____ required.

   A. only one identifying number is
   B. two identifying numbers are
   C. three identifying numbers are
   D. four identifying numbers are

9. A battery MUST be taken out of service if it has

   A. one dead cell   B. broken cell caps
   C. one reversed cell   D. a low water level

10. The battery water level should be brought up above the plates by _____ inches.

    A. 2.75   B. 1.370   C. 1.264   D. 0.600

11. Specific gravity readings are to be taken only on batteries which   11.___

    A. are removed from service
    B. have missing cell caps
    C. are weak
    D. have a high water level

12. Dead cells are sometimes caused by   12.___

    A. a slight turn of the connecting post
    B. taking unnecessary gravity readings
    C. adding too little battery oil
    D. adding too much water

Questions 13-14.

DIRECTIONS: Questions 13 and 14 are to be answered SOLELY on the basis of the following paragraph.

It cannot be stressed too strongly that the greatest care should be taken in handling tools. If they are handled carelessly, serious accidents may result. Many accidents can be avoided if the back of the trowel is kept clean and if the trowel is not allowed to contain too much mortar. Where there is an *excess* of mortar, some might drop or splash into the plasterer's eyes. Any mortar which is dropped onto the hands, wrists, ankles, or underclothing should be removed immediately.

13. The MAIN point of the above paragraph is that   13.___

    A. all accidents will be avoided if tools are kept clean
    B. most accidents can be avoided by the use of protective gloves
    C. many accidents are caused by careless handling of tools
    D. trowels should be kept free of mortar at all times

14. In the above paragraph, the word *excess* means MOST NEARLY   14.___

    A. surplus   B. minor   C. scant   D. short

Questions 15-18.

DIRECTIONS: Questions 15 through 18 are to be answered SOLELY on the basis of the following paragraph.

There are two unfounded ideas that must be discarded before tackling the lube-simplification job. *Oil is oil* was a common expression from the middle of the nineteenth century up to the early 1900s. Then, as the century got well underway, *the pendulum swung in a wide arc*. At present, we find many oils being used, each with supposedly special properties. The large number of lube oils used at present results from the rapid growth at the same time of machine development and oil refining. The refiner acts to market new oils for each machine developed, and the machine manufacturer feels that each new mechanical unit is different from the others and needs a special lube oil. These feelings may be well-founded, but in many cases they are based on misinformation or blind faith in certain lube oil qualities. At the present time, operators and even lube engineers are finding it tough to keep track of all the claimed properties of all the lube oils.

15. It follows from the sense of this paragraph that the idea that *oil is oil* is unfounded because

    A. it was conceived in the middle of the nineteenth century
    B. the basic and varying properties of lube oils have now been shown to exist
    C. lube oil properties, though fully known, were kept secret for economic reasons
    D. there was no need for but one basic lube oil in the latter part of the nineteenth century

16. In the above paragraph, the phrase *the pendulum swung in a wide arc* means MOST NEARLY

    A. oil refining was unable to keep up with machinery development
    B. before 1900, lube oil engineers found it difficult to keep track of lube oil characteristics
    C. the simplification of lube oils and their application was developed about 1900
    D. many different lube oils with varying characteristics were marketed

17. As indicated in this paragraph, the simplification of the characteristics and the uses of lube oils is needed because the

    A. manufacturers develop new machines to overcome competition
    B. change in process at the refineries for a new lube oil is costly
    C. present market is flooded with many so-called *special purpose* lube oils
    D. *blind faith* of the operators in lube oil qualities should be rewarded

18. A reason given for the claimed need for special lube oil, as indicated in this paragraph, is that

    A. development of new lube oils created the need for new machine units
    B. lube oil engineers developed new tests and standards
    C. basic crudes, from which lube oil is obtained, allow different refining methods
    D. newly developed machines are so very different from each other

Questions 19-22.

DIRECTIONS: Questions 19 through 22 are to be answered SOLELY on the basis of the following paragraph.

ACCIDENT PREVENTION

Many accidents and injuries can be prevented if employees learn to be more careful. The wearing of shoes with thin or badly worn soles or open toes can easily lead to foot injuries from tacks, nails, and chair and desk legs. Loose or torn clothing should not be worn near moving machinery. This is especially true of neckties, which can very easily become caught in the machine. You should not place objects so that they block or partly block hallways, corridors, or other passageways. Even when they are stored in the proper place, tools, supplies, and equipment should be carefully placed or piled so as not to fall, nor have anything stick out from a pile. Before cabinets, lockers, or ladders are moved, the tops should be cleared of anything which might injure someone or fall off. If necessary, use a dolly to move these or other bulky objects.

Despite all efforts to avoid accidents and injuries, however, some will happen. If an employee is injured, no matter how small the injury, he should report it to his supervisor and have the injury treated. A small cut that is not attended to can easily become infected and can cause more trouble than some injuries which at first seem more serious. It never pays to take chances.

19. According to the above passage, the one statement that is NOT true is that

    A. by being more careful, employees can reduce the number of accidents that happen
    B. women should wear shoes with open toes for comfort when working
    C. supplies should be piled so that nothing is sticking out from the pile
    D. if an employee sprains his wrist at work, he should tell his supervisor about it

20. According to the above passage, you should NOT wear loose clothing when you are

    A. in a corridor   B. storing tools
    C. opening cabinets   D. near moving machinery

21. According to the above passage, before moving a ladder, you should

    A. test all rungs
    B. get a dolly to carry the ladder at all times
    C. remove everything from the top of the ladder which might fall off
    D. remove your necktie

22. According to the above passage, an employee who gets a slight cut should

    A. have it treated to help prevent infection
    B. know that a slight cut becomes more easily infected than a big cut
    C. pay no attention to it as it can't become serious
    D. realize that it is more serious than any other type of injury

Questions 23-25.

DIRECTIONS: Questions 23 through 25 are to be answered SOLELY on the basis of the following paragraph.

Keeping the city operating day and night requires the services of more than 400,000 civil service workers – roughly the number of people who live in Syracuse. This huge army of specialists works at more than 2,000 different jobs. The city's civil service workers are able to do everything that needs doing to keep our city running. Their only purpose is the well-being, comfort, and safety of the citizens of the city.

23. Of the following titles, the one that MOST nearly gives the meaning of the above paragraph is

    A. CIVIL SERVICE IN SYRACUSE
    B. EVERYONE WORKS
    C. JOB VARIETY
    D. SERVING THE CITY

24. According to the above paragraph, in order to keep the city operating 24 hours a day, 24.____
    A. half of the civil service workers work days and half work nights
    B. more than 400,000 civil service workers are needed on the day shift
    C. the city needs about as many civil service workers as there are people in Syracuse
    D. the services of some people who live in Syracuse is required

25. According to the above paragraph, it is MOST reasonable to assume that in the city's civil 25.____
    service,
    A. a worker can do any job that needs doing
    B. each worker works at a different job
    C. some workers work at more than one job
    D. some workers work at the same jobs

KEY (CORRECT ANSWERS)

1.	C	11.	C
2.	B	12.	A
3.	B	13.	C
4.	D	14.	A
5.	C	15.	B
6.	D	16.	D
7.	D	17.	C
8.	C	18.	D
9.	B	19.	B
10.	A	20.	D

21. C
22. A
23. D
24. C
25. D

EXAMINATION SECTION
TEST 1

DIRECTIONS: Each question or incomplete statement is followed by several suggested answers or completions. Select the one that BEST answers the question or completes the statement. *PRINT THE LETTER OF THE CORRECT ANSWER IN THE SPACE AT THE RIGHT.*

1. It is the policy of the department to hold each inspector responsible for formal work assignments given to him.
   Of the following, the BEST reason for this is that it
   A. enables division personnel to keep track of the work schedule
   B. encourages inspectors to be careful with written documents
   C. increases the speed with which inspections are carried out
   D. provides a double check on the time sheet records of inspectors

2. Assume that you are faced with delays caused by absences of team members due to illness.
   Of the following, the BEST means of handling this problem is to
   A. have your team members keep an accurate record of their absences so that you will be able to identify anyone who is becoming accident-prone
   B. insist on prompt notification at all times when someone on your tea is absent because of illness
   C. require that your team members submit a memorandum informing you of the days on which they will be absent
   D. take over all tasks assigned to your team members when they are absent

3. Assume that one of the men on your team tells you that he has a problem and would like to discuss it with you privately. During the course of this meeting, it becomes apparent that the man's difficulty stems from conflicts he is having with his wife.
   Of the following, the BEST course of action that you, his supervisor, should take in this situation is to
   A. advise the employee to meet with your superior, who might be able to give him more objective advice
   B. gather enough facts to advise the man about definite solutions for his problem
   C. help the man analyze what the problem is but leave the decision to him
   D. tell the man that you can talk to him only about problems that are job-related

4. Sometimes it may be advantageous for a senior inspector to let the inspectors under his supervision participate in the development of decisions that must be made about the team's activities.
   The one of the following that is LEAST likely to result when team members participate in supervisory decisions is that the inspectors may

A. be able to show leadership
B. have a chance to feel creative
C. require closer supervision
D. take more responsibility for minor problems

5. Of the following, the CHIEF reason that the senior inspector should take disciplinary measures as soon as possible after a subordinate inspector's violation of department rules is that
    A. delay will make the senior inspector seem lax
    B. the inspector is more likely to accept the discipline a justified
    C. the supervisor may forget about the offense
    D. there is less likelihood that other inspectors will find out about the offense

5.____

6. Assume that you have been directed to institute a new procedure for writing reports about violations encountered during the inspections conducted by the team of which you are in charge. You have heard, through the grapevine, that several of the experienced inspectors on the team have objections to this new procedure.
Of the following, the BEST course of action for you to take FIRST in this situation is to
    A. issue a written order to put the new procedure into effect
    B. meet with all the inspectors on your team to discuss the procedure
    C. modify the procedure to make it acceptable to all of your inspectors
    D. postpone institution of the new procedure

6.____

7. Assume that the head of your unit expects to be out for a week because of illness. You are to act as head of the unit for that time.
In determining what to do about those inspection duties that you were originally scheduled to perform and which should not be postponed, it would be MOST advisable to
    A. assign them to the inspector who needs training in this area
    B. assign them to the inspector with the most seniority
    C. attempt to do as many of them as possible yourself
    D. divide them among all inspectors who have the time and ability

7.____

8. The one of the following situations that is LEAST likely to result from poor planning and organization of an inspection unit's work is that
    A. inspectors will be uncertain about their responsibilities
    B. job performance will be poor
    C. the work will be completed at a steady monotonous pace
    D. there will be a high turnover rate in the unit's staff

8.____

9. Of the following, the BEST course of action to take in order to avoid charges of favoritism when making job assignments is to
    A. delegate the authority to make assignments to a well-liked experienced inspector
    B. keep records which may demonstrate proper distribution and rotation of assignments

9.____

C. select the oldest inspectors for the most desirable assignments
D. tell the men that, if they have any gripes about their assignments, they should see the supervising inspector

10. Of the following, the MOST important reason for a senior inspector to receive communications from the supervising inspector before they are transmitted to the inspectors is that he can
    A. avoid discussing communications with his subordinates
    B. exercises close supervision over every detail of the inspectors' assignments
    C. limit the amount of information received by his subordinates
    D. maintains his position in the chain of command

10.____

11. If an organization has rules that are clear but excessively detailed and rigid, the one of the following which is MOST likely to occur is that
    A. employees will tend to ignore the rules
    B. records of performance will be more difficult to maintain
    C. supervisors will have more difficulty in applying the rules to individual situations
    D. use of individual judgment and discretion will be decreased

11.____

12. An effective senior inspector strives to build up the feeling that he and his men are on the same team. The imposition of discipline may serious endanger the relationship built up between him and his men.
    The one of the following steps that the senior inspector may take to insure that the imposition of discipline will NOT cause any deterioration of his relationship with his subordinates is to
    A. avoid disciplinary action, except for very serious offenses
    B. delegate simple disciplinary problems to a competent, experienced inspector
    C. discipline his men in groups so that they will feel as if they were part of a team
    D. impose discipline in as impersonal way as possible

12.____

13. Suppose that one of the inspectors under the supervision of a senior inspector is repeatedly late for work. Despite the inspector's habitual lateness, he manages to complete his work assignments on schedule.
    Of the following, the MOST advisable action for the senior inspector to take in this situation is to
    A. ask one of the other inspectors to speak to him about his attendance
    B. ignore the inspector's habitual lateness as long as he does his work properly
    C. reprimand the inspector privately and follow through to see whether his attendance improves
    D. tell him in the presence of the other inspectors that he must improve his attendance record

13.____

14. Assume that you are informed by your superior that all reports prepared by your team should be checked by you when possible before their submission to a supervising inspector.
    Of the following, the BEST course of action to take if you are too busy to look at all these reports and they have to be sent out right away is to
    A. delegate the responsibility for checking the reports to someone you have carefully instructed in the need for neat and accurate reports
    B. request additional staff from another unit to help you review these reports
    C. send the reports out without checking them and attach an explanatory note, telling your superior that you have not had time to look at them
    D. tell our men to review one another's reports and initial them

15. Assume that a senior inspector notices that another senior inspector divides his team's workload in what seems to him to be an inefficient manner. He decides to report this to the supervising inspector.
    Of the following, an accurate evaluation of the action taken by the senior inspector in this situation is that it is GENERALLY
    A. *good* practice, mainly because the supervising inspector is the only person authorized to make this senior inspector divide the work according to standard procedure
    B. *good* practice, mainly because the senior inspector needs close supervision to adequately carry out his responsibilities
    C. *poor* practice, mainly because the senior inspector should have consulted other senior inspectors about this situation
    D. *poor* practice, mainly because the senior inspector should understand that other senior inspectors may manage their operations differently

16. Assume that you have heard a rumor that department rules are about to be changed in a manner which will make certain types of inspections more complicated.
    Of the following, the BEST action for you to take in this situation is to
    A. ask the members of your staff, individually, if they have heard such a rumor
    B. call a meeting of your staff to tell them such a change is rumored
    C. make plans to change your unit's procedures to adapt to the new methods
    D. await official confirmation or denial of the rumor

17. Assume that one of the inspectors under your supervision has been doing an excellent job but no longer seems to have any interest in the work. He complains to you that he finds the work boring.
    Of the following, the MOST advisable action for you to take FIRST is to
    A. ask some of his fellow inspectors to discuss the matter with him
    B. attempt to vary his assignments and give him more complex assignments
    C. remind him that his evaluation by superiors may depend in part on the interest he shows in his work
    D. suggest that the inspector be transferred to another division

18. The BEST way for you to prepare the inspectors in your unit to handle special assignments speedily and make decisions in an emergency is to
    A. follow each employee's work very carefully so you know where he is least efficient
    B. give them the freedom to make decisions in their everyday work
    C. refuse to accept work that is turned in late
    D. set deadlines ahead of the time when regularly assigned work is actually due so they will learn to work efficiently

19. Suppose you are supervising several inspectors. One of the inspectors has recently transferred to your unit. You discover that although he generally prepares his reports in a fairly correct way, he does not follow the prescribed procedure that you have taught the other inspectors.
    In this situation, the one of the following that it would be BEST for you to do is to
    A. allow him to use his own procedure if it is accurate and efficient
    B. refer him to your supervisor
    C. discuss the matter with all the inspectors and let them decide which procedure they wish to follow
    D. tell him to follow the procedure used by the other inspectors

20. Assume that you have one of your most competent inspectors working on a new type of project. As you are reviewing his work, you notice he has made some errors.
    You should
    A. correct the errors yourself, otherwise the inspector will get discouraged
    B. ignore the errors; they are probably not important, especially when the inspector is first learning the job
    C. tell the inspector about the errors; he will probably learn from them
    D. tell the inspector about the errors; then he will be aware that he is careless

21. Assume that your unit has been given a special assignment to make an original study. You plan to give this assignment to two of your most competent inspectors.
    The BEST way to start them on this work is to
    A. ask the two inspectors how they think the work can be done in a most effective way
    B. do some of the work with the inspectors to make sure they do not make any mistakes
    C. tell the inspectors they will be held directly responsible for the success of the study
    D. write up detailed instructions and give them to the inspectors who will do the work

22. Of the following steps in setting up an employee training program, the one which should PRECEDE the others is to
    A. assemble all the materials needed in the training program
    B. decide what training methods would be most effective
    C. determine what facilities are available for training purposes
    D. outline the areas that would be covered in the training program

23. Assume that you find it necessary to retrain an older, experienced inspector because you are giving this inspector a different kind of assignment.
    Of the following, the problem that is MOST likely to arise when retraining such a staff member is that the
    A. instructor will have disciplinary problems with this employee
    B. instructor will know less than this staff member
    C. employee at this status often lacks motivation to be retrained
    D. younger men will be unable to keep up with the performance of this employee

24. Assume that an inspector has recently been transferred from another unit and is now on your team.
    Of the following, the BEST method for you to use to determine whether this man needs any additional instruction or training is to
    A. ask him whether he is having difficulty with the work you assign to him
    B. ask the man's former supervisor whether he was a competent inspector
    C. review the way he handles the various tasks that you assign to him
    D. send this man into the field with one of your inspectors and have him evaluate the newly assigned inspector

25. Instituting a program of on-the-job training may sometimes present problems for the supervisor because, when first initiated, such training
    A. does not take place under actual working conditions
    B. is less instructive than formal training sessions
    C. may result in a decrease in the authority of the supervisor
    D. may slow down the unit's work

26. Suppose that you are approached by a newly appointed inspector who asks you to make an inspection visit with him because he is unsure of the procedure.
    The one of the following that you should do FIRST is to
    A. agree to make the visit with him
    B. refer him to the supervisor for help
    C. report him to the supervisor for incorrect behavior
    D. tell him to do the best he can and offer to help him write up the report

27. Suppose that you are writing up your inspection reports in your office on a particular day. A fellow inspector, who has left his identification at home, asks if he may use your identification card and badge in order to perform his scheduled inspections.

Of the following, you should
- A. allow him to use your identification since he is an inspector
- B. offer to perform the inspections for him if he will write the reports
- C. refuse his request and suggest he explain the situation to the supervisor
- D. tell him you need your identification for yourself

28. Assume that you are assigned to handle telephone complaints. After you have attempted to handle a complaint from a belligerent caller, the caller asks your name, saying that he is going to report you to your superior for being insolent to him.
It would be BEST for you to
- A. give the caller a false name so he will stop bothering you
- B. give the caller your name and explain the circumstances to your superior afterwards
- C. refuse to give the caller your name
- D. tell the caller that you have not been insolent to him

28.____

29. As a senior inspector, you are permitted to hold an outside job as long as it is NOT
- A. dangerous
- B. in conflict with the performance of your inspection duties
- C. mentally or physically taxing
- D. paid at a rate higher than your inspector job

29.____

30. Of the following, the MOST important reason that graphs and charts are used in reports to present material that can be treated statistically is that such material
- A. is easier to understand when it is presented in graph or chart form
- B. looks more impressive when it is presented in graph or chart form
- C. requires less time to prepare when it is presented in a graph or chart form instead of written out
- D. take up less space in graph or chart form than when it is written out

30.____

KEY (CORRECT ANSWERS)

1.	A	11.	D	21.	A
2.	B	12.	D	22.	D
3.	C	13.	C	23.	C
4.	C	14.	A	24.	C
5.	B	15.	D	25.	D
6.	B	16.	D	26.	B
7.	D	17.	B	27.	C
8.	C	18.	B	28.	B
9.	B	19.	D	29.	B
10.	D	20.	C	30.	A

TEST 2

DIRECTIONS: Each question or incomplete statement is followed by several suggested answers or completions. Select the one that BEST answers the question or completes the statement. *PRINT THE LETTER OF THE CORRECT ANSWER IN THE SPACE AT THE RIGHT.*

1. If an inspector finds a discrepancy between the plans and specifications, he should
    A. always follow the plans
    B. ask for an interpretation
    C. always follow the specifications
    D. follow the plans if the difference is in dimensions

    1.____

2. In performing field inspectional work, an inspector is the contact man between the public and the agency, and it is his job to secure compliance through the maximum utilization of persuasion and education and the minimum application of coercion.
    According to this statement, an inspector performing inspectional duties should
    A. seek to obtain voluntary compliance and use coercion only as a last resort
    B. be conciliatory on all issues of non-compliance and not take an attitude of firmness and authority
    C. maintain a strictly impersonal attitude in the exercise of his duties at all times
    D. use the threat of legal action to secure conformance with specified requirements

    2.____

3. The BEST way for a supervising inspector to determine whether a new inspector is learning his work properly is to
    A. ask the other men how this man is making out
    B. question him directly on details of the work
    C. assume that if he asks no questions, he knows the work
    D. inspect and follow up on the work which is assigned to him

    3.____

4. In assigning his men to various jobs, the BEST principle for a supervising inspector to follow is to
    A. study the men's abilities and assign them accordingly
    B. rotate a man from job to job until you find one which he can do well
    C. assign each of them to a job and let them adjust to it in their own way
    D. assume that men appointed to the position can do all parts of the work equally well

    4.____

5. Good inspection methods require that the inspector
    A. be observant and check all details
    B. constantly check with the engineer who designed the job
    C. apply specifications according to his interpretations
    D. permit slight job variation to establish good public relations

    5.____

6. An inspector inspecting a large job under construction inspected plumbing at 9 A.M., heating at 10 A.M., and ventilation at 11 A.M., and did his officework in the afternoon. He followed the same pattern daily for months.
   This procedure is
   A. *bad*, because not enough time is devoted to plumbing
   B. *bad*, because the tradesmen know when the inspections will occur
   C. *good*, because it is methodical and he does not miss any of the trades
   D. *good*, because it gives equal amount of time to the important trades

6.____

7. The BEST way to evaluate the overall state of completion of a construction project is to check the progress estimate against the
   A. inspection worksheet
   B. construction schedule
   C. inspector's checklist
   D. equipment maintenance schedule

7.____

8. When a contractor fails to adhere to an approved progress schedule, he should
   A. revise the schedule without delay
   B. ask for an extension of time on account of delays
   C. adopt such additional means and methods of construction as will make up for time lost
   D. take no immediate action with the hope that sufficient time will be available later on that will assure the completion in accordance with the schedule

8.____

9. The usual contract for agency work includes a section entitled instructions to bidders, which states that the
   A. contractor agrees that he has made his own examination and will make no claim for damages on account of errors or omissions
   B. contractor shall not make claims for damages of any discrepancy, error or omission in any plans
   C. estimates of quantities and calculations are guaranteed by the agency to be correct and are deemed to be a representation of the conditions affecting the work
   D. plans, measurement, dimensions, and conditions under which the work is to be performed are guaranteed by the agency

9.____

10. A lump sum type of contract may require the contractor to submit a schedule of unit price.
    The BEST reason for this is that it
    A. prevents the lump sum from being too high
    B. simplifies the selection of the lowest bidder
    C. enables the estimators to check the total cost
    D. provides a means of making equitable partial payments

10.____

11. A contractor on a large construction project USUALLY receives partial payments based on
    A. estimates of completed work
    B. actual cost of materials delivered and work completed
    C. estimates of material delivered and not paid for by the contractor
    D. the breakdown estimate submitted after the contract was signed and prorated over the estimated duration of the contract

11.____

12. In order to avoid disputes over payments for extra work in a contract for construction, the BEST procedure to follow would be to
    A. have contractor submit work progress reports daily
    B. insert a special clause in the contract specifications
    C. have a representative on the job at all times to verify conditions
    D. allocate a certain percentage of the cost of the job to cover such expenses

12.____

13. A fixed amount of money is generally withheld from the contractor for a definite period after the completion of construction.
    The BEST reason for this is
    A. that the money will be available for taxes due
    B. to penalize the contractor for poor work
    C. that it is a security for the repair of any defective work
    D. that the money will be available for modifications in the design of the structure

13.____

14. Prior to the installation of equipment called for in the specifications, the contractor is USUALLY required to submit for approval
    A. sets of shop drawings
    B. a set of revised specifications
    C. a detailed description of the methods of work to be used
    D. a complete list of skilled and unskilled tradesmen he proposes to use

14.____

15. During the actual construction work, the CHIEF value of a construction schedule is to
    A. insure that the work will be done on time
    B. reveal whether production is falling behind
    C. show how much equipment and material is required for the project
    D. furnish data as to the methods and techniques of construction operations

15.____

16. Of the following items, the one which should NOT be included in a proposed work schedule is
    A. a schedule of hourly wage rates and supplementary benefits
    B. an estimated time required for delivery of materials and equipment
    C. the anticipated commencement and completion of the various operations
    D. the sequence and inter-relationship of various operations with those of related contracts

16.____

17. The frequency with which job reports are submitted should depend MAINLY on   17._____
    A. how comprehensive the report has to be
    B. the amount of information in the report
    C. the availability of an experienced man to write the report
    D. the importance of changes in the information included in the report

18. The CHIEF purpose in preparing an outline for a report is usually to insure   18._____
    that
    A. the report will be grammatically correct
    B. every point will be given equal emphasis
    C. principal and secondary points will be properly integrated
    D. the language of the report will be of the same level and include the same technical terms

19. The MAIN reason for requiring written job reports is to   19._____
    A. avoid the necessity of oral orders
    B. develop better methods of doing the work
    C. provide a permanent record of what was done
    D. increase the amount of work that can be done

20. Assume you are recommending in a report to your superior that a radical   20._____
    change in a standard maintenance procedure should be adopted.
    Of the following, the MOST important information to be included in this report is
    A. a list of the reasons for making this change
    B. the names of others who favor the change
    C. a complete description of the present procedure
    D. amount of training time needed for the new procedure

KEY (CORRECT ANSWERS)

1.	B	11.	A
2.	A	12.	C
3.	B	13.	C
4.	A	14.	A
5.	A	15.	B
6.	B	16.	A
7.	B	17.	D
8.	C	18.	C
9.	A	19.	C
10.	D	20.	A

ARITHMETICAL REASONING
EXAMINATION SECTION
TEST 1

DIRECTIONS: Each question or incomplete statement is followed by several suggested answers or completions. Select the one that BEST answers the question or completes the statement. *PRINT THE LETTER OF THE CORRECT ANSWER IN THE SPACE AT THE RIGHT.*

1.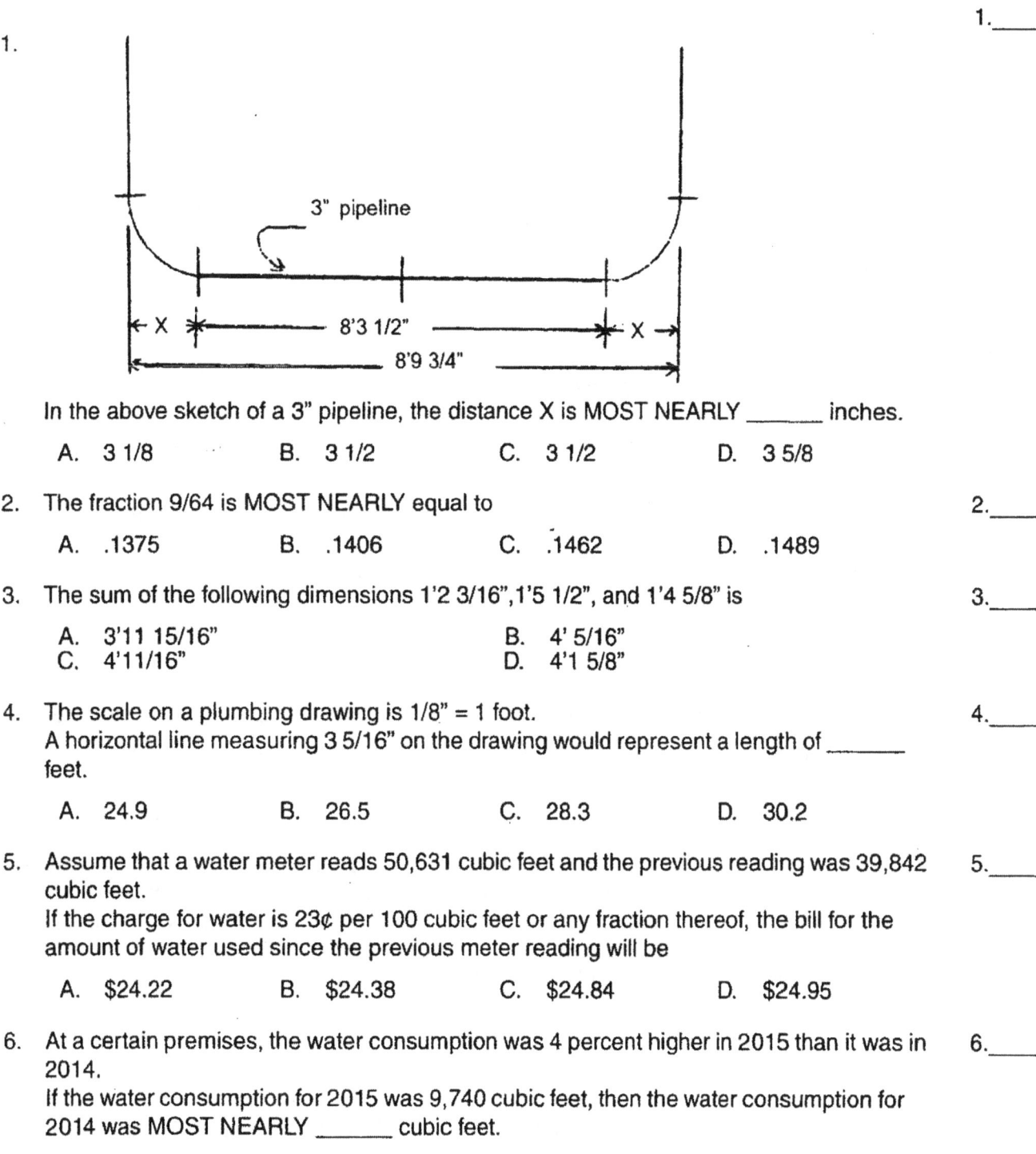

   In the above sketch of a 3" pipeline, the distance X is MOST NEARLY _____ inches.

   A. 3 1/8   B. 3 1/2   C. 3 1/2   D. 3 5/8

2. The fraction 9/64 is MOST NEARLY equal to

   A. .1375   B. .1406   C. .1462   D. .1489

3. The sum of the following dimensions 1'2 3/16", 1'5 1/2", and 1'4 5/8" is

   A. 3'11 15/16"   B. 4' 5/16"
   C. 4'11/16"   D. 4'1 5/8"

4. The scale on a plumbing drawing is 1/8" = 1 foot.
   A horizontal line measuring 3 5/16" on the drawing would represent a length of _____ feet.

   A. 24.9   B. 26.5   C. 28.3   D. 30.2

5. Assume that a water meter reads 50,631 cubic feet and the previous reading was 39,842 cubic feet.
   If the charge for water is 23¢ per 100 cubic feet or any fraction thereof, the bill for the amount of water used since the previous meter reading will be

   A. $24.22   B. $24.38   C. $24.84   D. $24.95

6. At a certain premises, the water consumption was 4 percent higher in 2015 than it was in 2014.
   If the water consumption for 2015 was 9,740 cubic feet, then the water consumption for 2014 was MOST NEARLY _____ cubic feet.

   A. 9,320   B. 9,350   C. 9,365   D. 9,390

7. A pump delivers water at a constant rate of 40 gallons per minute.
   If there are 7.5 gallons to a cubic foot of water, the time it will take to fill a tank 6 feet x 5 feet x 4 feet is MOST NEARLY _____ minutes.

   A. 15   B. 22.5   C. 28.5   D. 30

8. The total weight, in pounds, of three lengths of 3" cast-iron pipe 7'6" long, weighing 14.5 pounds per foot, and four lengths of 4" cast-iron pipe each 5'0" long, weighing 13.0 pounds per foot, is MOST NEARLY

   A. 540   B. 585   C. 600   D. 665

9. The water pressure at the bottom of a column of water 34 feet high is 14.7 lbs./sq.in. The water pressure in lbs./sq.in. at the bottom of the column of water 12 feet high is MOST NEARLY

   A. 3   B. 5   C. 7   D. 9

10. The number of cubic yards of earth that would be removed when digging a trench 8 feet wide x 9 feet deep x 63 feet long is

    A. 56   B. 168   C. 314   D. 504

11. On test, a meter registered one cubic foot for each 1 1/3 cubic feet of water that passed through it.
    If the meter had a reading of 1,200 cubic feet, we may conclude that the CORRECT amount should be _____ cubic feet.

    A. 800   B. 900   C. 1,500   D. 1,600

12. A water use meter reads 87,463 cubic feet.
    If the previous reading was 17,377 cubic feet and the rate charged is 15 cents per 100 cubic feet, the bill for water use during this period is about

    A. $45.00   B. $65.00   C. $85.00   D. $105.00

13. Under proper conditions, the one of the following groups of pipes that gives the same flow in gals/min as one 6" diameter pipe is (neglect friction) _____ pipes of _____ diameter each.

    A. 3; 3"   B. 4; 3"   C. 2; 4"   D. 3; 4"

14. A roof tank is used to furnish the domestic water supply to a ten story building. This tank has a capacity of 5,900 gallons. At 10:00 A.M. one morning, the tank is half full.
    If water is being used at the rate of 50 gals/min, the pump which is used to fill the tank has a rated capacity of 90 gals/min, the time it would take to fill the tank under these conditions is MOST NEARLY _____ hour(s), _____ minutes.

    A. 2; 8   B. 1; 14   C. 2; 32   D. 1; 2

15. The number of gallons of water contained in a cylindrical swimming pool 8 feet in diameter and filled to a depth of 3 feet 6 inches is MOST NEARLY (assume 7.5 gallons = 1 cubic foot)

    A. 30   B. 225   C. 1,320   D. 3,000

16. The charge for metered water is 52 1/2 cents per hundred cubic feet, with a minimum charge of $21 per annum. Of the following, the SMALLEST water usage in hundred cubic feet that would result in a charge GREATER than the minimum is

    A. 39 B. 40 C. 41 D. 42

17. The annual frontage rent on a one-story building 40 ft. in length is $735.00. For each additional story, $52.50 per annum is added to the frontage rent. For demolition, the charge for wetting down is 3/8 of the annual frontage charge.
    The charge for wetting down a building six stories in height, with a 40 ft. frontage, is MOST NEARLY

    A. $369 B. $371 C. $372 D. $374

18. If the drawing of a piping layout is made to a scale of 1/4" equals one foot, then a 7'9" length of piping would be represented by a scaled length on the drawing of APPROXIMATELY _____ inches.

    A. 2 B. 7 3/4 C. 23 1/4 D. 31

19. A plumbing sketch is drawn to a scale of eighth-size. A line measuring 3" on the sketch would be equivalent to _____ feet.

    A. 2 B. 6 C. 12 D. 24

20. If 500 feet of pipe weighs 800 lbs., the number of pounds that 120 feet will weigh is MOST NEARLY

    A. 190 B. 210 C. 230 D. 240

21. If a trench is excavated 3'0" wide by 5'6" deep and 50 feet long, the total number of cubic yards of earth removed is MOST NEARLY

    A. 30 B. 90 C. 150 D. 825

22. Assume that a plumber earns $86,500 per year.
    If eighteen percent of his pay is deducted for taxes and social security, his net weekly pay will be APPROXIMATELY

    A. $1,326 B. $1,365 C. $1,436 D. $1,457.50

23. Assume that a plumbing installation is made up of the following fixtures and groups of fixtures: 12 bathroom groups each containing one W.C., one lavatory, and one bathtub with shower; 12 bathroom groups each containing one W.C., one lavatory, one bathtub, and one shower stall; 24 combination kitchen fixtures; 4 floor drains; 6 slop sinks without flushing rim; and 2 shower stalls (or shower bath).
    The total number of fixtures for the above plumbing installation is MOST NEARLY

    A. 60 B. 95 C. 120 D. 210

24. A triangular opening in a wall forms a 30-60 degree right triangle.
    If the longest side measures 12'0", then the shortest side will measure

    A. 3'0" B. 4'0" C. 6'0" D. 8'0"

4 (#1)

25. You are directed to cut 4 pieces of pipe, one each of the following length: 2'6 1/4", 3'9 3/8", 4'7 5/8", and 5'8 7/8".
    The total length of these 4 pieces is

    A. 15'7 1/4"   B. 15'9 3/8"   C. 16'5 7/8"   D. 16'8 1/8"

25._____

KEY (CORRECT ANSWERS)

1. A
2. B
3. B
4. B
5. C

6. C
7. B
8. B
9. B
10. B

11. D
12. D
13. B
14. B
15. C

16. C
17. D
18. A
19. A
20. A

21. A
22. B
23. C
24. C
25. D

---

5 (#1)

SOLUTIONS TO PROBLEMS

1. 8'3 1/2" + x + x = 8'9 3/4" Then, 2x = 6 1/4", so x = 3 1/8"

2. 9/64 = .140625 = .1406

3. 1'2 3/16" + 1'5 1/2" +1'4 5/8" = 3'11 21/16" = 4'5/16"

4. 3 5/16" ÷ 1/8" =53/16 x 8/1 = 26.5. Then, (26.5)(1 ft.) = 26.5 feet

5. 50,631 - 39,842 = 10,789; 10,789 ÷ 100 = 107.89
   Since the cost is .23 per 100 cubic feet or any fraction thereof, the cost will be
   (.23)(107) + .23 = $24.84

6. 9740 ÷ 1.04 = 9365 cu.ft.

7. 40 ÷ 7.5 = 5 1/3 cu.ft. of water per minute. The volume = (6)(5)(4) = 120 cu.ft. Thus, the number of minutes needed to fill the tank is 120 ÷ 5 1/3 = 22.5

8. 3" pipe: 3 x 7'6" = 22 1/2' x 14.5 lbs. = 326.25
   4" pipe: 4 x 5' = 20' x 13 lbs. = 260
   326.25 + 260 = 586.25 (most nearly 585)

9. Let x = pressure. Then, 34/12 = 14.7/x. So, 34x = 176.4
   Solving, x ≈ 5 lbs./sq.in.

10. (8)(9)(63) = 4536 cu.ft. Since 1 cu.yd. = 27 cu.ft., 4536 cu.ft. is equivalent to 168 cu.yds.

11. Let x = correct amount. Then, $\frac{1}{1200} = \frac{1\frac{1}{3}}{x}$. Solving, x = 1600

12. 87,463 - 17,377 = 70,086; and 70,086 ÷ 100 = 700.86 ≈ 700 Then, (700)(.15) = $105.00

13. Cross-sectional area of a 6" diameter pipe = $(\pi)(3")^2 = 9\pi$ sq. in. Note that the combined cross-sectional areas of four 3" diameter pipes = $(4)(\pi)(1.5")^2 = 9\pi$ sq. in.

14. 90 - 50 = 40 gals/min. Then, 2950 ÷ 40 = 73.75 min. ≈ 1 hr. 14 min.

15. Volume = $(\pi)(4)^2(3\,1/2) = 56\pi$ cu.ft. Then, $(56\pi)(7.5)$ = 1320 gals.

16. For 4100 cu.ft., the charge of (.525)(41) = $21,525 > $21

17. Rent = $73,500 + (5)($52.50) = $997,50. For demolition, the charge = (3/8)($997.50) $374

18. (1/4")(7.75) = 2"

19. (3")(8) = 24" = 2 ft.

6 (#1)

20. Let x = weight. Then, 500/800 = 120/x . Solving, x = 192 190 lbs.

21. (3')(5 1/2')(50') = 825 cu.ft. Then, 825 ÷ 27 ≈ 30 cu.yds.

22. Net pay = (.82)($86,500) = $70,930/yr. Weekly pay = $70,930 ÷ 52 ≈ $1365

23. (12x3) + (12x4) +24+4+6+2= 120

24. The shortest side = (1/2)(hypotenuse) = (1/2)(12') = 6'

25. 2'6 1/4" + 3'9 3/8" + 4'7 5/8" + 5'8 7/8 " = 14'30 17/8" = 16'8 1/8"

TEST 2

DIRECTIONS: Each question or incomplete statement is followed by several suggested answers or completions. Select the one that BEST answers the question or completes the statement. *PRINT THE LETTER OF THE CORRECT ANSWER IN THE SPACE AT THE RIGHT.*

1. The sum of the following pipe lengths, 15 5/8", 8 3/4", 30 5/16" and 20 1/2", is

   A. 77 1/8"   B. 76 3/16"   C. 75 3/16"   D. 74 5/16"

2. If the outside diameter of a pipe is 6 inches and the wall thickness is 1/2 inch, the inside area of this pipe, in square inches, is MOST NEARLY

   A. 15.7   B. 17.3   C. 19.6   D. 23.8

3. Three lengths of pipe 1'10", 3'2 1/2", and 5'7 1/2", respectively, are to be cut from a pipe 14'0" long.
   Allowing 1/8" for each pipe cut, the length of pipe remaining is

   A. 3'1 1/8"   B. 3'2 1/2"   C. 3'3 1/4"   D. 3'3 5/8"

4. According to the building code, the MAXIMUM permitted surface temperature of combustible construction materials located near heating equipment is 76.5°C. (°F=(°Cx9/5)+32)
   Maximum temperature Fahrenheit is MOST NEARLY

   A. 170° F   B. 195° F   C. 210° F   D. 220° F

5. A pump discharges 7.5 gals/minutes.
   In 2.5 hours the pump will discharge _____ gallons.

   A. 1125   B. 1875   C. 1950   D. 2200

6. A pipe with an outside diameter of 4" has a circumference of MOST NEARLY _____ inches.

   A. 8.05   B. 9.81   C. 12.57   D. 14.92

7. A piping sketch is drawn to a scale of 1/8" = 1 foot.
   A vertical steam line measuring 3 1/2" on the sketch would have an ACTUAL length of _____ feet.

   A. 16   B. 22   C. 24   D. 28

8. A pipe having an inside diameter of 3.48 inches and a wall thickness of .18 inches will have an outside diameter of _____ inches.

   A. 3.84   B. 3.64   C. 3.57   D. 3.51

9. A rectangular steel bar having a volume of 30 cubic inches, a width of 2 inches, and a height of 3 inches will have a length of _____ inches.

   A. 12   B. 10   C. 8   D. 5

10. A pipe weighs 20.4 pounds per foot of length.
    The total weight of eight pieces of this pipe with each piece 20 feet in length is MOST NEARLY _____ pounds.

    A. 460   B. 1,680   C. 2,420   D. 3,260

11. Assume that four pieces of pipe measuring 2'1 1/4", 4'2 3/4", 5'1 9/16", and 6'3 5/8", respectively, are cut with a saw from a pipe 20"0" long.
    Allowing 1/16" waste for each cut, the length of the remaining pipe is

    A. 2'1 9/16"   B. 2'2 9/16"   C. 2'4 13/16"   D. 2'8 9/16"

12. If one cubic inch of steel weighs 0.28 pounds, the weight, in pounds, of a steel bar 1/2" x 6" x 2'0" long is MOST NEARLY

    A. 11   B. 16   C. 20   D. 24

13. If the circumference of a circle is equal to 31.416 inches, then its diameter, in inches, is equal to MOST NEARLY

    A. 8   B. 9   C. 10   D. 13

14. Assume that a steam fitter's helper receives a salary of $171.36 a day for 250 days is considered a full work year. If taxes, social security, hospitalization, and pension deducted from his salary amounts to 16 percent of his gross pay, then his net yearly salary will be MOST NEARLY

    A. $31,788   B. $35,982   C. $41,982   D. $42,840

15. If the outside diameter of a pipe is 14 inches and the wall thickness is 1/2 inch, then the inside area of the pipe, in square inches, is MOST NEARLY

    A. 125   B. 133   C. 143   D. 154

16. A steam leak in a pipe line allows steam to escape at a rate of 50,000 pounds each month.
    Assuming that the cost of steam is $2.50 per 1,000 pounds, the TOTAL cost of wasted steam from this leak for a 12-month period would amount to

    A. $125   B. $300   C. $1,500   D. $3,000

17. If 250 feet of 4" pipe weighs 400 pounds, the weight of this pipe per linear foot is _____ pounds.

    A. 1.25   B. 1.50   C. 1.60   D. 1.75

18. A set of heating plan drawings is drawn to a scale of 1/4" = 1 foot.
    If a length of pipe measures 4 5/8" on the drawing, the ACTUAL length of the pipe, in feet, is

    A. 16.3   B. 16.8   C. 17.5   D. 18.5

19. The TOTAL length of four pieces of pipe whose lengths are 3'4 1/2", 2'1 5/16", 4'9 3/8", and 2'3 1/4", respectively, is

    A. 11'5 7/16"   B. 11'6 7/16"
    C. 12'5 7/16"   D. 12'6 7/16"

20. Assume that a pipe trench is 3 feet wide, 3 feet deep, and 300 feet long.
    If the unit cost of excavating the trench is $120 per cubic yard, the TOTAL cost of excavating the trench is

    A. $1,200   B. $12,000   C. $27,000   D. $36,000

21. The TOTAL length of four pieces of 1 1/2" galvanized steel pipe whose lengths are 7 ft. + 3 1/2 inches, 4 ft. + 2 1/4 inches, 6 ft. + 7 inches, and 8 ft. +5 1/8 inches is   21._____

    A. 26 feet + 5 7/8 inches   B. 25 ft. + 6 7/8 inches
    C. 25 feet + 4 1/4 inches   D. 25 ft. + 3 3/8 inches

22. A swimming pool is 25' wide by 75' long and has an average depth of 5'. 1 cubic foot contains 7.5 gallons of water. The capacity, when filled to the overflow, is _____ gallons.   22._____

    A. 9,375   B. 65,625   C. 69,005   D. 70,312

23. The sum of 3 1/4, 5 1/8, 2 1/2 , and 3 3/8 is   23._____

    A. 14   B. 14 1/8   C. 14 1/4   D. 14 3/8

24. Assume that it takes 6 men 8 days to do a particular job. If you have only 4 men available to do this job and they all work at the same speed, then the number of days it would take to complete the job would be   24._____

    A. 11   B. 12   C. 13   D. 14

25. The total length of four pieces of 2" O.D. pipe, whose lengths are 7'3 1/2", 4'2 3/16", 5'7 5/16", and 8'5 7/8", respectively, is MOST NEARLY   25._____

    A. 24'6 3/4"   B. 24'7 15/16"
    C. 25'5 13/16"   D. 25'6 7/8"

KEY (CORRECT ANSWERS)

1.	C	11.	B
2.	C	12.	C
3.	D	13.	C
4.	A	14.	B
5.	A	15.	B
6.	C	16.	C
7.	D	17.	C
8.	A	18.	D
9.	D	19.	D
10.	D	20.	B

21.	A
22.	D
23.	C
24.	B
25.	D

SOLUTIONS TO PROBLEMS

1. 15 5/8" + 8 3/4" + 30 5/16" + 20 1/2" = 73 35/16" = 75 3/16"

2. Inside diameter = 6" - 1/2" - 1/2" = 5". Area = $(\pi)(5/2")^2 \approx$ 19.6 sq. in.

3. Pipe remaining = 14' - 1'10" - 3'2 1/2" - 5'7 1/2" - (3)(1/8") = 3'3 5/8"

4. 76.5 x 9/5 = 137.7 + 32 = 169.7

5. 7.5 x 150 = 1125

6. Radius = 2" Circumference = $(2\pi)(2") \approx$ 12.57"

7. 3 1/2" 1/8" = (7/2)(8/1) = 28 Then, (28)(1 ft.) = 28 feet

8. Outside diameter = 3.48" + .18" + .18" = 3.84"

9. 30 = (2)(3)(length). So, length = 5"

10. Total weight = (20.4)(8)(20) $\approx$ 3260 lbs.

11. 20' - 2'1 1/4" - 4'2 3/4" - 5'1 9/16" - 6'3 5/8" - (4)(1/16") = 2'2 9/16"

12. Weight = (.28)(1/2")(6")(24") = 20.16 $\approx$ 20 lbs.

13. Diameter = 31.416" $\div \pi \approx$ 10"

14. His net pay for 250 days = (.84)($171.36)(250) = $35,985.60 $\approx$ $35,928 (from answer key)

15. Inside diameter = 14" - 1/2" - 1/2" = 13". Area = $(\pi)(13/2")^2 \approx$ 133 sq.in

16. (50,000 lbs.)(12) = 600,000 lbs. per year. The cost would be ($2.50)(600) = $1500

17. 400 $\div$ 250 = 1.60 pounds per linear foot

18. 4 5/8" $\div$ 1/4" = 37/8 . 4/1 = 18.5 Then, (18.5)(1 ft.) = 18.5 feet

19. 3'4 1/2" + 2'1 5/16" + 4'9 3/8" + 2'3 1/4" = 11'17 23/16" = 12'6 7/16"

20. (3')(3')(300') = 2700 cu.ft., which is 2700 $\div$ 27 = 100 cu.yds. Total cost = ($120)(100) = $12,000

21. 7'3 1/2" + 4'2 1/4" + 6'7" + 8'5 1/8" = 25'17 7/8" = 26'5 7/8"

22. (25)(75)(5) = 9375 cu.ft. Then, (9375)(7.5) $\approx$ 70,312 gals.

23. 3 1/4 + 5 1/8 + 2 1/2 + 3 3/8 = 13 10/8 = 14 1/4

24. (6) (8) = 48 man-days. Then, 48 $\div$ 4 = 12 days

25. 7'3 1/2" + 4'2 3/16" + 5'7 5/16" + 8'5 7/8"= 24'17 30/16" = 25'6 7/8"

TEST 3

DIRECTIONS: Each question or incomplete statement is followed by several suggested answers or completions. Select the one that BEST answers the question or completes the statement. *PRINT THE LETTER OF THE CORRECT ANSWER IN THE SPACE AT THE RIGHT.*

1. The time required to pump 2,500 gallons of water out of a sump at the rate of 12 1/2 gallons per minutes would be _____ hour(s) _____ minutes. 1.____

    A. 1; 40   B. 2; 30   C. 3; 20   D. 6; 40

2. Copper tubing which has an inside diameter of 1 1/16" and a wall thickness of .095" has an outside diameter which is MOST NEARLY _____ inches. 2.____

    A. 1 5/32   B. 1 3/16   C. 1 7/32   D. 1 1/4

3. Assume that 90 gallons per minute flow through a certain 3-inch pipe which is tapped into a street main. 3.____
   The amount of water which would flow through a 1-inch pipe tapped into the same street main is MOST NEARLY _____ gpm.

    A. 90   B. 45   C. 30   D. 10

4. The weight of a 6 foot length of 8-inch pipe which weighs 24.70 pounds per foot is _____ lbs. 4.____

    A. 148.2   B. 176.8   C. 197.6   D. 212.4

5. If a 4-inch pipe is directly coupled to a 2-inch pipe and 16 gallons per minute are flowing through the 4-inch pipe, then the flow through the 2-inch pipe will be _____ gallons per minute. 5.____

    A. 4   B. 8   C. 16   D. 32

6. If the water pressure at the bottom of a column of water 34 feet high is 14.7 pounds per square inch, the water pressure at the bottom of a column of water 18 feet high is MOST NEARLY _____ pounds per square inch. 6.____

    A. 8.0   B. 7.8   C. 7.6   D. 7.4

7. If there are 7 1/2 gallons in a cubic foot of water and if water flows from a hose at a constant rate of 4 gallons per minute, the time it should take to COMPLETELY fill a tank of 1,600 cubic feet capacity with water from that hose is _____ hours. 7.____

    A. 300   B. 150   C. 100   D. 50

8. Each of a group of fifteen water meter readers read an average of 62 water meters a day in a certain 5-day work week. A total of 5,115 meters are read by this group the following week. 8.____
   The TOTAL number of meters read in the second week as compared to the first week shows a

    A. 10% increase   B. 15% increase
    C. 20% increase   D. 5% decrease

9. A certain water consumer used 5% more water in 1994 than he did in 1993. If his water consumption for 1994 was 8,375 cubic feet, the amount of water he consumed in 1993 was MOST NEARLY _____ cubic feet.

   A. 9,014 B. 8,816 C. 7,976 D. 6,776

10. Assume that a water meter reads 40,175 cubic feet and that the previous reading was 29,186 cubic feet.
    If the charge for water is 92 cents per 100 cubic feet or any fraction thereof, the bill for the amount of water used since the previous meter reading should be

    A. $100.28 B. $101.04 C. $101.08 D. $101.20

11. A leaking faucet caused a loss of 216 cubic feet of water in a 30-day month. If there are 7.5 gallons in a cubic foot of water, then the AVERAGE loss of water per hour for that month was _____ gallons.

    A. 2 1/4 B. 2 1/8 C. 2 D. 1 3/4

12. The fraction which is equal to .375 is

    A. 3/16 B. 5/32 C. 3/8 D. 5/12

13. A square backyard swimming pool, each side of which is 10 feet long, is filled to a depth of 3 1/2 feet.
    If there are 7 1/2 gallons in a cubic foot of water, the number of gallons of water in the pool is MOST NEARLY _____ gallons.

    A. 46.7 B. 100 C. 2,625 D. 3,500

14. When 1 5/8, 3 3/4, 6 1/3, and 9 1/2 are added, the resulting sum is

    A. 21 1/8 B. 21 1/6 C. 21 5/24 D. 21 1/4

15. When 946 1/2 is subtracted from 1,035 1/4, the result is

    A. 87 1/4 B. 87 3/4 C. 88 1/4 D. 88 3/4

16. When 39 is multiplied by 697, the result is

    A. 8,364 B. 26,283 C. 27,183 D. 28,003

17. When 16.074 is divided by .045, the result is

    A. 3.6 B. 35.7 C. 357.2 D. 3,572

18. To dig a trench 3'0" wide, 50'0" long, and 5'6" deep, the total number of cubic yards of earth to be removed is MOST NEARLY

    A. 30 B. 90 C. 140 D. 825

19. The TOTAL length of four pieces of 2" pipe, whose lengths are 7'3 1/2", 4'2 3/16", 5'7 5/16", and 8'5 7/8", respectively, is

    A. 24'6 3/4"
    B. 24'7 15/16"
    C. 25'5 13/16"
    D. 25'6 7/8"

20. A hot water line made of copper has a straight horizontal run of 150 feet and, when installed, is at a temperature of 45° F. In use, its temperature rises to 190° F. If the coefficient of expansion for copper is 0.0000095" per foot per degree F, the TOTAL expansion, in inches, in the run of pipe is given by the product of 150 multiplied by 0.0000095 by

    A. 145
    B. 145 x 12
    C. 145 divided by 12
    D. 145 x 12 x 12

21. A water storage tank measures 5' long, 4' wide, and 6' deep and is filled to the 5 1/2' mark with water.
    If one cubic foot of water weighs 62 pounds, the number of pounds of water required to COMPLETELY fill the tank is

    A. 7,440   B. 6,200   C. 1,240   D. 620

22. Assume that a pipe worker earns $83,125.00 per year.
    If seventeen percent of his pay is deducted for taxes, social security, and pension, his net weekly pay will be APPROXIMATELY

    A. $1598.50   B. $1504.00   C. $1453.00   D. $1325.00

23. If eighteen feet of 4" cast iron pipe weighs approximately 390 pounds, the weight of this pipe per lineal foot will be MOST NEARLY _____ lbs.

    A. 19   B. 22   C. 23   D. 25

24. If it takes 3 men 11 days to dig a trench, the number of days it will take 5 men to dig the same trench, assuming all work is done at the same rate of speed, is MOST NEARLY

    A. 6 1/2   B. 7 3/4   C. 8 1/4   D. 8 3/4

25. If a trench is dug 6'0" deep, 2'6" wide, and 8'0" long, the area of the opening, in square feet, is MOST NEARLY

    A. 48   B. 32   C. 20   D. 15

KEY (CORRECT ANSWERS)

1. C
2. D
3. D
4. A
5. B

6. B
7. D
8. A
9. C
10. D

11. A
12. C
13. C
14. C
15. D

16. C
17. C
18. A
19. D
20. A

21. D
22. D
23. B
24. A
25. C

SOLUTIONS TO PROBLEMS

1. 2500 ÷ 12 1/2 = 200 min. = 3 hrs. 20 min.

2. 1 1/16" + .095" + .095" = 1.0625 + .095 + .095 = 1.2525" ≈ 1 1/4"

3. Cross-sectional areas for a 3-inch pipe and a 1-inch pipe are $(\pi)(1.5)^2$ and $(\pi)(.5)^2$ = 2.25 π and .25 π, respectively. Let x = amount of water flowing through the 1-inch pipe. Then, $\frac{90}{x} = \frac{2.25\pi}{.25\pi}$. Solving, x = 10 gals/min

4. (24.70)(6) = 148.2 lbs.

5. $\frac{4" \text{ pipe}}{16 \text{ gallons}} = \frac{2" \text{ pipe}}{x \text{ gallons}}$, 4x = 32, x = 8

6. Let x = pressure. Then, 34/18 = 14.7/x. Solving, x ≈ 7.8

7. (1600)(7.5) = 12,000 gallons. Then, 12,000 ÷ 4 = 3000 min. = 50 hours

8. (15)(62)(5) = 4650. Then, (5115-4650)/4650 = 10% increase

9. 8375 ÷ 1.05 ≈ 7976 cu.ft.

10. 40,175 - 29,186 = 10,989 cu.ft. Then, 10,989 100 = 109.89. Since .92 is charged for each 100 cu.ft. or fraction thereof, total cost = (.92)(110) = $101.20

11. (216)(7.5) = 1620 gallons. In 30 days, there are 720 hours. Thus, the average water loss per hour = 1620 ÷ 720 = 2 1/4 gallons.

12. .375 = 375/1000 = 3/8

13. Volume = (10)(10)(3 1/2) = 350 cu.ft. Then, (350)(7 1/2) = 2625 gallons

14. 1 5/8 + 3 3/4 + 6 1/3 + 9 1/2 = 19 53/24 = 21 5/24

15. 1035 1/4 - 946 1/2 = 88 3/4

16. (39)(697) = 27,183

17. 16.074 .045 = 357.2

18. (3')(50')(5 1/2') = 825 cu.ft. ≈ 30 cu.yds., since 1 cu.yd. = 27 cu.ft.

19. 7'3 1/2" + 4'2 3/16" + 5'7 5/16" + 8'5 7/8" = 24'17 30/16" = 25'6 7/8"

20. Total expansion = (150)(.0000095)(145)

21. Number of pounds needed = (5) (4)(6-5 1/2)(62) = 620

22. Net annual pay = ($83,125)(.83) ≈ $69000. Then, the net weekly pay = $69000 ÷ 52 ≈ $1325 (actually about $1327)

23. 390 lbs. ÷ 18 = 21.6 lbs. per linear foot

24. (3)(11) = 33 man-days. Then, 33 ÷ 5 = 6.6 ≈ 6 1/2 days

25. Area = (8')(2 1/2') = 20 sq.ft.

PLUMBING ELEMENTS OF A HOUSING INSPECTION

CONTENTS

	PAGE
I. Background Factors	1
II. Definitions	1
III. Main Features of an Indoor Plumbing System	3
IV. Elements of a Plumbing System	3

PLUMBING ELEMENTS OF A HOUSING INSPECTION

Plumbing may be defined as practice, materials, and fixtures used in the installation, maintenance, and alteration of all piping, fixtures, appliances, and appurtenances in connection with sanitary or storm drainage facilities, the venting system, and the public or private water supply systems. **Plumbing** does not include the trade of drilling water wells, installing water softening equipment, or the business of manufacturing or selling plumbing fixtures, appliances, equipment, or hardware. A plumbing system consists of three separate parts: an adequate potable water supply system; a safe, adequate drainage system; and ample fixtures and equipment.

I. Background Factors

The generalized inspector of housing is concerned with a safe water supply system, an adequate drainage system, and ample and proper fixtures and equipment. This chapter covers the major features of a residential plumbing system and the basic plumbing terms the inspector must know and understand to identify properly housing code violations involving plumbing and the more complicated defects that he will refer to the appropriate agencies.

II. Definitions

1. **Air Chambers** — Air Chambers are pressure absorbing devices that eliminate water hammer. They should be installed as close as possible to the valves or faucet and at the end of long runs of pipe.

2. **Air Gap (Drainage System)** — The unobstructed vertical distance through the free atmosphere between the outlet of a water pipe and the flood level rim of the receptacle into which it is discharging.

3. **Air Gap (Water Distribution System)** — The unobstructed vertical distance through the free atmosphere between the lowest opening from any pipe or faucet supplying water to a tank, plumbing fixture, or other device and the flood level rim of the receptacle.

4. **Air Lock** — An air lock is a bubble of air which restricts the flow of water in a pipe.

5. **Backflow** — Backflow is the flow of water or other liquids, mixtures, or substances into the distributing pipes of a potable water supply from any source or sources other than the intended source. Back siphonage is one type of backflow.

6. **Back Siphonage** — Back siphonage is the flowing back of used, contaminated, or polluted water from a plumbing fixture or vessel into a potable water supply due to a negative pressure in the pipe.

7. **Branch** — A branch is any part of the piping system other than the main, riser, or stack.

8. **Branch Vent** — A vent connecting one or more individual vents with a vent stack.

9. **Building Drain** — The building (house) drain is the part of the lowest piping of a drainage system that receives the discharge from soil, waste, or other drainage pipes inside the walls of the building (house) and conveys it to the building sewer beginning 3 feet outside the building wall.

10. **Cross Connection** — Any physical connection or arrangement between two otherwise separate piping systems, one of which contains potable water and the other either water of unknown or questionable safety or steam, gas, or chemical whereby there may be a flow from one system to the other, the direction of flow depending on the pressure differential between the two systems. (See Backflow and Back siphonage.)

11. **Disposal Field** — An area containing a series of one or more trenches lined with coarse aggregate and conveying the effluent from the septic tank through vitrified clay pipe or

perforated, non-metallic pipe, laid in such a manner that the flow will be distributed with reasonable uniformity into natural soil.

12 **Drain** — A drain is any pipe that carries waste water or water-borne waste in a building (house) drainage system.

13 **Flood Level Rim** — The top edge of a receptacle from which water overflows.

14 **Flushometer Valve** — A device that discharges a predetermined quantity of water to fixtures for flushing purposes and is closed by direct water pressures.

15 **Flush Valve** — A device located at the bottom of the tank for flushing water closets and similar fixtures.

16 **Grease Trap** — See Interceptor

17 **Hot Water** — Hot water means potable water that is heated to at least 120°F and used for cooking, cleaning, washing dishes, and bathing.

18 **Insanitary** — Contrary to sanitary principles — injurious to health.

19 **Interceptor** — A device designed and installed so as to separate and retain deleterious, hazardous, or undesirable matter from normal wastes and permit normal sewage or liquid wastes to discharge into the drainage system by gravity.

20 **Leader** — An exterior drainage pipe for conveying storm water from roof or gutter drains to the building storm drain, combined building sewer, or other means of disposal.

21 **Main Vent** — The principal artery of the venting system, to which vent branches may be connected.

22 **Main Sewer** — See Public Sewer.

23 **Pneumatic** — The word pertains to devices making use of compressed air as in pressure tanks boosted by pumps.

24 **Potable Water** — Water having no impurities present in amounts sufficient to cause disease or harmful physiological effects and conforming in its bacteriological and chemical quality to the requirements of the Public Health Service drinking water standards or meeting the regulations of the public health authority having jurisdiction.

25 **P & T (Pressure and Temperature) Relief Valve** — A safety valve installed on a hot water storage tank to limit temperature and pressure of the water.

26 **P Trap** — A trap with a vertical inlet and a horizontal outlet.

27 **Public Sewer** — A common sewer directly controlled by public authority.

28 **Relief Vent** — An auxiliary vent that permits additional circulation of air in or between drainage and vent systems.

29 **Septic Tank** — A watertight receptacle that receives the discharge of a building's sanitary drain system or part thereof and is designed and constructed so as to separate solid from the liquid, digest organic matter through a period of detention, and allow the liquids to discharge into the soil outside of the tank through a system of open-joint or perforated piping, or through a seepage pit.

30 **Sewerage System** — A sewerage system comprises all piping, appurtenances, and treatment facilities used for the collection and disposal of sewage, except plumbing inside and in connection with buildings served, and the building drain.

31 **Soil Pipe** — The pipe that directs the sewage of a house to the receiving sewer, building drain, or building sewer.

32 **Soil Stack** — The vertical piping that terminates in a roof vent and carries off the vapors of a plumbing system.

33 **Stack Vent** — An extension of a solid or waste stack above the highest horizontal drain connected to the stack. Sometimes called a waste vent or a soil vent.

34 **Storm Sewer** — A sewer used for conveying rain water, surface water, condensate, cooling water, or similar liquid waste.

35 **Trap** — A trap is a fitting or device that provides a liquid seal to prevent the emission of sewer gases without materially affecting the flow of sewage or waste water through it.

36 **Vacuum Breaker** — A device to prevent backflow (back siphonage) by means of an opening through which air may be drawn to relieve negative pressure (vacuum).

37 **Vent Stack** — The vertical vent pipe installed to provide air circulation to and from the drainage system and that extends through one or more stories.

38 **Water Hammer** — The loud thump of water in a pipe when a valve or faucet is suddenly closed.

39 **Water Service Pipe** — The pipe from the water main or other sources of potable water supply to the water-distributing system of the building served.

40 **Water Supply System** — The water supply system consists of the water service pipe, the water-distributing pipes, the necessary connecting pipes, fittings, control valves, and all appurtenances in or adjacent to the building or premises.

41 **Wet Vent** — A vent that receives the discharge of waste other than from water closets.

42 **Yoke Vent** — A pipe connecting upward from a soil or waste stack to a vent stack for the purpose of preventing pressure changes in the stacks.

III. Main Features of an Indoor Plumbing System

The primary functions of the plumbing system within the house are as follows:

1 To bring an adequate and potable supply of hot and cold water to the users of the dwelling.

2 To drain all waste water and sewage discharged from these fixtures into the public sewer, or private disposal system.

It is, therefore, very important that the housing inspector familiarize himself fully with all elements of these systems so that he may recognize inadequacies of the structure's plumbing as well as other code violations. In order to aid the inspector in understanding the plumbing system, a series of drawings and diagrams has been included at the end of this chapter.

IV. Elements of a Plumbing System

A Supply System

1 **Water Service:** The piping of a house service line should be as short as possible. Elbows and bends should be kept to a minimum since these reduce the pressure and therefore the supply of water to fixtures in the house.

The house service line should also be protected from freezing. The burying of the line under 4 feet of soil is a commonly accepted depth to prevent freezing. This depth varies, however, across the country from north to south. The local or state plumbing code should be consulted for the recommended depth in your area of the country.

A typical house service installation is pictured in Figure 1.

The materials used for a house service may be copper, cast iron, steel or wrought iron. The connections used should be compatible with the type of pipe used.

a **Corporation stop** — The corporation stop is connected to the water main. This connection is usually made of brass and can be connected to the main by use of a special tool without shutting off the municipal supply. The valve incorporated in the corporation stop permits the pressure to be maintained in the main while the service to the building is completed.

b **Curb stop** — The curb stop is a similar valve used to isolate the building from the main for repairs, nonpayment of water bills, or flooded basements.

Since the corporation stop is usually under the street and would necessitate breaking the pavement to reach the valve, the curb stop is used as the isolation valve.

c **Curb stop box** — The curb stop box is an access box to the curb stop for opening and closing the valve. A long-handled wrench is used to reach the valve.

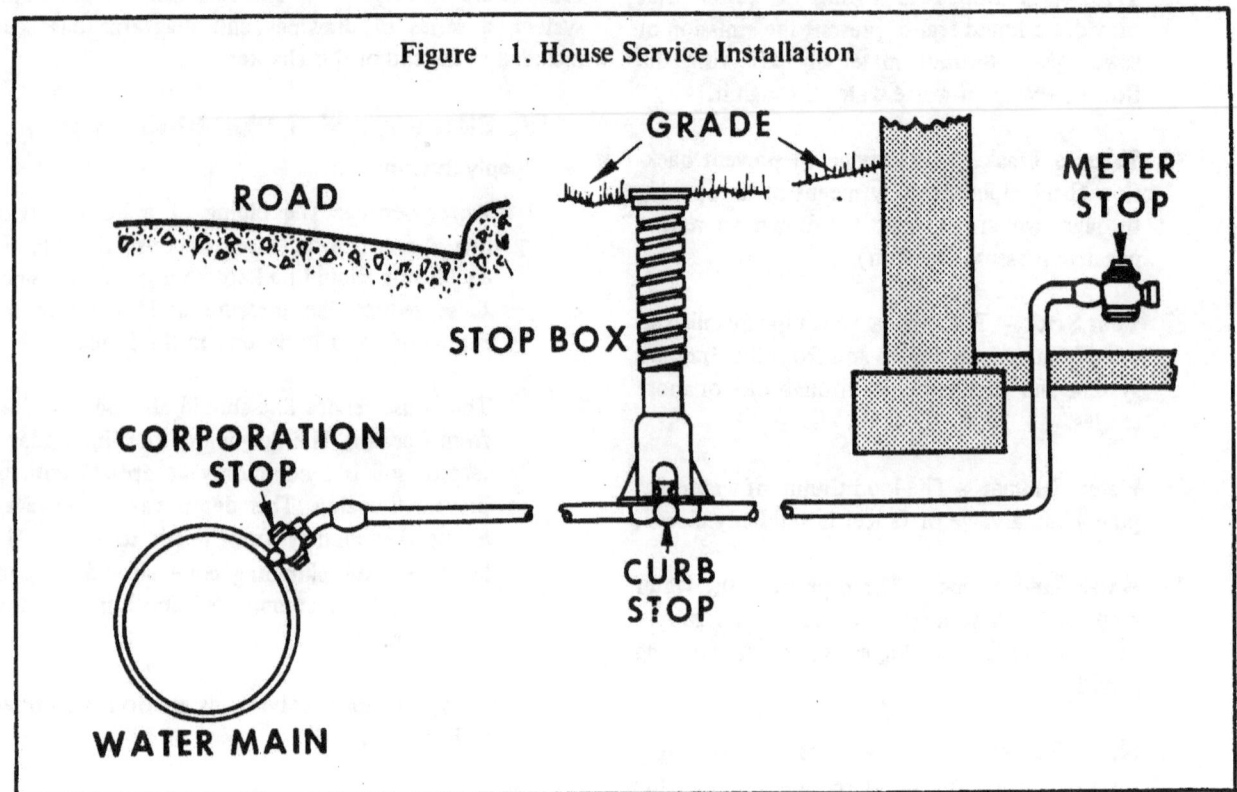

Figure 1. House Service Installation

    d **Meter stop** — The meter stop is a valve placed on the street side of the water meter to isolate the meter for installation or maintenance. Many codes require a gate valve on the house side of the meter to shut off water for house plumbing repairs. The curb and meter stops are not to be used frequently and can be ruined in a short time if used very frequently.

    e **Water meter** — The water meter is a device used to measure the amount of water used in the house. It is usually the property of the city and is a very delicate instrument that should not be abused.

       Since the electric system is usually grounded to the water line, a grounding loop-device should be installed around the meter. Many meters come with a yoke that maintains electrical continuity even though the meter is removed.

2 **Hot and Cold Water Main Lines:** The hot and cold water main lines are usually hung from the basement ceiling and are attached to the water meter and hot-water tank on one side and the fixture supply risers on the other.

These pipes should be installed in a neat manner and should be supported by pipe hangers or straps of sufficient strength and number to prevent sagging.

Hot and cold water lines should be approximately 6 inches apart unless the hot water line is insulated. This is to insure that the cold water line does not pick up heat from the hot water line.

The supply mains should have a drain valve or stop and waste valve in order to remove water from the system for repairs. These valves should be on the low end of the line or on the end of each fixture riser.

    a The **fixture risers** start at the basement main and rise vertically to the fixtures on the upper floors. In a one-family dwelling, riser branches will usually proceed from the main riser to each fixture grouping. In any event the fixture risers should not depend on the branch risers for support but should be supported with a pipe bracket.

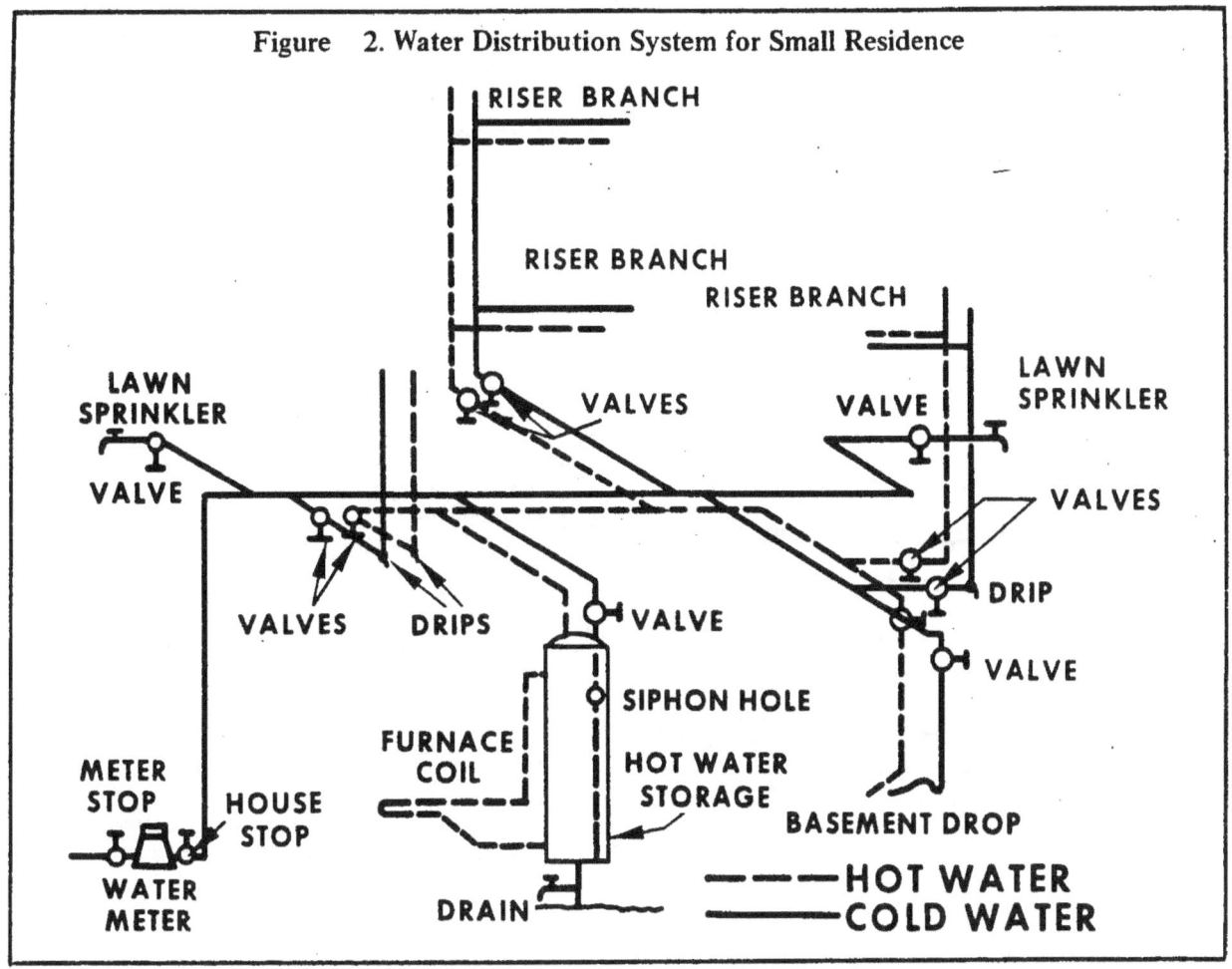

Figure 2. Water Distribution System for Small Residence

b Each fixture is then connected to the branch riser by a separate line. The last fixture on a line is usually connected directly to the branch riser. Figure 2 is a diagram of a typical single-family-residence water supply system.

3 **Hot Water Heaters:** Hot water heaters are usually powered by electricity, fuel oil, gas, or in rare cases, coal or wood. They consist of a space for heating the water and a storage tank for providing hot water over a limited period of time.

All hot water heaters should be fitted with a temperature-pressure relief valve no matter what fuel is used.

This valve will operate when either the temperature or the pressure becomes too high due to an interruption of the water supply or a faulty thermostat.

Figure 3 shows the correct installation of a hot water heater.

4 **Pipe Sizes:** The size of basement mains and risers depends on the number of fixtures supplied. However, a ¾ inch pipe is usually the minimum size used. This allows for deposits on the pipe due to hardness in the water and will usually give satisfactory volume and pressure.

B **Drainage System**

The water supply brought into the house and used is discharged through the drainage system. This system is either a sanitary drainage system carrying just interior waste water or a combined system carrying interior waste and roof runoff. The sanitary system will be discussed first.

1 **Sanitary Drainage System:** The proper sizing of the sanitary drain or house drain depends on the number of fixtures it serves. The usual

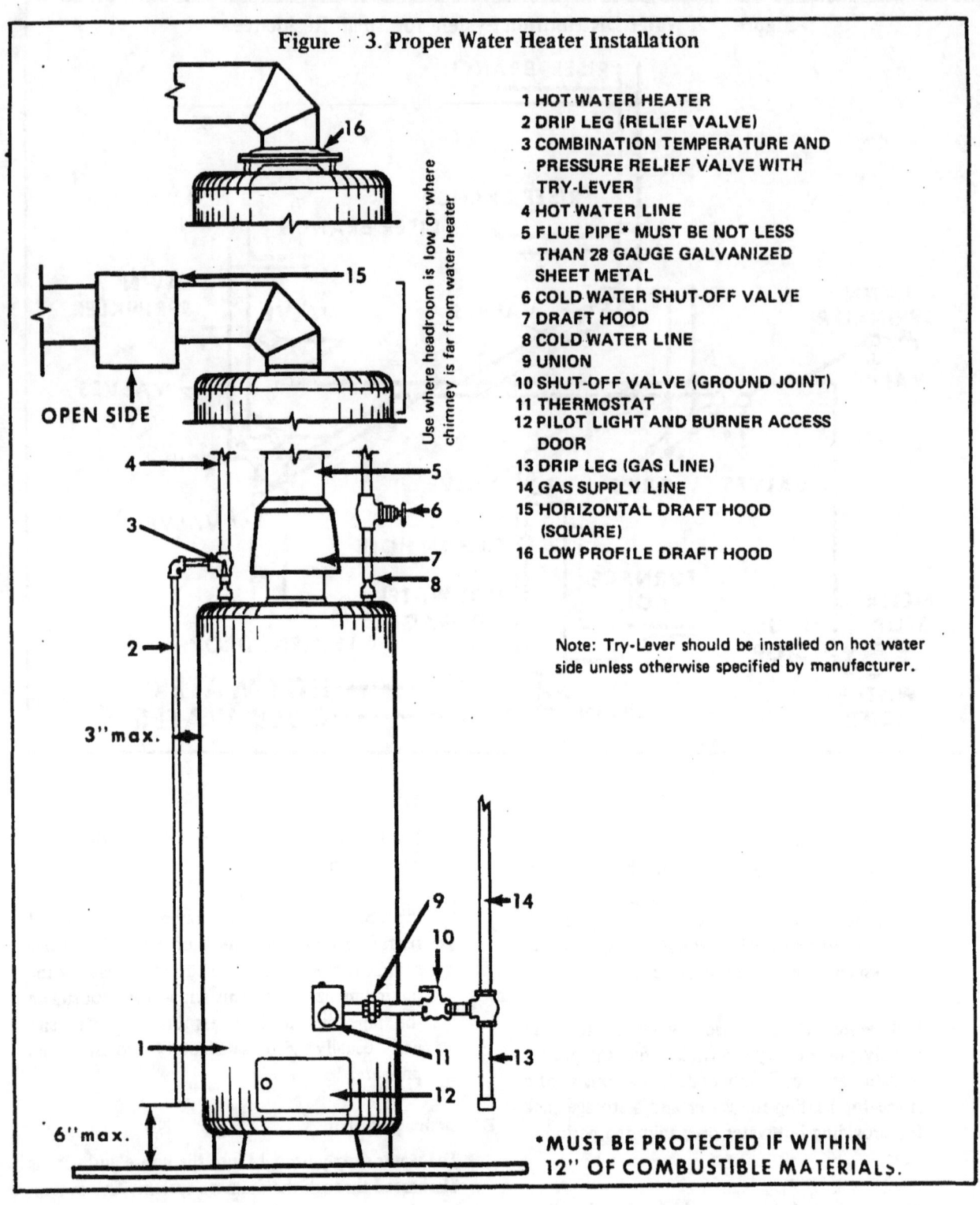

Figure 3. Proper Water Heater Installation

minimum size is 6 inches in diameter. The materials used are usually cast iron, vitrified clay, plastic, and in rare cases, lead. For proper flow in the drain the pipe should be sized so that it flows approximately one-half full. This ensures proper scouring action so that the solids contained in the waste will not be deposited in the pipe.

a **Sizing of house drain** — The Uniform Plumbing Code Committee has developed a method of sizing of house drains in terms of "fixture units." One "fixture unit" equals approximately 7½ gallons of water per minute. This is the surge flow-rate of water discharged from a wash basin in 1 minute. All other fixtures have been related to this unit.

A table fixture unit values is shown in Table 1.

The maximum number of fixture units attached to a sanitary drain is shown in Table 2.

b **Grade of house drain** — A house drain or building sewer should be sloped toward the sewer to ensure scouring of the drain. Figure 4 shows the results of proper and improper pitch of a house drain.

The usual pitch of a house or building sewer is ¼ inch fall in 1 foot of length.

Table 1. FIXTURE UNIT VALUES

Fixture	Units
Lavatory/wash basin	1
Kitchen sink	2
Bathtub	2
Laundry tub	2
Combination fixture	3
Urinal	5
Shower bath	2
Floor drain	1
Slop sinks	3
Water closet	6
One bathroom group (water closet, lavatory, bathtub, and shower; or water closet, lavatory, and shower)	8
180 square feet of roof drained	1

c **House drain installation** — A typical house drain installation is shown in Figure 5. Typical branch connections to the main are shown in Figure 6.

d **Fixture and branch drains** — A branch drain is a waste pipe that collects the waste from two or more fixtures and conveys it to the building or house sewer. It is sized in the same way as the house sewer, taking into account that all water closets must have a minimum 3-inch diameter drain, and

Table 2. SANITARY DRAIN SIZES

Maximum number of fixture units

Diameter of pipe, in.	Slope 1/8"/Ft.	Slope 1/4"/Ft.	Slope 1/2"/Ft.
1¼	1	1	1
1½	2	2	3
2	5	6	8
3	15	18	21
4	84	96	114
6	300	450	600
8	990	1,392	2,220
12	3,084	4,320	6,912

*A water closet must enter a 3 inch diameter drain and no more than 2 water closets may enter a 3 inch horizontal branch.

Figure 4. Results of Proper and Improper Pitch of a House Drain

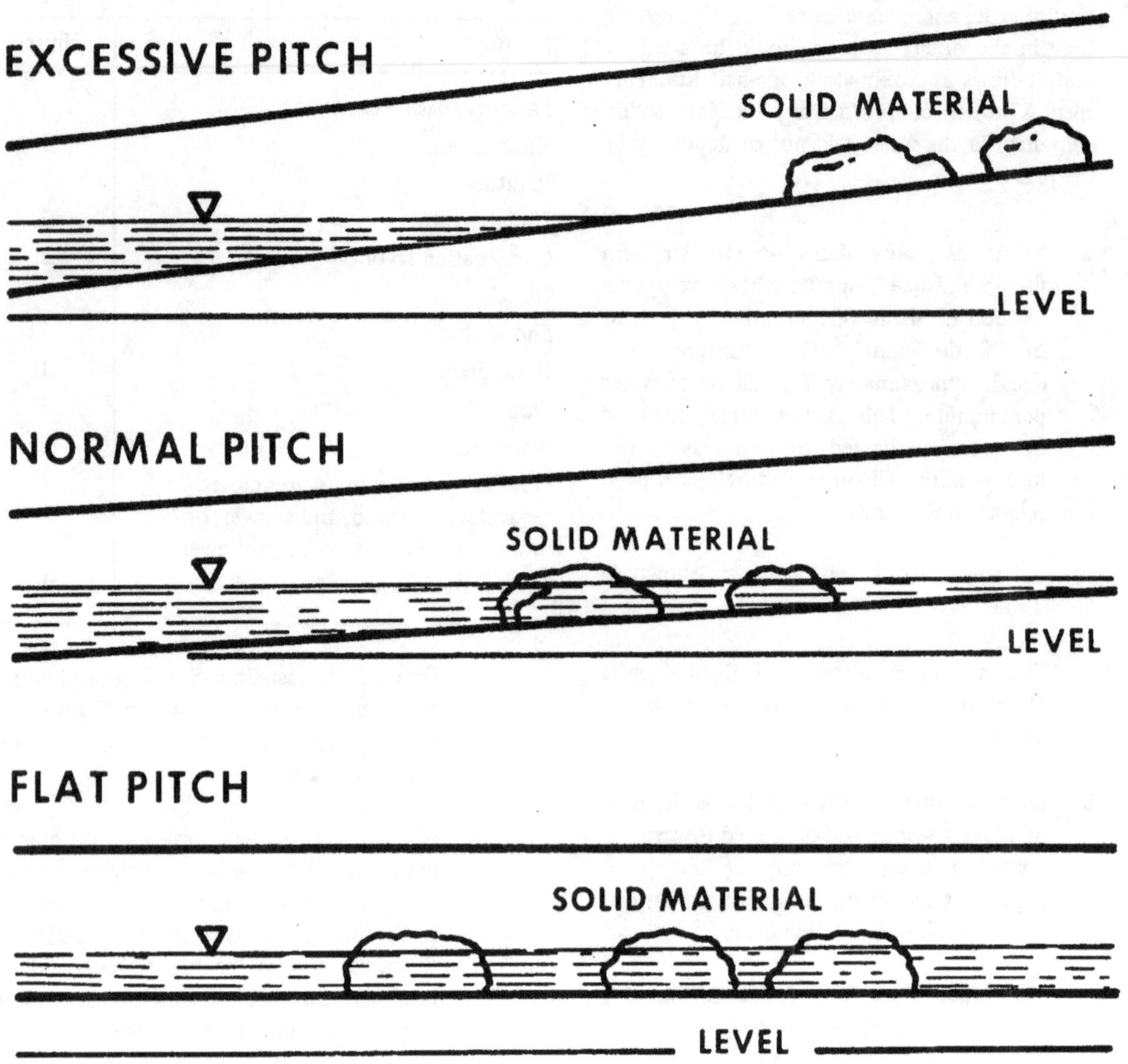

EXCESSIVE PITCH

NORMAL PITCH

FLAT PITCH

only two water closets may connect into one 3-inch drain.

All branch drains must join the house drain with a "Y"-type fitting as shown in Figure 6. The same is true for fixture drains joining branch drains.

The "Y" fitting is used to eliminate, as much as possible, the deposit of solids in or near the connection. A build-up of these solids will cause a blockage in the drain.

The recommended minimum size of fixture drain is shown in Table 3.

e **Traps** — A plumbing trap is a device used in a waste system to prevent the passage of sewer gas into the structure and yet not hinder the fixture's discharge to any great extent. All fixtures connected to a household plumbing system should have a trap installed in the line.

Table 3. MINIMUM FIXTURE SERVICE

Fixture	Supply line, in.	Vent line, in.	Drain line, in.
Bathtub	½	1½	1½-2
Kitchen sink	½	1½	1½
Lavatory	3/8	1¼	1¼
Laundry sink	½	1½	1½
Shower	½	2	2
Water closet (tank)	3/8	3	3

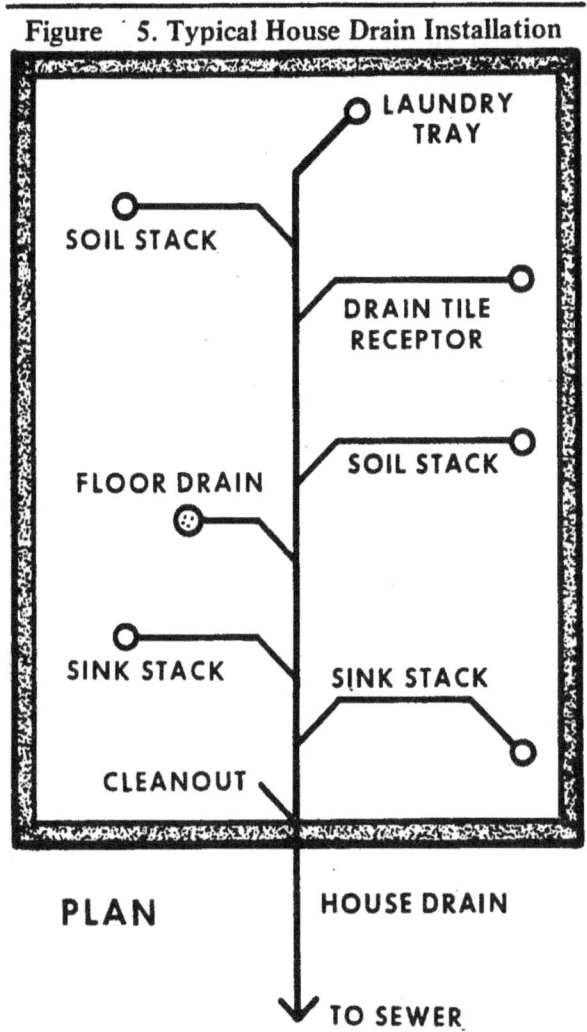

Figure 5. Typical House Drain Installation

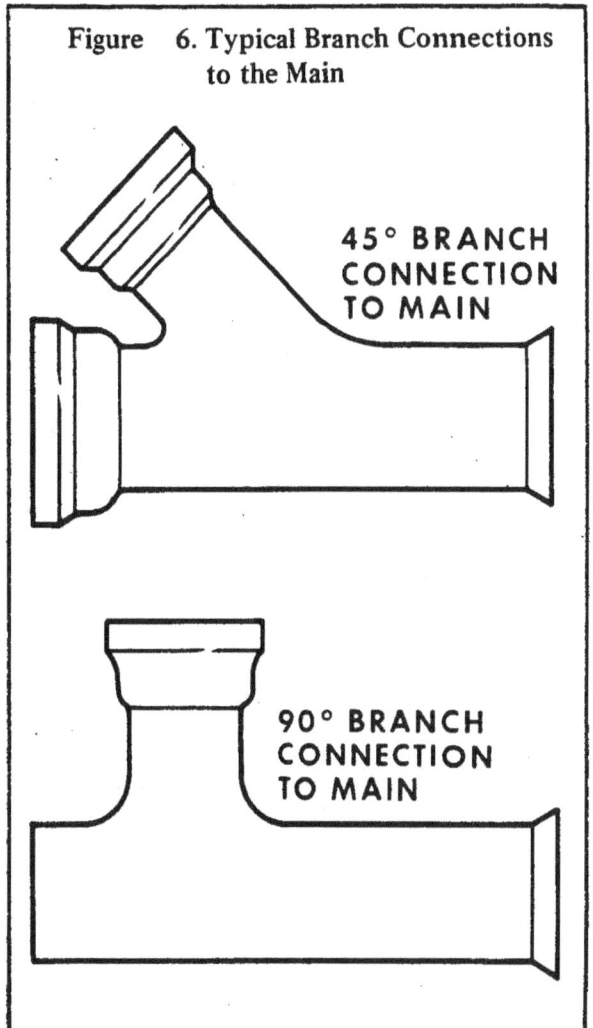

Figure 6. Typical Branch Connections to the Main

The effect of sewer gases on the human body are known; many are extremely harmful. Additionally, certain sewer gases are explosive. A trap will prevent these gases from passing into the structure.

1) "P" trap — The most common trap found today is the "P" trap. Figure 6-7 is a drawing of a "P" trap.

The depth of the seal in a trap is usually 2 inches. A deep seal trap has a 4-inch seal.

As was mentioned earlier, the purpose of a trap is to seal out sewer gases from the structure. Since a plumbing system is subject to wide variations in flow, and this flow originates in many different sections of the system, there is a wide variation in pressures in the waste lines. These pressure differences tend to destroy the water seal in the trap.

To counteract this problem mechanical traps were introduced. It has been found, however, that the corrosive liquids flowing in the system corrode or jam these mechanical traps. It is for this reason that most plumbing codes prohibit mechanical traps.

There are many manufacturers of traps, and all have varied the design somewhat. Figures 8 and 9 show various types of "P" traps. The "P" trap is usually found in lavatories, sinks, urinals, drinking fountains, showers, and other installations that do not discharge a great deal of water.

10

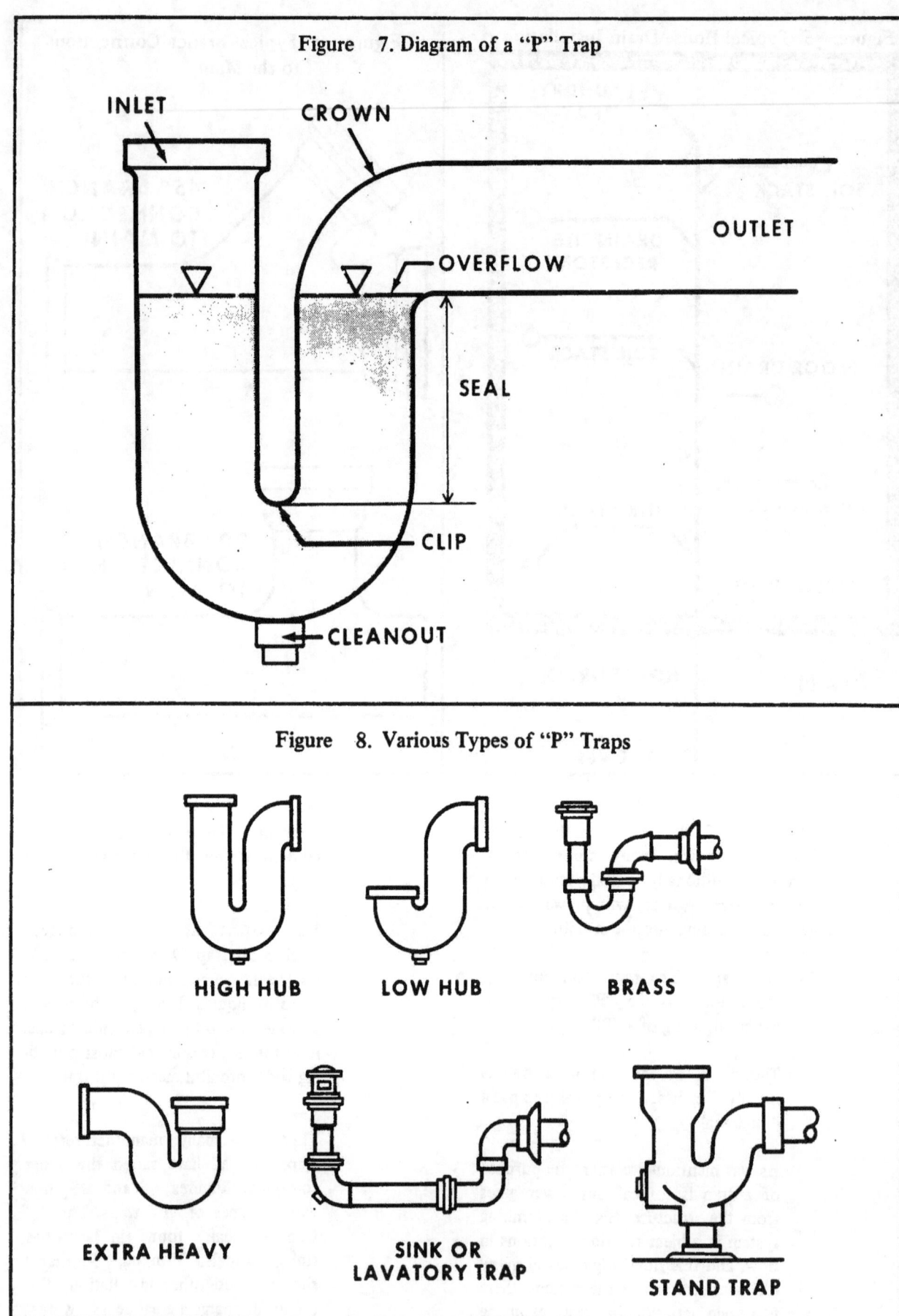

Figure 7. Diagram of a "P" Trap

Figure 8. Various Types of "P" Traps

2) Drum trap — The drum trap is another water seal-type trap. They are usually used in the 4- x 5-inch or 4- x 8-inch sizes. These traps have a greater sealing capacity than the "P" trap and pass large amounts of water quickly. Figure 10 shows a drum trap.

Drum traps are commonly connected to bathtubs, foot baths, sitz baths, and modified shower baths. Figure 11 shows a drum trap connected to a bathtub and shower.

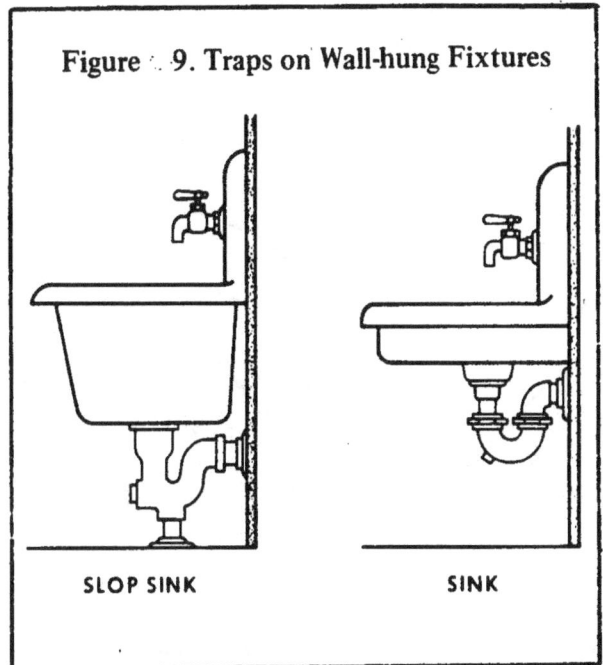

Figure 9. Traps on Wall-hung Fixtures

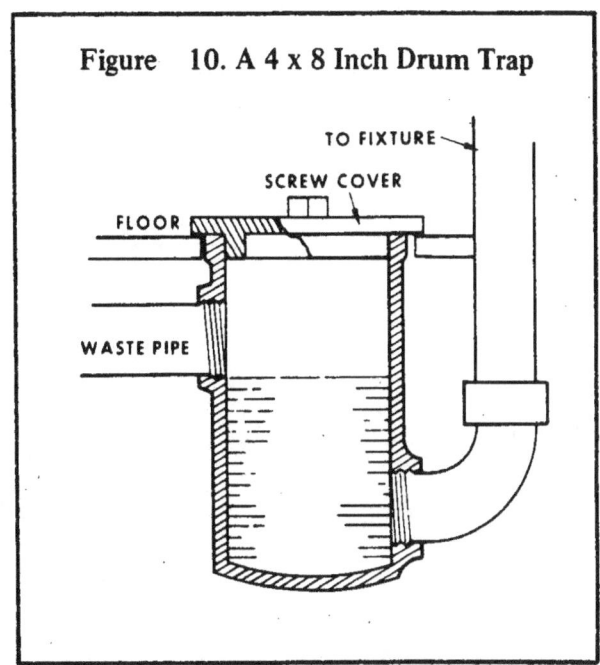

Figure 10. A 4 x 8 Inch Drum Trap

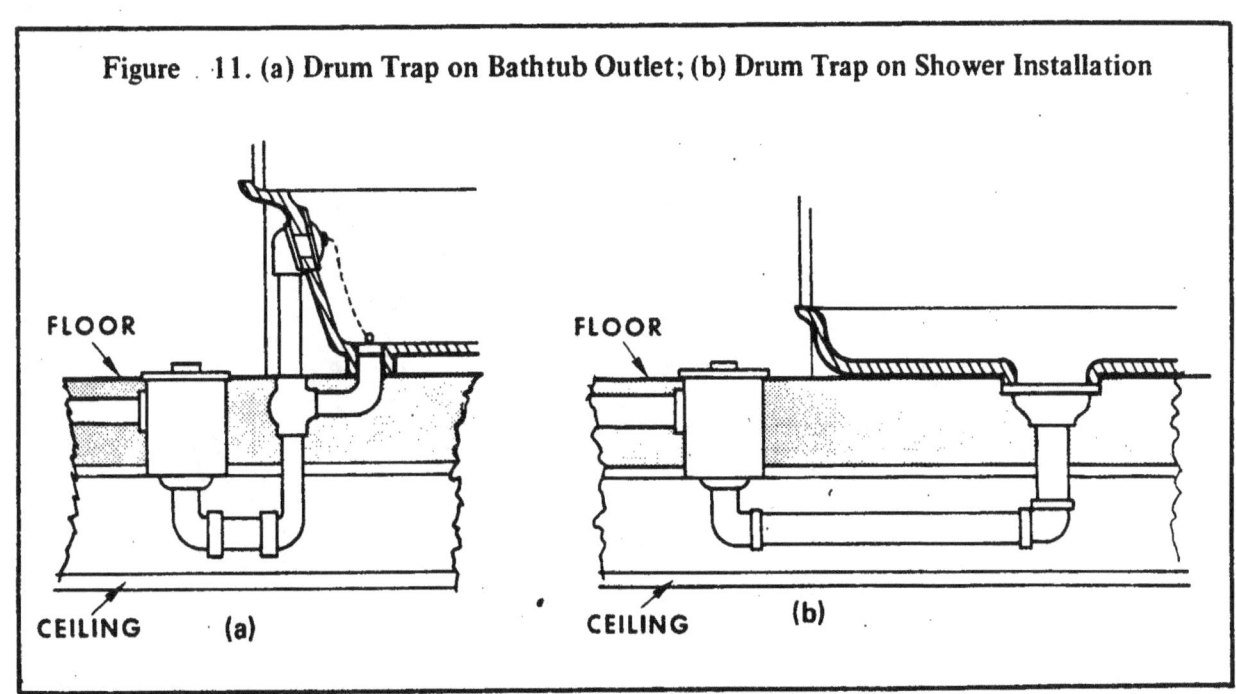

Figure 11. (a) Drum Trap on Bathtub Outlet; (b) Drum Trap on Shower Installation

3) Objectionable traps — The "S" trap and the ¾ "S" trap should not be used in plumbing installations. They are almost impossible to ventilate properly, and the ¾ "S" trap forms a perfect siphon.

The bag trap, an extreme form of "S" trap, is seldom found. Figure 12 shows these types of "S" traps.

Figure 13 shows one type of mechanically sealed trap. Any trap that depends on a moving part for its effectiveness is usually inadequate and has been prohibited by the local plumbing codes.

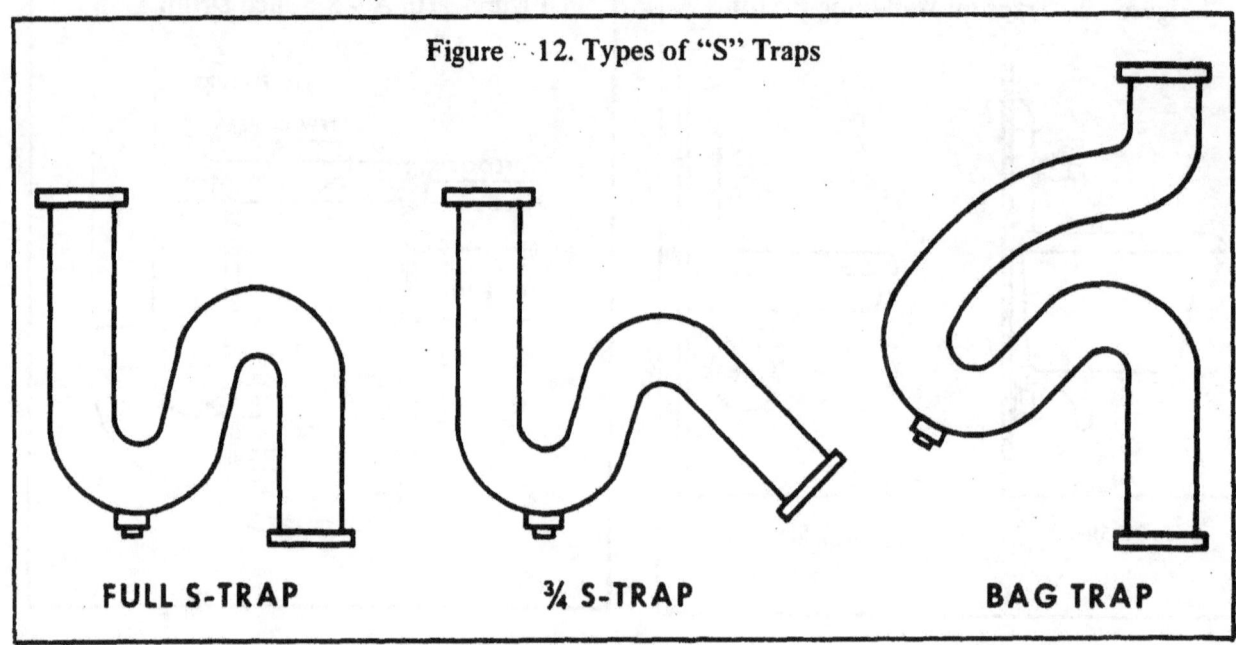

Figure 12. Types of "S" Traps

FULL S-TRAP   ¾ S-TRAP   BAG TRAP

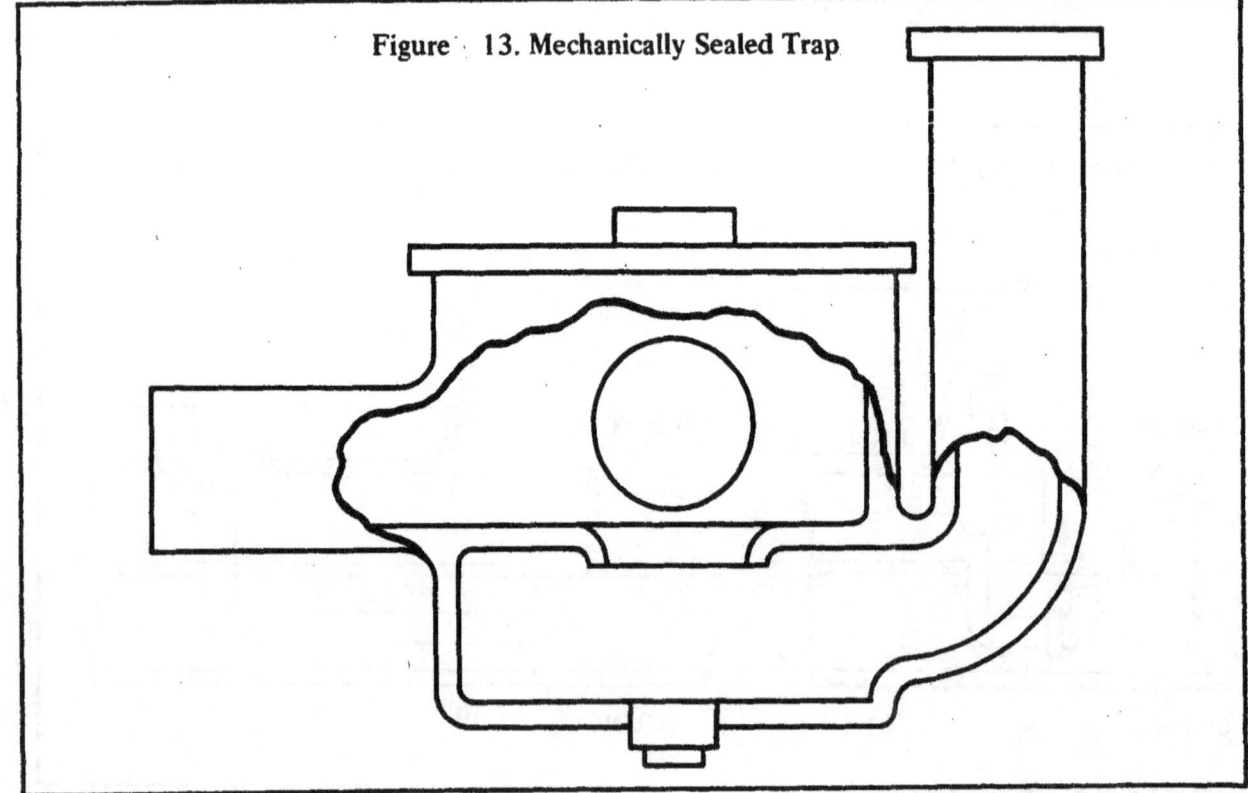

Figure 13. Mechanically Sealed Trap

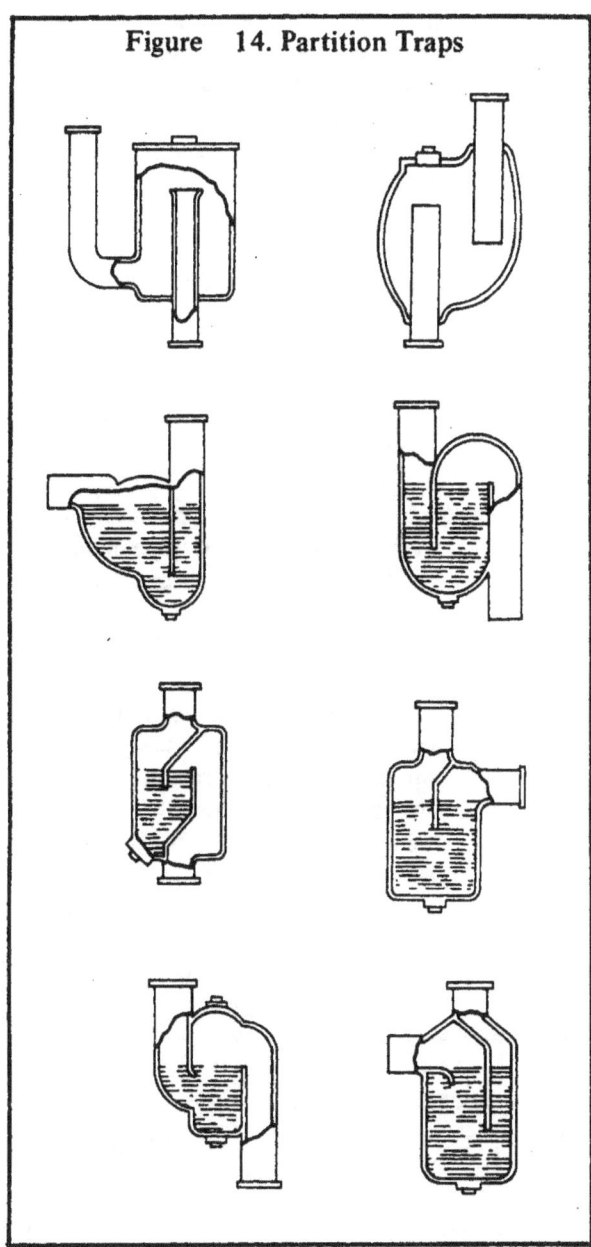

Figure 14. Partition Traps

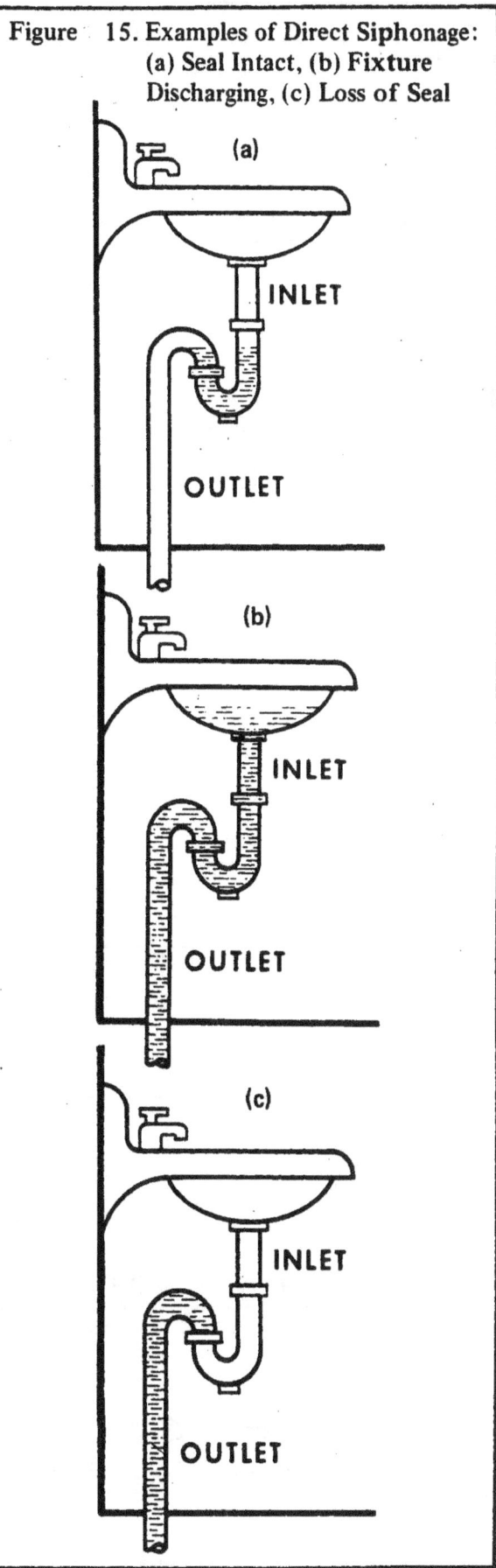

Figure 15. Examples of Direct Siphonage: (a) Seal Intact, (b) Fixture Discharging, (c) Loss of Seal

Figure 14 shows various types of internal partition traps. These traps work, but their design usually results in their being higher priced than the "P" or drum traps.

It should be remembered that traps are used only to prevent the escape of sewer gas into the structure. They do not compensate for pressure variations. Only proper venting will eliminate pressure problems.

f   Ventilation — A plumbing system is ventilated to prevent trap seal loss, material deterioration, and flow retardation.

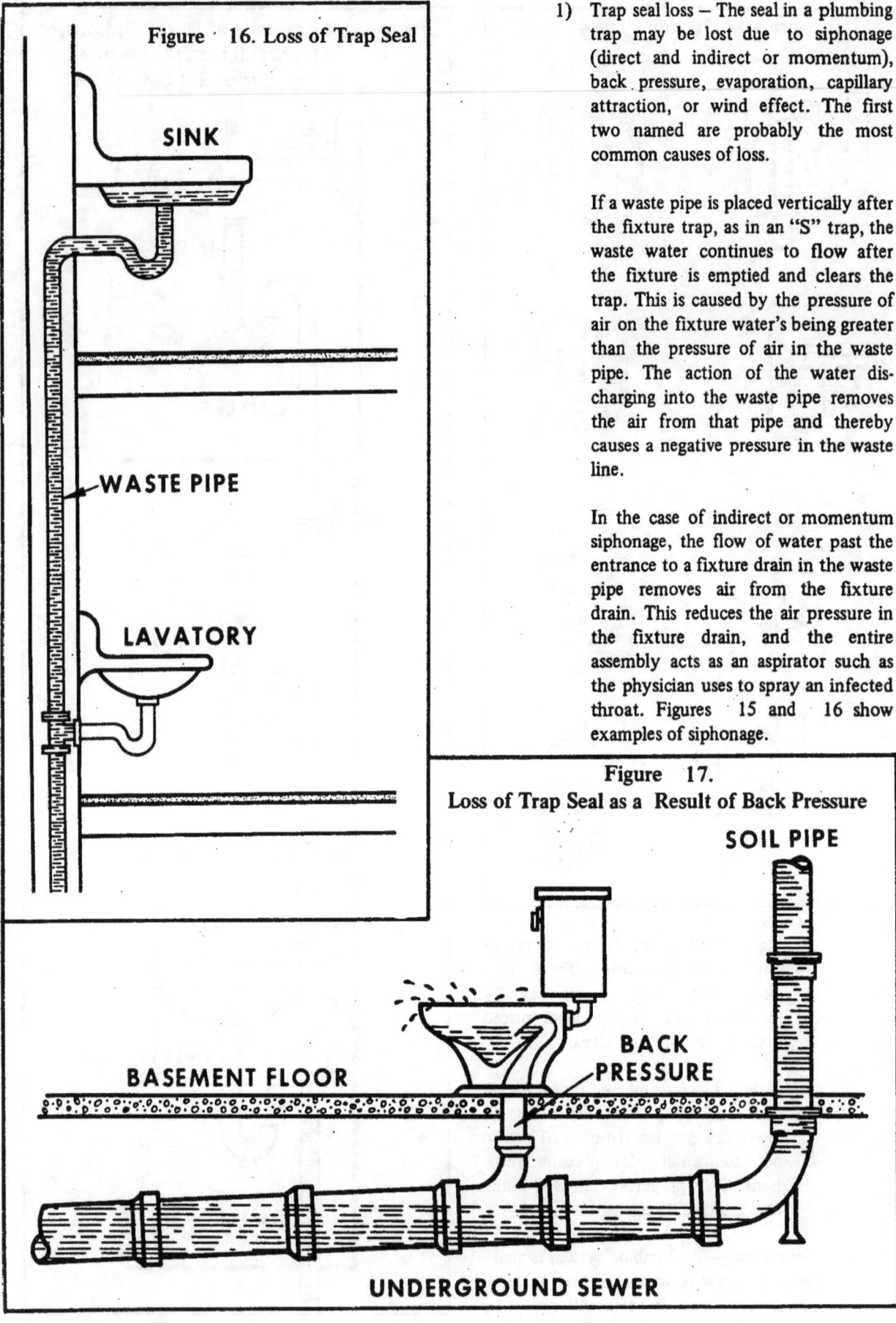

Figure 16. Loss of Trap Seal

1) Trap seal loss — The seal in a plumbing trap may be lost due to siphonage (direct and indirect or momentum), back pressure, evaporation, capillary attraction, or wind effect. The first two named are probably the most common causes of loss.

If a waste pipe is placed vertically after the fixture trap, as in an "S" trap, the waste water continues to flow after the fixture is emptied and clears the trap. This is caused by the pressure of air on the fixture water's being greater than the pressure of air in the waste pipe. The action of the water discharging into the waste pipe removes the air from that pipe and thereby causes a negative pressure in the waste line.

In the case of indirect or momentum siphonage, the flow of water past the entrance to a fixture drain in the waste pipe removes air from the fixture drain. This reduces the air pressure in the fixture drain, and the entire assembly acts as an aspirator such as the physician uses to spray an infected throat. Figures 15 and 16 show examples of siphonage.

Figure 17. Loss of Trap Seal as a Result of Back Pressure

2) Back pressure — The flow of water in a soil pipe varies according to the fixtures being used. A lavatory gives a small flow and a water closet a large flow. Small flows tend to cling to the sides of the pipe, but large ones form a slug of waste as they drop. As this slug of water falls down the pipe the air in front of it becomes pressurized. As the pressure builds it seeks an escape point. This point is either a vent or a fixture outlet. If the vent is plugged or there is no vent, the only escape for this air is the fixture outlet. The air pressure forces the trap seal up the pipe into the fixture. If the pressure is great enough the seal is blown out of the fixture entirely. Figures 17 and 18 illustrate this type of problem.

3) Vent sizing — Vent pipe installation is similar to that of soil and waste pipe. The same fixture unit criteria are used. Table 3 shows minimum vent pipe sizes.

Vent pipes of less than 1¼ inches in diameter should not be used. Vents smaller than this diameter tend to clog and do not perform their function.

4) Individual fixture ventilation — Figure 19 shows a typical installation of a wall-hung plumbing unit. This type of ventilation is generally used for sinks, lavatories, drinking fountains, and so forth.

Figure 20 shows a typical installation of a bathtub or shower ventilation system.

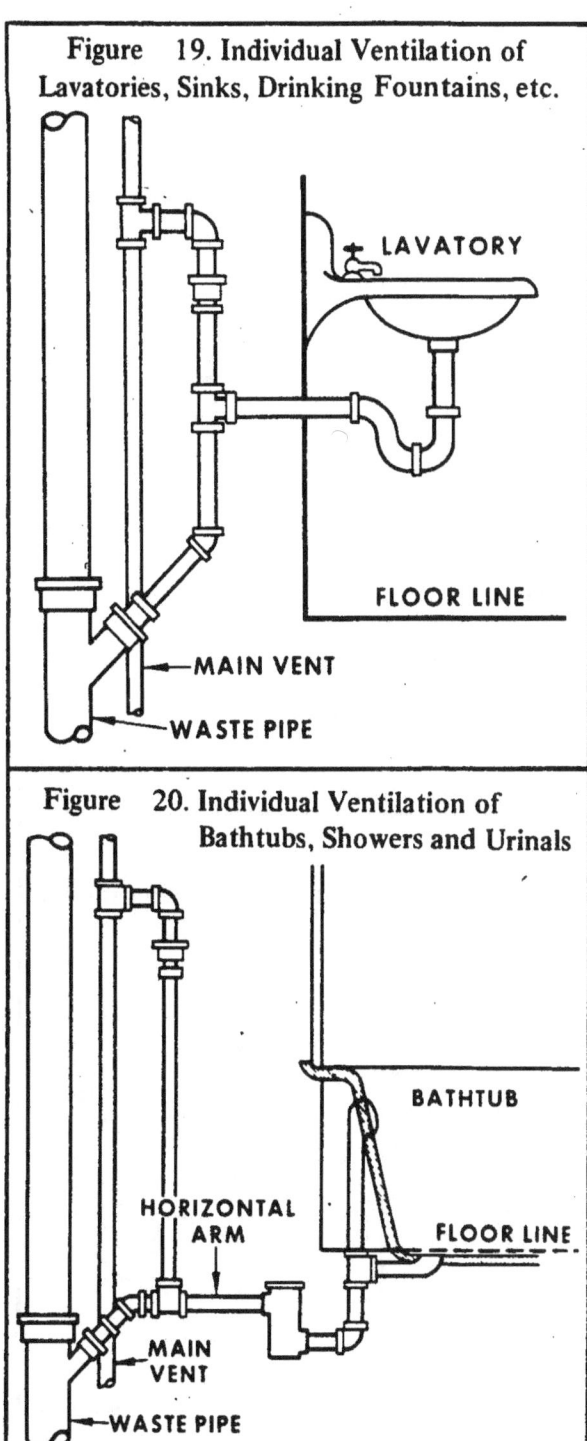

Figure 19. Individual Ventilation of Lavatories, Sinks, Drinking Fountains, etc.

Figure 20. Individual Ventilation of Bathtubs, Showers and Urinals

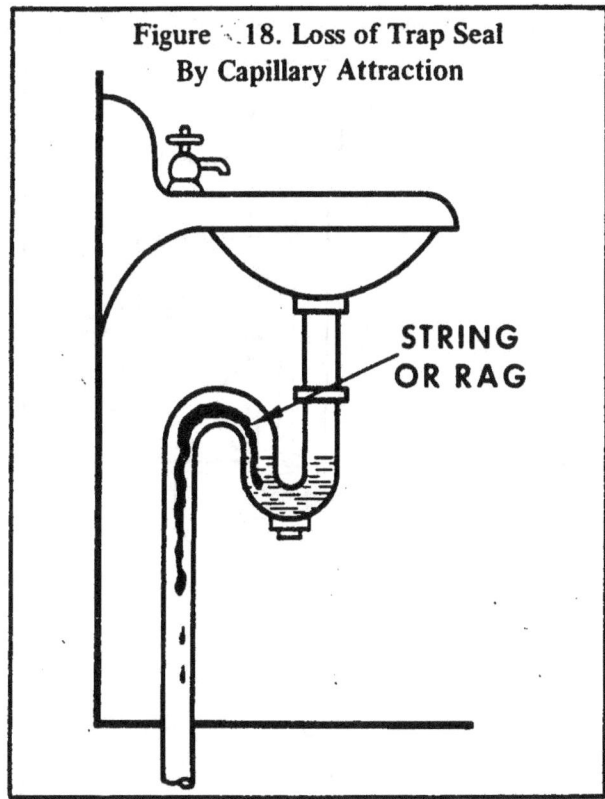

Figure 18. Loss of Trap Seal By Capillary Attraction

Figure 21 shows the proper vent connection for a water closet or slop sink. The water closet can be either a tank type or a flushometer valve type.

5) Unit venting — Figures 22 to 24 picture a back-to-back ventilation system for various common plumbing fixtures. The unit venting system is commonly used in apartment buildings. This type of system saves a great deal of money and space when fixtures are placed back to back in separate apartments.

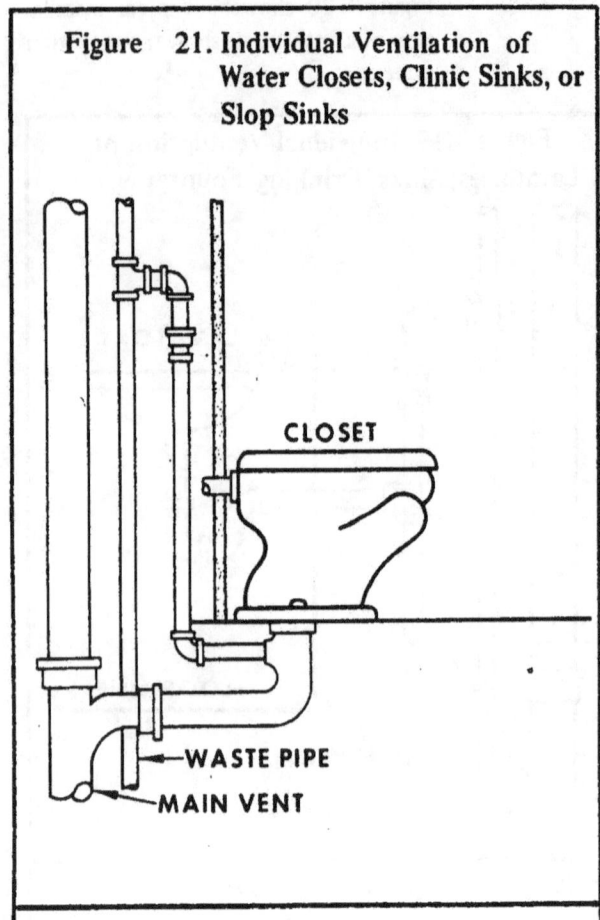

Figure 21. Individual Ventilation of Water Closets, Clinic Sinks, or Slop Sinks

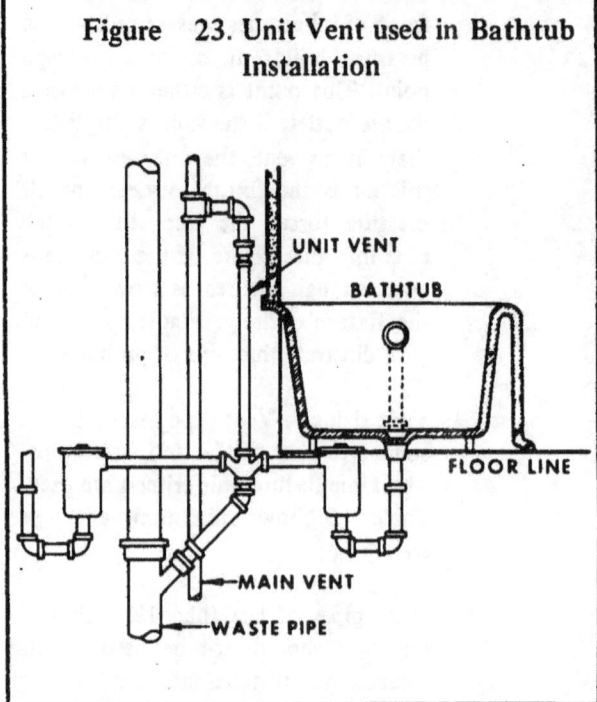

Figure 23. Unit Vent used in Bathtub Installation

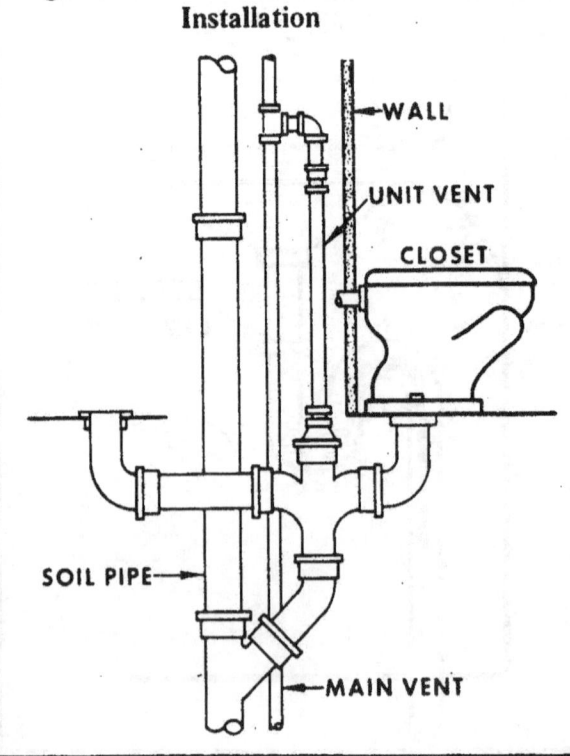

Figure 22. Unit Vent Method of Ventilating Wall-hung Fixture Traps

Figure 24. Unit Vent used in Water Closet Installation

Figure 25 shows a double combination "Y" used for joining the fixtures to the common soil pipe. The deflectors are to prevent waste from one fixture flowing back up into the waste in the attached fixture on the other side of the wall.

6) Wet venting — Wet venting of a plumbing system is common in household bathroom fixture grouping. It is exactly what the name implies: the vent pipe is used as a waste line. Figure 26 shows a typical wet-vent installation in a home.

7) Total drainage system — Up to now we have talked about the drain, soil waste, and vent systems of a plumbing system separately. For a working system, however, they must all be connected. Figures 27 through 32 show some typical drainage systems that are found in homes and small apartment buildings.

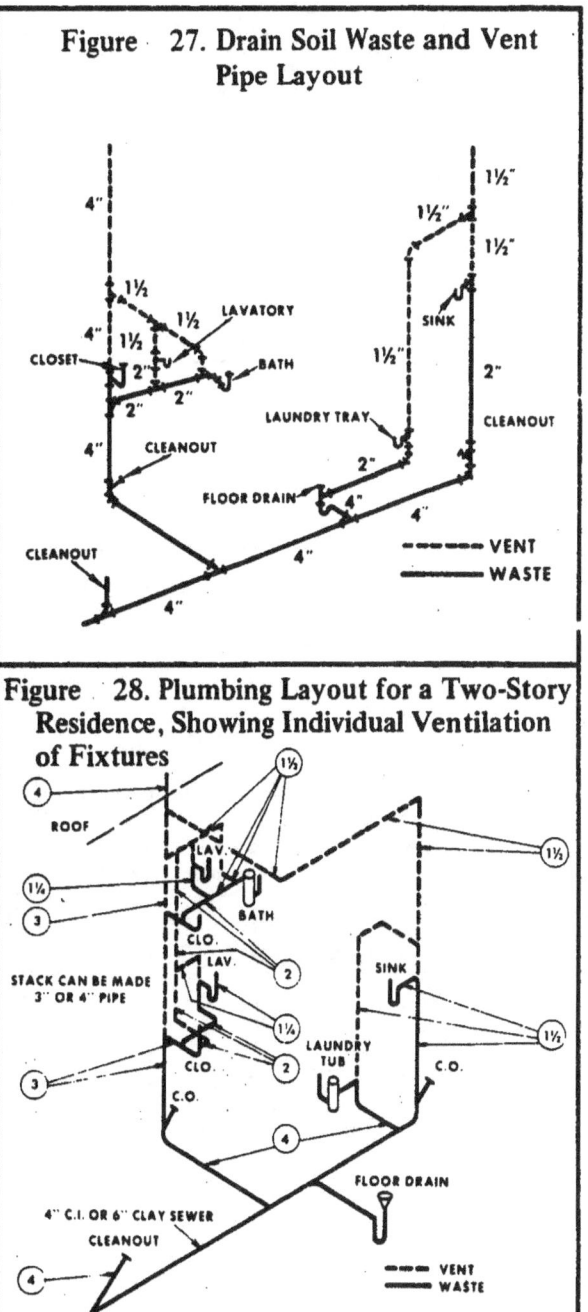

Figure 25. Double Combination Y and 1/8 Bend with Deflectors

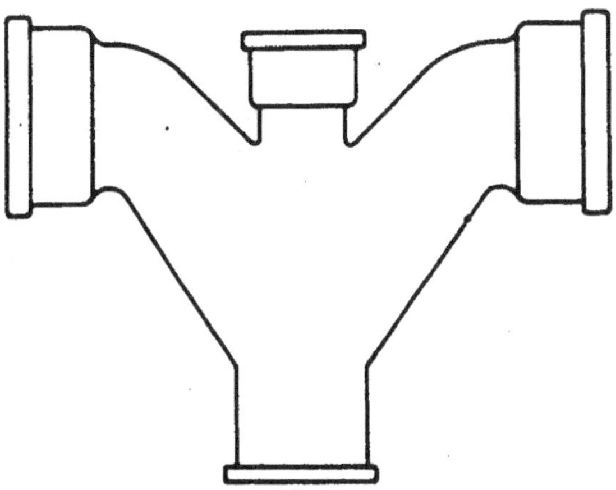

Figure 26. West Vent Used in Connection With Bathroom Group of Fixtures

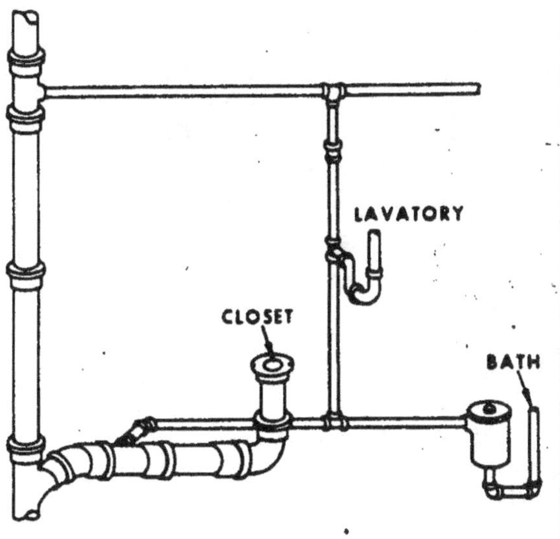

Figure 27. Drain Soil Waste and Vent Pipe Layout

Figure 28. Plumbing Layout for a Two-Story Residence, Showing Individual Ventilation of Fixtures

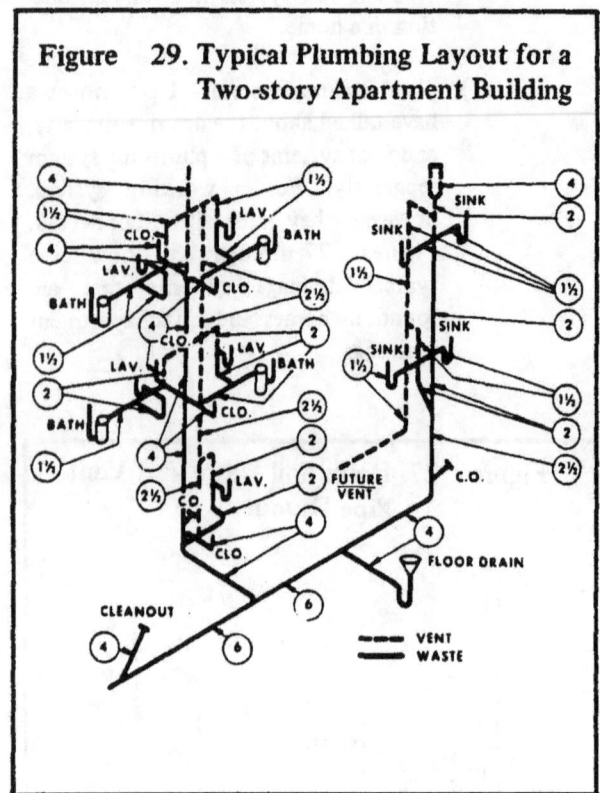

Figure 29. Typical Plumbing Layout for a Two-story Apartment Building

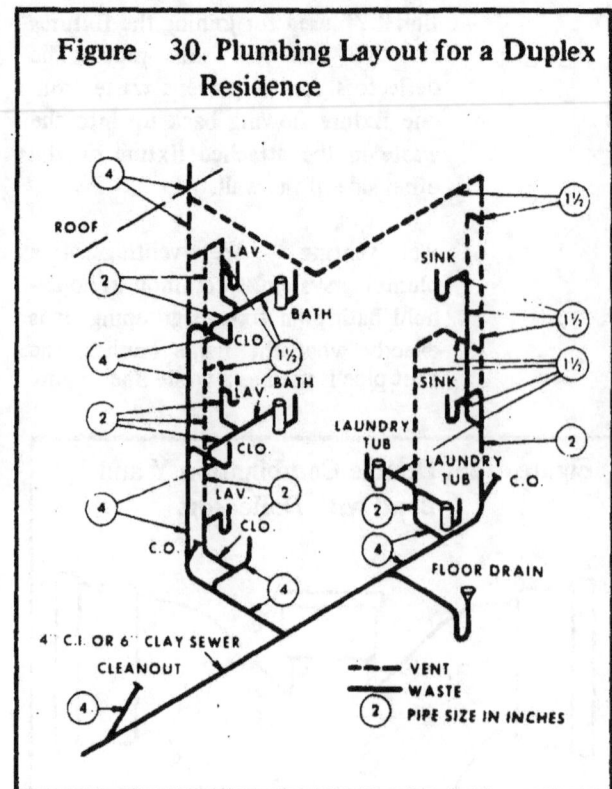

Figure 30. Plumbing Layout for a Duplex Residence

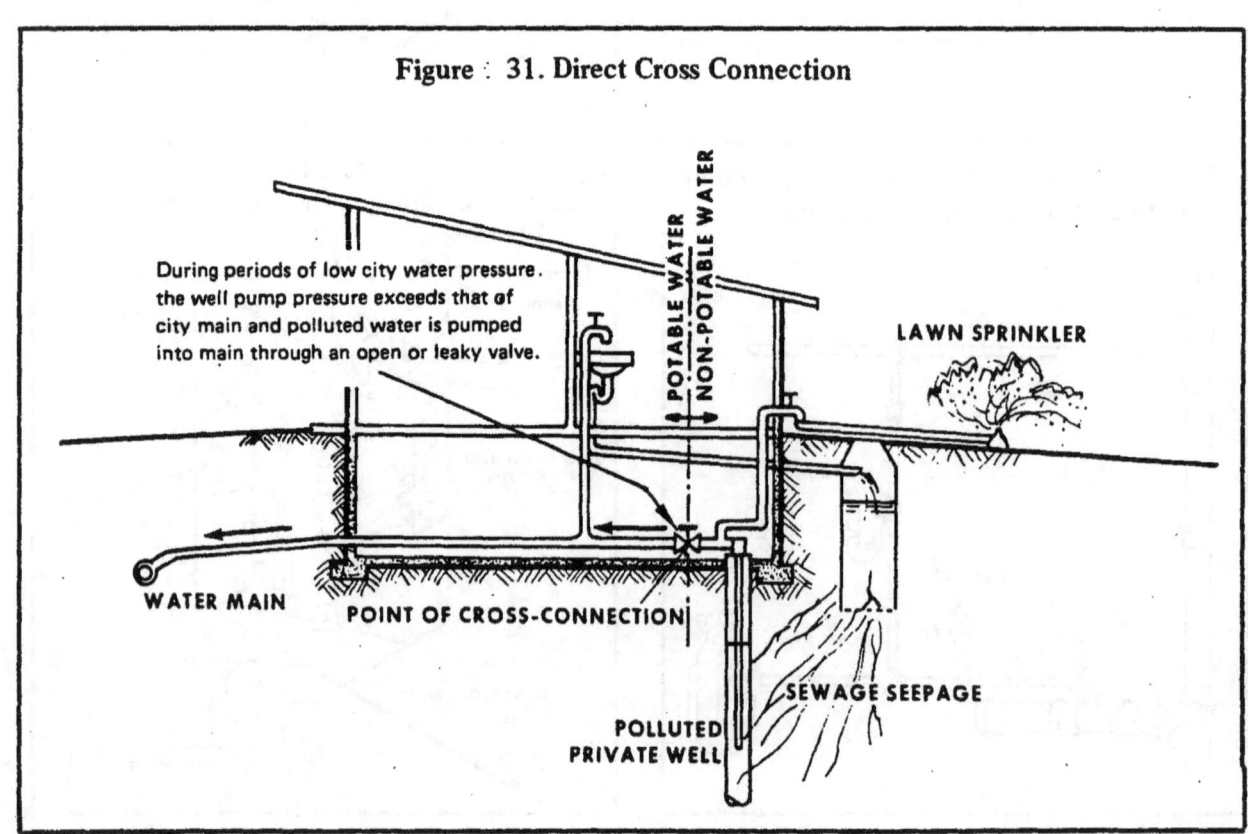

Figure 31. Direct Cross Connection

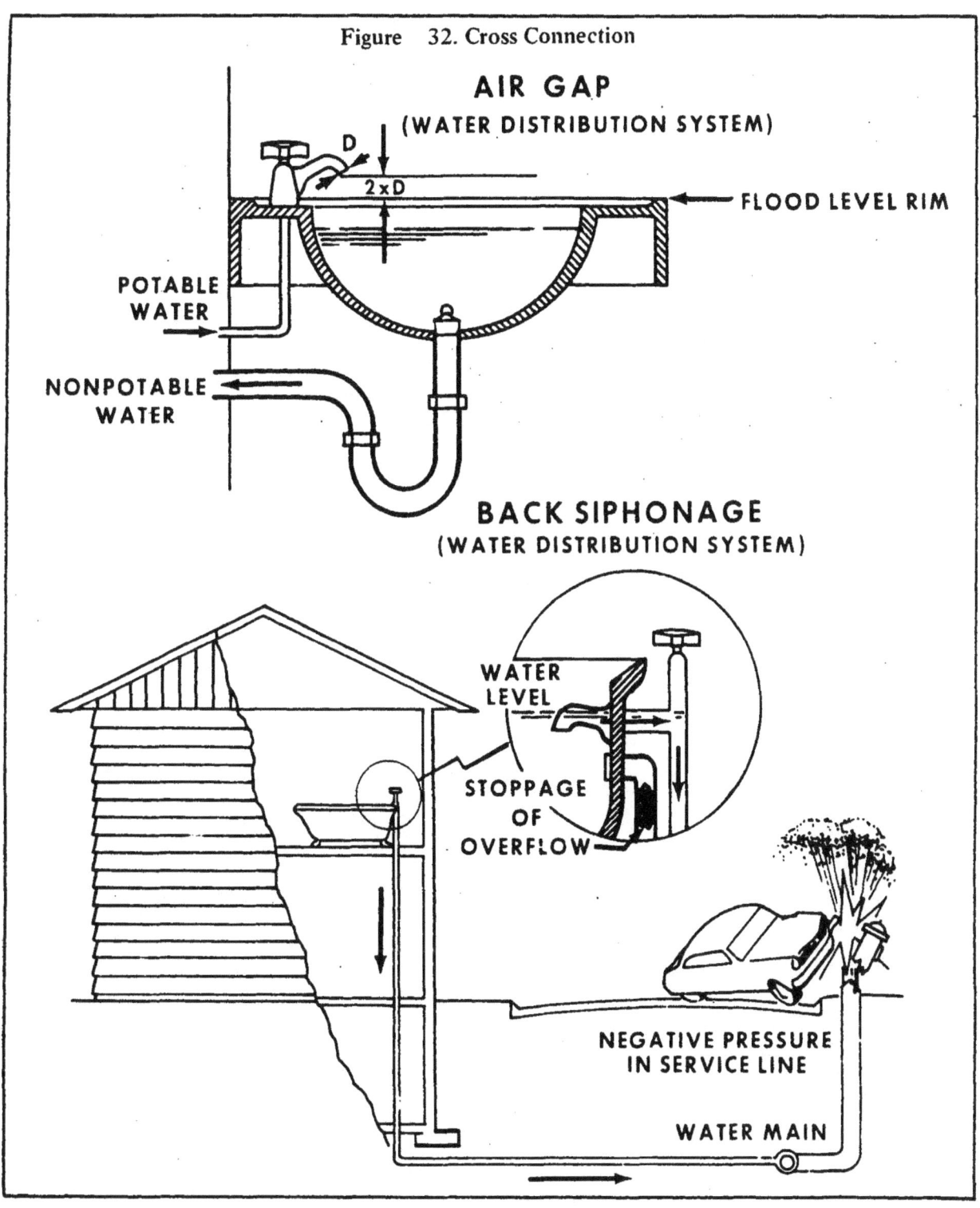

Figure 32. Cross Connection

BASIC FUNDAMENTALS OF PLUMBING
CONTENTS

		Page
CHAPTERS		
I.	DEFINITIONS	1
II.	GENERAL REGULATIONS	4
III.	QUALITY, WEIGHT, AND THICKNESS OF MATERIALS	5
IV.	JOINTS AND CONNECTIONS	6
V.	TRAPS AND CLEAN-OUTS	7
VI.	WATER SUPPLY AND DISTRIBUTION	8
VII.	PLUMBING FIXTURES	9
VIII.	SOIL AND WASTE PIPES FOR SANITARY SYSTEMS	9
IX.	STORM DRAINS	10
X.	VENTS AND VENTING	11
XI.	INDIRECT CONNECTIONS TO WASTE PIPES	13
XII.	MAINTENANCE	13
XIII.	INSPECTION AND TESTS	13
FIGURES		
1.	STANDARD PLUMBING SYMBOLS	15
2.	ILLUSTRATION OF DEFINITIONS	16

BASIC FUNDAMENTALS OF PLUMBING

CHAPTER I. DEFINITIONS

SEC. 101.—DEFINITIONS.

Accepted standards.—Accepted standards are the standards cited in this manual, or other standards approved by the authority having jurisdiction over plumbing.

Air gap.—The air gap in a water-supply system for plumbing fixtures is the vertical distance between the supply-fitting outlet (spout) and the highest possible water level in the receptor when flooded.

If the plane of the end of the spout is at an angle to the surface of the water, the mean gap is the basis for measurement.

Approved.—Approved means accepted as satisfactory to the authority having jurisdiction over plumbing.

Area drain.—An area drain is a drain installed to collect surface or rain water from an open area.

Backflow.—Backflow means the flow of water into a water-supply system from any source except its regular one. Back siphonage is one type of backflow.

Backflow connection.—A backflow connection is any arrangement whereby backflow can occur.

Back vent.—A back vent is a branch vent installed primarily for the purpose of protecting fixture traps from self-siphonage.

Branch.—A branch is any part of a piping system other than a main. (See *Main.*)

Branch interval.—A branch interval is a length of soil or waste stack corresponding in general to a story height, but in no case less than 8 feet, within which the horizontal branches from one floor or story of the building are connected to the stack.

Branch vent.—A branch vent is any vent pipe connecting from a branch of the drainage system to the vent stack.

Building drain.—The building (house) drain is that part of the lowest horizontal piping of a building-drainage system which receives the discharge from soil, waste, and other drainage pipes inside the walls of the building and conveys it to the building (house) sewer beginning 5 feet outside the inner face of the building wall.

Building-drainage system.—The building-drainage system consists of all piping provided for carrying waste water, sewage, or other drainage from the building to the street sewer or place of disposal.

Building main.—The building main is the water-supply pipe, including fittings and accessories, from the water (street) main or other source of supply to the first branch of the water-distributing system.

Building sewer.—The building (house) sewer is that part of the horizontal piping of a building-drainage system extending from the building drain 5 feet outside of the inner face of the building wall to the street sewer or other place of disposal (a cesspool, septic tank, or other type of sewage-treatment device or devices) and conveying the drainage of but one building site.

Building subdrain.—A building (house) subdrain is that portion of a drainage system which cannot drain by gravity into the building sewer.

Circuit vent.—A circuit vent is a group vent extending from in front of the last fixture connection of a horizontal branch to the vent stack.

Combination fixture.—Combination fixture is a trade term designating an integral combination of one sink and one or two laundry trays in one fixture.

Continuous-waste-and-vent.—A continuous-waste-and-vent is a vent that is a continuation of and in a straight line with the drain to which it connects. A continuous-waste-and-vent is further defined by the angle the drain and vent at the point of connection make with the horizontal; for example, vertical continuous-waste-and-vent, 45° continuous-waste-and-vent, and flat (small-angle) continuous-waste-and-vent.

Continuous waste.—A waste from two or more fixtures connected to a single trap.

Cross-connection.—See *Interconnection.*

Developed length.—The developed length of a pipe is its length along the center line of the pipe and fittings.

Diameter.—Unless specifically stated, the term diameter means the nominal diameter as designated commercially.

Distance.—The distance or difference in elevation between two sloping pipes is the distance between the intersection of their center lines with the center line of the pipe to which both are connected.

Double offset.—A double offset is two offsets installed in succession or series in the same line.

Drain.—A drain or drain pipe is any pipe which carries water or water-borne wastes in a building-drainage system.

Drainage piping.—Drainage piping is all or any part of the drain pipes of a plumbing system.

Dry vent.—A dry vent is any vent that does not carry water or water-borne wastes.

Dual vent.—A dual vent (sometimes called a unit vent) is a group vent connecting at the junction of two fixture branches and serving as a back vent for both branches.

Effective opening.—The effective opening is the minimum cross-sectional area between the end of the supply-fitting outlet (spout) and the inlet to the controlling valve or faucet. The basis of measurement is the diameter of a circle of equal cross-sectional area.

If two or more lines supply one outlet, the effective opening is the sum of the effective openings of the individual lines or the area of the combined outlet, whichever is the smaller.

Fixture branch.—A fixture branch is the supply pipe between the fixture and the water-distributing pipe.

Fixture drain.—A fixture drain is the drain from the trap of a fixture to the junction of the drain with any other drain pipe.

Fixture unit.—A fixture unit is a factor so chosen that the load-producing values of the different plumbing fixtures can be expressed approximately as multiples of that factor.

Flood level.—Flood level in reference to a plumbing fixture is the level at which water begins to overflow the top or rim of the fixture.

Grade.—The grade of a line of pipe is its slope in reference to a horizontal plane. In plumbing it is usually expressed as the fall in inches per foot length of pipe.

Group vent.—A group vent is a branch vent that performs its functions for two or more traps.

Horizontal branch.—A horizontal branch is a branch drain extending laterally from a soil or waste stack or building drain, with or without vertical sections or branches, which receives the discharge from one or more fixture drains and conducts it to the soil or waste stack or to the building (house) drain.

Indirect waste pipe.—An indirect waste pipe is a waste pipe which does not connect directly with the building-drainage system, but discharges into it through a properly trapped fixture or receptacle.

Interconnection.—An interconnection, as the term is used in this manual, is any physical connection or arrangement of pipes between two otherwise separate building water-supply systems whereby water may flow from one system to the other, the direction of flow depending upon the pressure differential between the two systems.

Where such connection occurs between the sources of two such systems and the first branch from either, whether inside or outside the building, the term cross-connection (American Water Works terminology) applies and is generally used.

Jumpover.—See *Return offset.*

Leader.—A leader or downspout is the water conductor from the roof to the storm drain or other means of disposal.

Loop vent.—A loop vent is the same as a circuit vent except that it loops back and connects with a soil- or waste-stack-vent instead of the vent stack.

Main.—The main of any system of continuous piping is the principal artery of the system to which branches may be connected.

Main vent.—See *Vent stack.*

Nonpressure drainage.—Nonpressure drainage refers to a condition in which a static pressure cannot be imposed safely on the building drain. This condition is sometimes referred to as gravity flow and implies that the sloping pipes are not completely filled.

Offset.—An offset in a line of piping is a combination of elbows or bends which brings one section of the pipe out of line with but into a line parallel with another section.

Plumbing.—Plumbing is the work or business of installing in buildings the pipes, fixtures, and other apparatus for bringing in the water supply and removing liquid and water-borne wastes. The term is also used to denote the installed fixtures and piping of a building.

Plumbing fixtures.—Plumbing fixtures are receptacles which receive and discharge water, liquid, or water-borne wastes into a drainage system with which they are connected.

Plumbing system.—The plumbing system of a building includes the water-supply distributing pipes; the fixtures and fixture traps; the soil, waste, and vent pipes; the building (house) drain and building (house) sewer; and the storm-drainage pipes; with their devices, appurtenances, and connections all within or adjacent to the building.

Pool.—A pool is a water receptacle used for swimming or as a plunge or other bath, designed to accommodate more than one bather at a time.

Pressure drainage.—Pressure drainage, as used in this manual, refers to a condition in which a static pressure may be imposed safely on the entrances of sloping building drains through soil and waste stacks connected thereto.

Primary branch.—A primary branch of the building (house) drain is the single sloping drain from the base of a soil or waste stack to its junction with the main building drain or with another branch thereof.

Relief vent.—A relief vent is a branch from the vent stack, connected to a horizontal branch between the first fixture branch and the soil or waste stack, whose primary function is to provide for circulation of air between the vent stack and the soil or waste stack.

Return offset.—A return offset or jumpover is a double offset installed so as to return the pipe to its original line.

Riser.—A riser is a water-supply pipe which extends vertically one full story or more to convey water to branches or fixtures.

Sand interceptor (Sand trap).—A sand interceptor (sand trap) is a watertight receptacle designed and constructed to intercept and prevent the passage of sand or other solids into the drainage system to which it is directly or indirectly connected.

Sanitary sewer.—A sanitary sewer is a sewer designed or used only for conveying liquid or water-borne waste from plumbing fixtures.

Secondary branch.—A secondary branch of the building drain is any branch of the building drain other than a primary branch.

Sewage-treatment plant.—A sewage-treatment plant consists of structures and appurtenances which receive the discharge of a sanitary drainage system, designed to bring about a reduction in the organic and bacterial content of the waste so as to render it less offensive or dangerous, including septic tanks and cesspools.

Side vent.—A side vent is a vent connecting to the drain pipe through a 45° wye.

Size of pipe and tubing.—The size of pipe or tubing, unless otherwise stated, is the nominal size by which the pipe or tubing is commercially designated. Actual dimensions of the different kinds of pipe and tubing are given in the specifications applying.

Soil pipe.—A soil pipe is any pipe which conveys the discharge of water closets or fixtures having similar functions, with or without the discharges from other fixtures.

Stack.—Stack is a general term for the vertical main of a system of soil, waste, or vent piping.

Stack-vent.—A stack-vent is the extension of a soil or waste stack above the highest horizontal or fixture branch connected to the stack.

Storm drain.—A storm drain is a drain used for conveying rain water, subsurface water, condensate, cooling water, or other similar discharges.

Storm sewer.—A storm sewer is a sewer used for conveying rain water, subsurface water, condensate, cooling water, or other similar discharges.

Subsoil drain.—A subsoil drain is a drain installed for collecting subsurface or seepage water and conveying it to a place of disposal.

Trap.—A trap is a fitting or device so designed and constructed as to provide a liquid trap seal which will prevent the passage of air through it.

Trap seal.—The trap seal is the vertical distance between the crown weir and the dip of the trap.

Vent.—A vent is a pipe installed to provide a flow of air to or from a drainage system or to provide a circulation of air within such system to protect trap seals from siphonage and back pressure.

Vent stack.—A vent stack, sometimes called a main vent, is a vertical vent pipe installed primarily for the purpose of providing circulation of air to or from any part of the building-drainage system.

Waste pipe.—A waste pipe is a drain pipe which receives the discharge of any fixture other than water closets or other fixtures receiving human excreta.

Water main.—The water (street) main is a water-supply pipe for public or community use.

Water-service pipe.—The water-service pipe is that part of a building main installed by or under the jurisdiction of a water department or company.

Water-supply system.—The water-supply system of a building consists of the water-service pipe, the water-distributing pipes, and the necessary connecting pipes, fittings, and control valves.

Wet vent.—A wet vent is a soil or waste pipe that serves also as a vent.

Yoke vent.—A yoke vent is a vertical or 45° relief vent of the continuous-waste-and-vent type formed by the extension of an upright wye-branch or 45° wye-branch inlet of the horizontal branch to the stack. It becomes a dual yoke vent when two horizontal branches are thus vented by the same relief vent. (See fig. 2, pt. III.)

CHAPTER II. GENERAL REGULATIONS

Sec. 201. INSTALLATION OF PIPING.—Horizontal drainage piping shall be run in practical alinement and shall be supported at intervals not exceeding 10 feet. The minimum slopes shall be as follows: Not less than ¼-inch fall per foot for 1¼- to 2-inch diameters, inclusive; not less than ⅛-inch fall per foot for 2½- to 4-inch diameters, inclusive; not less than ¹⁄₁₆-inch fall per foot for 5- to 8-inch diameters, inclusive; and a slope that will maintain a velocity of at least 2.0 fps in a pipe of 10-inch diameter or larger as computed by the pipe formula given in paragraph 201, part III. Stacks shall be supported at their bases, and shall be rigidly secured. Piping shall be installed without undue stresses or strains, and provision made for expansion, contraction, and structural settlement. No structural member shall be weakened or impaired beyond a safe limit by cutting, notching, or otherwise, unless provision is made for carrying the structural load.

Sec. 202. CHANGES IN DIRECTION.—Changes in direction in drainage piping shall be made by the appropriate use of cast-iron 45° wyes, half wyes, long-sweep quarter bends, sixth, eighth, or sixteenth bends, or by combinations of these fittings, or by use of equivalent fittings or their combinations; except that sanitary tees may be used in vertical sections of drains or stacks, and short quarter bends may be used in drainage lines where the change in direction of flow is from the horizontal to the vertical. Tees and crosses may be used in vent pipes and in water-distributing pipes. No change in direction greater than 90° in a single turn shall be made in drainage pipes.

Sec. 203. PROHIBITED FITTINGS.—No double hub, or double-tee branch, shall be used on soil or waste lines. The drilling and tapping of building drains, soil, waste, or vent pipes, and the use of saddle hubs or bands, are prohibited. Any fitting or connection which has an enlargement, chamber, or recess with a ledge, shoulder, or reduction of the pipe area, that offers an obstruction to flow through the drain, is prohibited.

Sec. 204. PROHIBITED CONNECTIONS.—(*a*) No fixture, device, or construction shall be installed which will provide a backflow connection between a distributing system of water for drinking and domestic purposes and a drainage system, soil, or waste pipe so as to permit or make possible the backflow of sewage or waste into the water-supply system.

(*b*) No interconnection or cross-connection shall be made between a water-supply system carrying water meeting accepted standards of purity and any other water-supply system.

Sec. 205. PROTECTION OF PIPES.—Pipes passing under or through walls shall be protected from breakage. Pipes passing through or under cinder concrete or other corrosive material shall be protected against external corrosion.

No soil or waste stack shall be installed or permitted outside a building or in an exterior wall unless adequate provision is made to protect it from freezing.

Sec. 206. PROTECTION OF ELECTRICAL MACHINERY.—No water or drainage piping shall be located over electrical machinery or equipment unless adequate protection is provided against drip caused by condensation on the piping.

Sec. 207. PROTECTION OF WATER TANKS.—Drainage piping shall not pass directly over water-supply tanks or reservoirs unless such tanks or reservoirs are tightly closed.

Sec. 208. WORKMANSHIP.—Workmanship shall be of such character as fully to secure the results sought in all sections of this manual.

CHAPTER III. QUALITY, WEIGHT, AND THICKNESS OF MATERIALS

Sec. 301. QUALITY OF MATERIALS.—Materials used in any plumbing system, or part thereof, shall meet accepted standards and shall be free from defects.

Refere ces made in the following sections to standards and specifications shall be taken to mean the latest issues thereof. (See par. 301, pt. III, for information about such issues and for similar and equivalent specifications.)

Sec. 302. IDENTIFICATION OF MATERIALS.—Each length of pipe, and each fitting, trap, fixture, and device used in a plumbing system shall be cast, stamped, or indelibly marked with the maker's mark or name; and also with the weight and quality thereof, when this is required in the specification that applies.

Sec. 303. VITRIFIED-CLAY PIPE.—Vitrified-clay pipe shall conform to Federal Specification for Pipe; Clay, Sewer.

Sec. 304. CONCRETE PIPE.—Concrete pipe shall conform to Federal Specification for Pipe; Concrete, Non-Pressure, Non-Reinforced and Reinforced.

Sec. 305. CAST-IRON SOIL PIPE.—Cast-iron soil pipe and fittings (calked joints) shall conform to Federal Specification for Pipe and Pipe-Fittings; Soil, Cast-Iron, provided that, when approved by the authority having jurisdiction over plumbing, lighter pipe and fittings of equal quality may be used.

Sec. 306. CAST-IRON WATER PIPE.—Cast-iron water pipe shall conform to Federal Specification for Pipe; Water, Cast-Iron (Bell and Spigot and Bolted Joint).

Sec. 307. CAST-IRON SCREWED PIPE.—Cast-iron screwed pipe shall conform to Federal Specification for Pipe, Cast-Iron; Drainage, Vent, and Waste (Threaded).

Sec. 308. WROUGHT-IRON PIPE.—Wrought-iron pipe shall conform to Federal Specification for Pipe; Wrought-Iron, Welded, Black and Galvanized.

Sec. 309. STEEL PIPE.—Steel pipe shall conform to Federal Specification for Pipe; Steel, Seamless and Welded, Black and Zinc-Coated.

Sec. 310. BRASS AND COPPER PIPE.—Brass and copper pipe (I. P. S.) shall conform to Federal Specifications for Pipe, Brass, Seamless, Iron-Pipe-Size, Standard and Extra-Strong; and for Pipe, Copper, Seamless, Iron-Pipe-Size, Standard, respectively.

Sec. 311. BRASS TUBING.—Brass tubing for fixture connections and fittings shall conform to Federal Specification for Plumbing Fixtures; (for) Land Use.

Sec. 312. COPPER TUBING.—Copper tubing for use with flared or soldered fittings shall conform to Federal Specification for Tubing; Copper, Seamless (for Use with Soldered or Flared Fittings) (types K, L, and M). Copper tubing for use with flanged fittings or with silver-brazed joints shall conform to Federal Specification for Tubing, Copper, Seamless (for General Use with I. P. S. Flanged Fittings) (types A, B, C, and D).

Sec. 313. LEAD PIPE.—Lead pipe shall conform to accepted standards. (See table 313–III, pt. III.)

Sec. 314. SHEET LEAD.—Sheet lead shall conform to Federal Specification for Lead; Sheet, and shall weigh not less than 4 pounds per square foot.

Sec. 315. CALKING LEAD.—Calking lead shall conform to Federal Specification for Lead, Calking.

Sec. 316. SHEET COPPER AND BRASS.—Sheet copper and brass shall conform to Federal Specifications for Copper; Bars, Plates, Rods, Shapes, Sheets, and Strips, and for Brass, Commercial; Bars, Plates, Rods, Shapes, Sheets, and Strips, respectively, and shall be not lighter than No. 18 AWG (Brown & Sharpe gage).

Sec. 317. ZINC-COATED (GALVANIZED) SHEET IRON AND STEEL.—Zinc-coated (galvanized) sheet iron and steel shall conform to Federal Specification for Iron and Steel; Sheet, Black and Zinc-Coated (Galvanized); and shall be not lighter than the following AWG (Brown & Sharpe gage):

- No. 26 for 2- to 12-inch pipe.
- No. 24 for 13- to 20-inch pipe.
- No. 22 for 21- to 26-inch pipe.

Sec. 318. SCREWED FITTINGS.—(a) Screwed fittings shall be of cast iron, malleable iron, or brass. Cast-iron fittings shall conform to Federal Specification for Pipe Fittings; Cast-Iron (Threaded). Malleable-iron fittings shall conform to Federal Specification for Pipe-Fittings; Malleable-Iron (Threaded). Brass fittings shall conform to Federal Specification for Pipe-Fittings; Brass or Bronze (Threaded), 125-lb.

(b) Drainage fittings shall be of cast iron, malleable iron, or brass. Cast-iron fittings shall conform to Federal Specification for Pipe-Fittings; Cast-Iron, Drainage. Malleable-iron and brass fittings shall conform to the applicable requirements of the same specification.

Sec. 319. SOLDERED FITTINGS.—Soldered fittings shall conform to American Standards Association Standard for Soldered-Joint Fittings.

Sec. 320. CALKING FERRULES.—Brass calking ferrules shall be of the best quality cast red brass of approved weights and dimensions (see table 320–III, pt. III). Iron-body ferrules shall conform to Federal Specification for Pipe and Pipe-Fittings; Soil, Cast-Iron.

Sec. 321. SOLDERING NIPPLES AND BUSHINGS.—(a) Soldering nipples shall be of red brass pipe, iron-pipe size, or of heavy cast red brass of approved weights. (See table 321 (a)–III, pt. III.)

(b) Soldering bushings shall be of red brass pipe, iron-pipe size, or of heavy cast red brass.

Sec. 322. FLOOR FLANGES.—Floor flanges for plumbing fixtures shall conform to Federal Specification for Plumbing Fixtures; (for) Land Use.

Sec. 323. PACKING.—Packing for hub-and-spigot joints shall conform to Federal Specification for Packing; Jute, Twisted.

Sec. 324. SETTING COMPOUND.—Setting compound for connecting fixtures to floor flanges shall conform to Federal Specification for Compound; Plumbing-Fixture-Setting.

Sec. 325. GASKETS.—Gaskets for connecting fixtures to floor flanges shall conform to Federal Specification for Gaskets; Plumbing-Fixture-Setting.

Sec. 326. ALTERNATE MATERIALS.—Any material other than that specified in this manual which the authority having jurisdiction over plumbing approves may be used.

CHAPTER IV. JOINTS AND CONNECTIONS

Sec. 401. TIGHTNESS.—Joints and connections shall be made gastight and watertight.

Sec. 402. VITRIFIED-CLAY AND CONCRETE PIPE.—Joints in vitrified-clay and concrete pipe, or between such pipe and metals, shall be hot-poured or cemented joints. Hot-poured joints shall be packed with approved packing and filled with an approved jointing compound at one pouring (see par. 402, pt. III). Cemented joints shall be packed with approved packing and secured with portland cement (see par. 402, pt. III).

Sec. 403. CALKED JOINTS.—Calked joints shall be firmly packed with approved packing, secured with well-calked lead, not less than 1 inch deep; and no paint, varnish, or putty shall be permitted until after the joint is tested.

Sec. 404. SCREWED JOINTS.—Screwed joints shall be made with a lubricant on the male thread only. All burrs or cuttings shall be removed.

Sec. 405. JOINTS IN CAST-IRON PIPE.—Joints in cast-iron pipe may be either calked or screwed and shall be made as required in this chapter.

Sec. 406. JOINTS BETWEEN CAST-IRON AND OTHER PIPING.—Joints between cast-iron and wrought-iron, steel, or brass piping may be either screwed or calked joints made as required in this chapter. The end of threaded pipe for calking shall have a ring or half coupling screwed on to form a spigot end.

Sec. 407. WIPED JOINTS.—Wiped joints in lead pipe, or between lead pipe and brass or copper pipes, ferrules, soldering nipples, bushings, or traps, in all cases on the sewer side of the trap and in concealed joints on the inlet side of the trap, shall be full-wiped joints, with an exposed surface of the solder on each side of the joint not less than three-quarters of an inch, and a minimum thickness at the thickest part of the joint of not less than three-eighths of an inch. Where a round joint is made, a thickness of not less than ⅜ of an inch for bushings and flange joints shall be provided.

Sec. 408. JOINTS BETWEEN LEAD AND OTHER PIPING.—Joints between lead and cast-iron, steel, or wrought-iron piping shall be made by means of a calking ferrule, soldering nipple, or bushing.

Sec. 409. JOINTS IN COPPER TUBING.—Copper-tubing joints shall be made in accordance with approved practice. (See par. 409, pt. III.)

Sec. 410. SLIP JOINTS AND UNIONS.—Slip joints and unions shall be used only in trap seals or on the inlet side of the trap, except that expansion joints of approved type may be permitted. Unions on the sewer side of the trap shall be ground faced, and shall not be concealed or enclosed.

Sec. 411. ROOF FLASHINGS.—Joints at the roof shall be made watertight by use of copper, lead, or zinc-coated (galvanized) iron flashings, cast-iron plates, or other approved materials.

Sec. 412. FLOOR CONNECTIONS.—Floor connections for water-closets and other fixtures shall be made by means of an approved brass or cast-iron floor flange soldered securely or calked to the drain pipe. The joint between the fixture and floor flange shall be made tight by means of an approved fixture-setting compound or gasket.

Sec. 413. INCREASERS AND REDUCERS.—Where different sizes of drainage pipes or pipes and fittings are to be connected, proper sizes of standard increasers and reducers shall be employed. Reduction of size of drain pipes in the direction of flow is prohibited, except as indicated in paragraph 413, part III.

Sec. 414. SUPPORTS.—Connections of wall hangers, pipe supports, or fixture settings to masonry or concrete backing shall be made with approved bolts without the use of wooden plugs.

CHAPTER V. TRAPS AND CLEAN-OUTS

Sec. 501. TYPES AND SIZES OF TRAPS.—Every trap shall be self-cleaning, shall be of the same nominal size as the drain to which it is connected, and shall conform to accepted standards. (See par. 501, pt. III.)

The minimum size (nominal inside diameter) of trap and fixture drain for a given fixture shall be not less than shown in the following table:

Fixture:	Size of trap and fixture drain, inches
Bathtubs	1½
Combination fixtures	1½
Drinking fountains	1¼
Floor drains	2
Laundry trays	1½
Lavatories	1¼
Shower stalls	2
Sinks, kitchen, residence	1½
Sinks, hotel or public	2
Sinks, small, pantry or bar	1¼
Sinks, dishwasher	1½
Sinks, service	2
Urinals, trough	2
Urinals, stall	2

For water closets and other fixtures with integral traps, the fixture drains shall be not smaller than the fixture-trap outlet. (See par. 501, pt. III.)

Sec. 502. PROHIBITED TRAPS.—No form of trap which depends for its seal upon the action of movable parts, or partitions that cannot be exposed for inspection, except in a trap integral with a fixture, shall be used for fixtures. No fixture shall be double-trapped. (See par. 502, pt. III.)

Sec. 503. TRAPS REQUIRED.—Each fixture shall be separately trapped by an approved trap placed as near to the fixture as possible or integral therewith, except that a set of not more than three fixtures such as lavatories or laundry trays, or a set of two laundry trays and one sink, may connect with a single trap, provided the trap for three fixtures is placed centrally. (See fig. 3, pt. III.)

Sec. 504. TRAP SEAL.—Each fixture trap shall have a water seal of not less than 2 inches and not more than 4 inches. (See fig. 4, pt. III.)

Sec. 505. TRAP CLEAN-OUTS.—Each trap, except those in combination with fixtures in which the trap seal is plainly visible and accessible, shall be provided with an approved clean-out plug conforming to Federal Specification for Plumbing Fixtures; (for) Land Use.

Sec. 506. INSTALLATION OF TRAPS.—Traps shall be set true with respect to their water seals and protected from freezing.

Sec. 507. PIPE CLEAN-OUTS.—Pipe clean-outs, ferrules, and plugs shall conform to Federal Specification for Pipe and Pipe-Fittings; Soil, Cast-Iron.

Sec. 508. PIPE CLEAN-OUTS REQUIRED.—Accessible clean-outs shall be provided at or near the foot of each vertical waste or soil stack and each inside leader that connects to the building drain, and at each change in direction of the building drain greater than 45°. The distance between clean-outs in horizontal soil lines shall not exceed 50 feet. Clean-outs shall be of the same nominal size as the pipes up to 4 inches and not less than 4 inches for larger pipes.

Sec. 509. CLEAN-OUT EQUIVALENTS.—Any floor or wall connection of fixture traps when bolted or screwed to the floor or wall shall be regarded as a pipe clean-out.

Sec. 510. ACCESSIBILITY OF TRAPS AND CLEAN-OUTS.—Underground traps and clean-outs of a building, except where clean-outs are flush with the floor, and exterior underground traps that are not readily accessible shall be made accessible by manholes with proper covers.

Sec. 511. GREASE INTERCEPTORS.—Grease interceptors shall be installed when required by and in accordance with the regulations of the authority having jurisdiction over plumbing.

Sec. 512. OIL INTERCEPTORS.—Oil interceptors shall be installed when required by and in accordance with the regulations of the authority having jurisdiction over plumbing.

Sec. 513. SAND INTERCEPTORS.—Sand interceptors, when installed, shall be so designed and placed as to be readily accessible for cleaning.

Sec. 514. FLOOR DRAINS.—Floor and area drains shall conform to Federal Specification for Plumbing Fixtures; (for) Land Use, where applicable.

Sec. 515. BACKWATER VALVES.—Backwater valves shall have all bearing parts of corrosion-resisting metal, and be so constructed as to provide a positive mechanical seal against backwater. The area of valve seat shall be equal to the cross-sectional area of the pipe connection.

CHAPTER VI. WATER SUPPLY AND DISTRIBUTION

Sec. 601. QUALITY OF WATER.—The quality of the water supply to each building shall meet accepted standards of purity. Development of private sources of supply shall be in accordance with approved practice. (See par. 601, pt. III.)

Sec. 602. PROTECTION OF WATER SUPPLY.—

(a) Potable and nonpotable water supplies shall be distributed through systems entirely independent of each other.

(b) Water pumps, wells, hydrants, filters, softeners, appliances, and devices shall be protected from surface water and outside contamination by approved covers, walls, or copings.

(c) Potable water-supply tanks, whether storage, pressure, or suction tanks, shall be properly covered to prevent entrance of foreign material into the water supply. (See also sec. 207.)

(d) Every supply outlet or connection to a fixture or appliance shall be protected from backflow by means of an approved air gap or backflow preventer between the control valve of the outlet and the fixture or appliance. (See par. 602 (d), pt. III.)

Sec. 603. PROTECTION FROM FREEZING.—Water pipes, storage tanks, flushing cisterns, and appliances, when subject to freezing temperatures, shall be protected. Water pipes underground shall be placed below freezing level, or shall be otherwise insulated to protect them from freezing. Interior piping shall be insulated, when necessary, for protection.

Sec. 604. SIZE OF BUILDING MAIN.—The building main, including the water-service pipe, shall be of sufficient size to permit a continuous ample flow of water to the building under the average daily minimum service pressure in the street main. The required size for each building shall be determined by the rules given in paragraph 604, part III. No building main of less than ¾-inch diameter shall be installed. If flush valves are installed, the building main shall be of not less than 1-inch diameter.

Sec. 605. Quantity of Water.—Plumbing fixtures shall be provided with a sufficient supply of water for flushing and keeping them in a sanitary condition.

Sec. 606. Size of Fixture Branches.—The minimum size of fixture branches and other supply outlets shall be as follows:

	Inch
Sill cocks	½
Domestic water heaters	½
Laundry trays	½
Sinks	½
Lavatories	⅜
Bathtubs	½
Water-closet tanks	⅜
Water-closet flush valves	1
Flush valves for pedestal urinals	1
Flush valves for wall or stall urinals	½

Sec. 607. Shut-Offs.—Accessible shut-offs with drains shall be provided on the building main and on branches for each dwelling unit and in freezing climates for each outdoor connection. Additional shut-offs may be installed.

Sec. 608. Material for Water Piping and Tubing.—Material for building water-supply pipes and tubes shall be of brass, copper, cast or wrought iron, lead, or steel, with approved fittings. All threaded ferrous pipe and fittings shall be galvanized (zinc-coated). No pipe, tubing, or fittings that have been previously used shall be used for distributing water except for replacement in the same system.

Lead piping in water-supply lines shall not be used unless it has been definitely determined that no poisonous lead salts are produced by contact of lead with the particular water supply.

Sec. 609. Relief Valves.—An approved relief valve shall be installed in each hot-water system and so located that there is no shut-off or check valve between the tank and the relief valve.

CHAPTER VII. PLUMBING FIXTURES

Sec. 701. Quality of Fixtures.—Plumbing fixtures shall conform to accepted standards. (See par. 701, pt. III.)

Sec. 702. Installation of Fixtures.—Plumbing fixtures shall be installed in a manner to afford access for cleaning. Where practicable, pipes from fixtures shall be run to the wall, and no lead trap or lead pipe shall extend nearer to the floor than 12 inches unless protected by casing.

Sec. 703. Frostproof Closets.—Frostproof closets may be installed only in compartments which have no direct access to a building used for human habitation or occupancy. The soil pipe between the hopper and the trap shall be of not less than 3-inch diameter and shall be of lead, or cast iron enameled on the inside. The waste tube from the valve shall not be connected to the soil pipe or sewer.

Sec. 704. Floor Drains.—A floor drain or a shower drain shall be considered a fixture and provided with a strainer.

Sec. 705. Fixture Strainers. — Fixtures other than water closets and pedestal and blow-out urinals shall be provided with approved strainers. (See par. 705, pt. III.)

Sec. 706. Fixture Overflow.—The overflow pipe from a fixture shall be connected on the inlet side of the trap and be so arranged that it may be cleaned.

Sec. 707. Swimming Pools. — Swimming pools shall be constructed in accordance with accepted practice. (See par. 707, pt. III.)

Sec. 708. Miscellaneous Fixtures.—Baptistries, ornamental and lily ponds, aquaria, ornamental fountain basins, and similar constructions shall have supplies thereto protected from backflow as required in section 602.

Sec. 709. Ventilation.—No plumbing fixtures shall be located in any room not provided with proper ventilation. Ventilating pipes from toilet rooms shall form an independent system.

CHAPTER VIII. SOIL AND WASTE PIPES FOR SANITARY SYSTEMS [2]

Sec. 801. Materials.—(*a*) Soil and waste piping for sanitary drainage systems within a building shall be of brass, copper, iron, steel, or lead.

(*b*) The building drain when underground shall be of cast iron.

(*c*) The building sewer shall be of cast iron, vitrified clay, or concrete.

Sec. 802. Minimum Sizes.—The minimum required sizes of soil and waste pipes, depending on location and conditions of service, shall be in accordance with the following sections and tables of this chapter and the principles, rules, and tables relating to drains and sewers in part III. (See par. 802, pt. III.)

Sec. 803. Fixture Units. — The following table of fixture-unit values designating the relative load weights of different kinds of fixtures shall be employed in estimating the total load carried by a soil or waste pipe and shall be used in connection with tables of size for waste and drain pipes in which the permissible load is given in terms of fixture units.

Table 803.—*Fixture units per fixture or group* [1]

Fixture and type of installation	Number of fixture units
Lavatory or washbasin:	
Public	2
Private	1
Water closet:	
Public	10
Private	6
Bathtub, public	4
Shower head:	
Public	4
Private	2
Pedestal urinal, public	10
Wall or stall urinal, public	5
Service sink [2]	3
Kitchen sink, private [2]	2
Bathtub, private	2
Bathroom group, private	8
Bathroom group with separate shower stall, private	10
Two or three laundry trays with single trap, private [2]	3
Combination sink and laundry tray, private [2]	3
Sewage ejector or sump pump, for each 25 gpm	50

[1] See par. 803, pt. III for fixture-unit weights not included in table 803.
[2] These fixtures and groups may be omitted in determining the total fixture units to be applied for soil pipes but the fixture-unit weights assigned must be applied for separate waste lines for groups of these fixtures.

Sec. 804. Stacks To Be Vertical.—Soil and waste stacks shall extend in a vertical line from the highest to the lowest horizontal branch or fixture branch connected thereto, except as provided for in section 806, and shall be vented in accordance with the requirements of chapter X.

Sec. 805. Size of Soil and Waste Pipes.—(*a*) Except as provided in (*b*) of this section, the total number of fixture units installed on a soil or waste stack or horizontal branch of given diameter shall be in accordance with table 805. No soil or waste stack shall be smaller than the largest horizontal branch connected thereto.

(*b*) If the total fixture units are distributed on horizontal branches in three or more branch intervals of the stack, the total number of fixture units on a straight soil or waste stack of a given diameter may be increased from the values given in table 805 within the limits of table 805(*b*)–III, part III, provided the maximum fixture units for one branch interval as computed in accordance with table 805(*b*)–III is not exceeded in any branch interval of the system.

Table 805.—*Permissible number of fixture units on horizontal branches and stacks*

Diameter of pipe (inches)	Fixture units on 1 horizontal branch	Fixture units on 1 stack
	Number	*Number*
1¼	1	2
1½	3	4
2	6	10
3 waste only	32	48
3 soil	20	30
4	160	240
5	360	540
6	640	960
8	1,200	2,240
10	1,800	3,780
12	2,800	6,000

Sec. 806. Offsets.—(*a*) A single offset, a double offset, or a return offset, with no change in direction greater than 45°, may be installed in a soil or waste stack with the stack and branches vented as required for a straight stack, provided that the total number of fixture units on such stack does not exceed one-half the limit permitted by section 805(*a*) and table 805, and no horizontal branch connects to the stack in or within 4 diameters (stack) above or below a sloping section of the offset.

(*b*) If an offset is made at an angle greater than 45°, the required diameter of that portion of the stack above the offset shall be determined as for a separate stack. The diameter of the offset including fittings shall be determined as for a primary branch, and the portion above the offset shall be considered as a horizontal branch in determining the diameter of that portion of the stack below the offset. A relief vent shall be installed in accordance with the requirements of section 1017 at the offset or between it and the next lower horizontal branch.

(*c*) An offset above the highest horizontal branch in a soil or waste stack system is an offset in the stack-vent and shall not be considered in this connection other than as to its effect on the developed length of vent.

(*d*) In case of an offset in a soil or waste stack below the lowest horizontal branch, no change in diameter of the stack because of the offset shall be required if it is made at an angle of not greater than 45°. If such an offset is made at an angle greater than 45°, the required diameter of the offset and the stack below it shall be determined as for a primary branch.

Sec. 807. HORIZONTAL AND PRIMARY BRANCHES.—(a) The required sizes of horizontal branches and primary branches of the building drain shall be in accordance with table 807, except that the permissible number of fixture units in table 807 may be increased as provided for in section 807(d).

TABLE 807.—*Capacities of horizontal branches and primary branches of the building drain*

Diameter of pipe (inches)	Horizontal branch at minimum permissible slope or greater	Primary branch [1]						
		⅛-inch fall per foot		¼-inch fall per foot		½-inch fall per foot		¾-inch fall per foot
	Number	Number		Number		Number		Number
1¼	....	....		....		2		3
1½	3	....		....		5		7
2 waste only	6	....		....		21		26
3 soil	20	....		36		42		50
4	180	....		216		240		290
5	360	....		480		540		560
6	600	360		660		720		940
8	1,800	1,400		1,600		1,920		2,240
10	1,200	2,400		2,700		3,240		3,780
12	2,800	3,000		4,200		4,800		6,000

[1] See par. 807, pt. III, for method of computing permissible number of fixture units for other slopes than those given in this table.

(b) In case the sanitary system consists of one soil stack only or of one soil stack and one or more waste stacks of less than 3-inch diameter, drainage may apply when the prescribed conditions are complied with.

(c) In case the plumbing system has two or more soil stacks each having its separate primary branch or has one or more soil stacks and one or more waste stacks of 3-inch diameter or larger, each soil and waste stack having its separate primary branch, the number of fixture units for a secondary branch, the main building drain, or the building sewer of a given diameter and slope may be increased from the value given in table 807 for a primary branch of the same diameter and slope to the value given in table 807(c), part III, of this manual, provided that the increase is made strictly within the principles and rules of paragraph 807, part III.

(d) In case there is no fixture drain or horizontal branch connecting directly with the building drain or a branch thereof and the lowest fixture branch or horizontal branch connected to any soil or waste stack of the system is 3 feet or more above the grade line of the building drain, the permissible number of fixture units on primary branches, secondary branches, main building drain, and building sewer, may be increased within the limits given by table 807(d), part III, provided the increases are made in accordance with the principles and rules given in paragraph 807, part III.

(e) The provisions of sections 807(c) and 807(d) shall not apply unless plans drawn to scale showing the proposed installation in detail in regard to the diameter, direction, length, and slope of the building drain and its branches and of the building sewer have been submitted to and approved by the authority having jurisdiction over plumbing.

Sec. 808. SUMPS AND RECEIVING TANKS.—All building subdrains shall discharge into an airtight sump or receiving tank so located as to receive the sewage by gravity, from which sump or receiving tank the sewage shall be lifted and discharged into the building sewer by pumps, ejectors, or any equally efficient method. Such sumps shall either be automatically discharged or be of sufficient capacity to receive the building sewage and wastes for not less than 24 hours.

CHAPTER IX. STORM DRAINS

Sec. 901. GENERAL.—Roofs and paved areas, yards, courts, and courtyards shall be drained into the storm-sewerage system or the combined sewerage system, but not into sewers intended for sanitary sewage only. When connected with a combined sewerage system, storm drains, the intakes of which are within 12 feet of any door, window, or ventilating opening, if not at least 3 feet higher than the top of such opening, shall be effectively trapped. One trap on the main storm drain may serve for all such connections. Traps shall be set below the frost line or on the inside of the building. Where there is no sewer accessible, storm drainage shall discharge into the public gutter, unless otherwise permitted by the proper authorities, and in such case need not be trapped.

Sec. 902. LEADERS AND GUTTERS.—(a) Leaders, when placed within the walls of a building or run in a vent or pipe shaft, shall be of cast-iron, zinc-coated (galvanized) wrought-iron or steel, brass, copper, or lead pipe, or of copper tubing.

(b) Outside leaders may be of sheet metal. When of sheet metal and connected with a building storm drain or storm sewer, they shall be connected to a cast-iron drain extending not less than 1 foot above the finish grade. A sheet metal leader along a public driveway without sidewalk shall be properly protected against injury.

(c) Roof gutters shall be of metal or other materials suitable for forming an effective open channel for collecting water and conducting it to the leaders and suitable for making a tight connection with the leaders. (See par. 902, pt. III.)

Sec. 903. SIZE OF STORM DRAINS AND LEADERS.—(a) Storm drains of a building shall be of ample size to convey the estimated storm water from the roof gutters to the street sewer or other approved place of discharge without overflow and without producing dangerously high pressures in any building drain or leader. The estimated flow shall be based on the maximum expected rate of rainfall and estimated rate of flow of storm sewage from other sources. The tables in this section pertaining to leaders and building storm drains are based on the horizontal projection of the roof area, a rate of rainfall of 4 inches per hour and limited slopes as indicated in the tables. (See par. 903, pt. III, for methods of computing the requirements for conditions not covered by or in these tables.)

(b) The area drained into or by a vertical leader or a sloping leader or connecting pipe having a slope of ½-inch fall per foot or greater shall not exceed the values given in table 903(b).

(c) The roof area drained into a building storm sewer or into a main storm drain or any of its branches shall not exceed the values given in table 903(c).

(d) Roof area or drained area as applying in the preceding tables of this section, shall be the horizontal projection of the area, except that where a building wall extends above the roof or court in such a manner as to drain additional run-off shall be made. (See par. 903(d), pt. III, for methods of computing additional run-off shall be made.)

Sec. 904. SEPARATE AND COMBINED DRAINS.—(a) The sanitary and storm-drainage systems of a building shall be entirely separate, except that a combined sanitary-and-storm street sewer is available the storm drains may connect to a combined sanitary-and-storm building drain or sewer at least 10 feet downstream from any primary branch of the sanitary system. Connections between the sanitary and storm systems shall be made at the same grade by means of a single wye fitting. (See par. 904, pt. III, for explanation of this requirement.)

(b) Up to the point of combining into one system, the sizes of the storm and sanitary

TABLE 903(b).—*Maximum roof area for leaders*

Diameter of leader or pipe	Maximum roof area
Inches	*Square feet*
2	500
2½	900
3	1,500
4	3,100
5	5,400
6	8,800
8	17,400

* Drainage fittings are not generally available.

TABLE 903(c).—*Maximum roof area for building storm sewers or drains*

Diameter of pipe (inches)	Maximum roof area for drains of various slopes			
	⅛-inch fall per foot	¼-inch fall per foot	½-inch fall per foot	¾-inch fall per foot
	Square feet	*Square feet*	*Square feet*	*Square feet*
*2	....	....	520	550
3	....	750	870	1,500
*3½	....	1,050	1,200	2,200
4	1,600	1,550	2,150	3,100
5	....	2,900	4,200	5,800
6	3,900	4,700	6,000	8,000
8	5,900	8,700	10,000	17,400
10	....	15,200	19,000	20,400
12	15,900	24,700	31,800	40,400

* 2½-inch and 3½-inch cast-iron soil pipe and fittings and 3½-inch drainage fittings are not generally available.

branches shall be as required for separate storm and sanitary systems.

In the case of a combined sanitary-and-storm building drain or sewer, or of a branch formed by the junction of a single storm drain or sewer and a single sanitary drain or sewer when neither the storm nor the sanitary drain carries more than one-half of its allowable load as given in table 903(c), part II, and table 807(c)–III, part III, the diameter of the combined drain or combined sewer shall be at least equal to that of the larger of the two branches emptying into it, except that in no case shall a combined sanitary-and-storm building drain or building sewer be less than 4 inches in diameter. If either or both of the storm or sanitary branch drains carry more than one-half the allowable load, the combined drain or combined building sewer shall be in accordance with table 904–III and rules of paragraph 904, part III.

Sec. 905. Closed System Required.—When connected with a combined sanitary-and-storm sewerage system, the building storm-drainage piping shall form a closed system with water-tight joints, except for its outlet and intake openings.

Sec. 906. Overflow Pipes.—Overflow pipes from cisterns, supply tanks, expansion tanks, and drip pans shall connect with any building sewer, building drain, or soil pipe only by means of an indirect connection.

Sec. 907. Subsoil Sumps.—Subsoil drains below the main-sewer level shall discharge into a sump or receiving tank, the contents of which shall be automatically lifted and discharged into the drainage system through a properly trapped fixture or drain.

Sec. 908. Construction of Subsoil Drains.—Where subsoil drains are placed under the cellar floor or used to encircle the outer walls of a building, they shall be made of open-jointed drain tile or earthenware pipe, not less than 4 inches in diameter. When the building drain is subject to backwater the subsoil drain shall be protected by an accessibly located automatic back-pressure valve before entering the building sewer or drain. If such drains are connected with the sanitary sewer or with a combined system they shall be properly trapped. They may discharge to an area drain.

CHAPTER X. VENTS AND VENTING

Sec. 1001. Material.—Vent pipes or tubing shall be of cast iron, zinc-coated (galvanized) wrought iron or steel, brass, copper, or lead.

Sec. 1002. Protection of Trap Seals.—The seal of every fixture trap in a plumbing system shall be adequately protected by a properly installed vent or system of venting. A stack-vent, back vent, relief vent, dual vent, circuit or loop vent, or a combination of two or more of these forms installed in the manner and within the limitations specified in sections 1006 to 1012, inclusive, shall be considered as adequate protection of trap seals in the sense of this section. (See par. 1002, pt. III.)

Sec. 1003. Stack-Vents Required.—Every soil or waste stack shall be extended vertically as a stack-vent to at least 6 inches above the highest horizontal branch and then to the open air above the roof or otherwise terminated in the open air outside the building; or the stack-vent and vent stack may be connected together within the building at least 6 inches above the flood level of the highest fixture, with a single extension from the connection to the open air.

Sec. 1004. Vent Stacks Required.—A vent stack or main vent shall be installed with a soil or waste stack whenever relief vents, back vents, or other branch vents are required in two or more branch intervals. The vent stack shall terminate independently in the open air outside the building or may be connected with the stack-vent as prescribed in section 1003, and shall connect with the soil or waste stack through, at, or below the lowest horizontal branch or with the primary branch of the building drain.

Sec. 1005. Distance of Trap From Vent.—Except as provided for particular fixtures and forms of construction in sections 1010 and 1011, and excepting water closets, pedestal urinals, trap-standard service sinks, and other fixtures which depend on siphon action for the proper functioning of the fixture, each fixture trap shall have a protecting vent located so that the total fall in the fixture drain from the trap weir to the vent fitting is not more than 1 pipe diameter, and the developed length of drain from trap weir to vent fitting is not less than 2 nor more than 48 pipe diameters. A back vent or

relief vent, preferably in the form of a continuous-waste-and-vent, shall be installed within these limits as may be necessary for compliance with this requirement. (See par. 1005, and fig. 13, pt. III.)

Sec. 1006. Dual Vents Permitted.—A dual vent for two fixture traps installed as a vertical continuous-waste-and-vent, or a stack-vent in a dual capacity, may be employed under the following conditions and no additional vents for the traps thus vented shall be required:

(a) When both fixture drains connect with a vertical drain or stack at the same level, and the developed length and total fall of each of the two fixture drains are within the limits given in section 1005. (See fig. 14A, pt. III.)

(b) When the two fixture drains connect with the vertical drain or stack at different levels, the difference in level of the two connections is not greater than five times the diameter of the vertical section of drain or stack, the diameter of the vertical section or stack up to and including the higher connection is not less than that required for the horizontal drain for both fixtures, the cross-section of the higher of the two fixture drains is not greater than one-half that of the vertical drain, and the developed length and total fall of each of the two fixture drains is within the limits given in section 1005. (See fig. 14B, pt. III.)

Sec. 1007. Group Vents Permitted.—(a) A lavatory trap and a bathtub or shower-stall trap may be installed on the same horizontal branch with a back vent for the lavatory trap and with no back vent for the bathtub or shower-stall trap, provided the vertical section of the lavatory drain is of not less than 1¼-inch diameter, connects with the tub or shower-stall drain in a vertical plane, and the developed lengths of both fixture drains are within the limits of permissible fixture units (sec. 805(b)), provided that a relief vent is installed from the water-closet branch drain in the third branch interval from the top and in each lower branch interval. (See fig. 15A, pt. III.)

(b) Two lavatory traps and two bathtub or shower-stall traps may be installed on the same horizontal branch with a dual vent for the lavatory traps and with no back vents for the bathtub or shower-stall traps, provided that the horizontal branch, except the separate fixture drains, shall be at least 2 inches in diameter and the fixture drains for bathtubs or shower stalls connect as closely as practicable

upstream from the vent by means of a drainage wye. (See fig. 15B, pt. III.)

(c) A lavatory trap, kitchen-sink trap, and a bathtub or shower-stall trap may be installed on the same horizontal branch, as in (a), provided the dual vent for the lavatory and sink traps is installed in accordance with section 1006. (See fig. 15C, pt. III.)

Sec. 1008. Yoke and Relief Vents.—Bathroom groups, or one bathroom group with lavatory, and a shower stall or bathtub with or without shower head, may be installed on a soil stack with any of the following forms of group venting:

(a) Two bathroom groups, or one bathroom group and kitchen sink or kitchen-sink-and-tray combination, may be installed in the highest branch interval of the soil stack or on a vertical yoke-vented branch not less than 3 inches in diameter with no branch vents other than the yoke vent, provided each fixture drain connects independently to the soil stack or with the water-closet drain (closet bend) in the highest branch interval and each fixture drain in all except the highest branch interval connects independently with the yoke-vented branch or with the water-closet drains (closet bends) within the limits given in section 1005. (See fig. 16, pt. III.)

(b) One bathroom group with group venting in accordance with section 1007(a) and with the horizontal branch connected to the soil stack at the same level as the water-closet drain or connected to the water-closet drain (closet bend), or a bathroom group and kitchen sink with connections to the stack in the same manner and with group venting in accordance with section 1007(c), may be installed in the same branch interval of a soil stack within the limits of permissible fixture units for one soil stack and branch intervals (sec. 805(b)), provided that a relief vent is installed from the water-closet branch drain in the third branch interval from the top and in each lower branch interval. (See fig. 19, pt. III.)

(c) Two bathroom groups with group venting in accordance with section 1007(a) or 1007(b), or two bathroom groups and two kitchen sinks with group venting in accordance with section 1007(c), may be installed in the same branch interval of a soil stack, provided a relief vent is installed for the second and lower branch intervals from the top. (See figs. 18 and 20, pt. III.)

(d) In all cases the relief vent required under (a), (b), or (c), may be a dual vent and the size shall be in accordance with section 1015. Fittings that combine the effects of two or more standard fittings in one casting may be permitted. (See also par. 1008 and figs. 13 to 20, pt. III.)

Sec. 1009. CIRCUIT VENTS AND LOOP VENTS.—(a) A group of fixtures in line (battery) on the same floor or level may be installed on one horizontal branch with a circuit or loop vent connected to the horizontal branch in front of the last fixture drain, within the limits given in table 1009(a), provided relief vents connected to the horizontal branch in front of the first fixture drain are installed as follows:

In each branch interval, if the total fixture units installed in the branch exceeds one-half the number given in table 1009(a), except that no relief vent shall be required in the highest branch interval of the system or in any branch interval if the total number of fixture units on the stack above the horizontal branch does not exceed the limits for one stack given in table 805 and the number of fixtures on the circuit- or loop-vented horizontal branch does not exceed two for a 2- or 3-inch horizontal branch or does not exceed one-half the permissible number in column 2 of table 1009(a) for 4-inch and larger horizontal branches. A dual relief vent for two circuit- or loop-vented horizontal branches in the same branch interval may be installed.

TABLE 1009(a).—*Limits for circuit and loop venting*

(1)	(2)	(3)
Diameter of horizontal branch	Water closets, pedestal urinals, or trap-standard fixtures	Fixture units for fixtures other than designated in column 2
Inches	Number	Number
2	None	6
3	2	20
4	8	60
5	16	120
6	24	180

(b) The limits for circuit- or loop-vented horizontal branches may be increased to one and one-half times the values given in table 1009(a) for 3-inch and larger branches when relief vents are installed so that there is a relief vent inside the first fixture drain, the number of fixtures or fixture units outside the last relief vent does not exceed the limits given in columns 2 and 3 of table 1009(a), and the number of fixture drains between any two successive relief vents does not exceed two for a 3-inch, three for a 4-inch, five for a 5-inch, or eight for a 6-inch or larger horizontal branch.

(c) Two lines of fixtures back-to-back (double battery) shall not be circuit- or loop-vented on one branch, but each line may be installed on a separate branch and circuit- or loop-vented. (See figs. 21 and 22, pt. III.)

Sec. 1010. VENTS FOR FLAT-BOTTOMED FIXTURES.—The trap and fixture drain not exceeding 2 inches in diameter of a single fixture having a relatively flat bottom at least 200 square inches of which slopes toward the outlet with a fall not exceeding ⅛ inch per foot, or the trap and fixture drain from a group of not more than three such fixtures, may be installed with a vertical section of the fixture drain not exceeding 24 pipe diameters in length at a distance not exceeding 10 pipe diameters from the trap weir, with a total length of sloping drain not exceeding 72 pipe diameters, with no back vent, provided that the fixture drain is the highest drain on the soil or waste stack or on a yoke-vented vertical section of a horizontal branch. If the total developed length of the sloping sections of the drain from the fixture to the stack-vent or relief vent exceeds 72 pipe diameters (9 feet for 1¼-inch diameter or 12 feet for 2-inch diameter), a back vent to the first vertical section of the drain or a continuous waste-and-vent relief vent at or within this prescribed maximum distance shall be installed.

Sec. 1011. VENTS FOR RESEALING TRAPS.—If a resealing trap of approved design is installed for a fixture or a group of not more than three fixtures, the limits given for venting in section 1010 shall apply. (See par. 1011, pt. III.)

Sec. 1012. FIXTURES AT BASE OF MAIN VENT.—A group of not more than three fixtures, none of which discharge greasy wastes, may be installed on a main vent or vent stack below the lowest branch vent, provided the load does not exceed one-half the allowable load by table 807 on a horizontal branch of the same diameter as the main vent. (See par. 1012, pt. III.)

Sec. 1013. SIZE AND LENGTH OF MAIN VENTS.—Vent stacks or main vents shall have a diameter of at least one-half that of the soil or waste stack, and shall be of larger diameter in accordance with the limits of length and number of fixture units as given in table 1013. The length of the main vent for application with table 1013 shall be the total developed length as follows:

(a) From the lowest connection of the vent system with the soil stack, waste stack, or primary branch to the terminal of the vent, if it terminates separately to the open air;

(b) From the lowest connection of the vent system with the soil stack, waste stack, or primary branch to the stack-vent plus the developed length of the stack-vent to its terminal in the open air, if the stack-vent and vent stack are joined with a single extension to the open air.

TABLE 1013.—*Size and length of main vents*

Diameter of soil or waste stack (inches)	Number of fixture units on soil or waste stack	Maximum permissible developed length of vent						
		1¼-inch vent	1½-inch vent	2-inch vent	2½-inch vent	3-inch vent	4-inch vent	5-inch vent	6-inch vent
		Feet	Feet	Feet	Feet	Feet	Feet	Feet	Feet
1¼	2	75							
1½	8	50	150						
1½	10	30	100						
2	12	25	75	200					
2	20	20	50	150					
2	40		30	100					
3	10		30	100	600				
3	30			60	500				
3	60			50	400				
4	100			35	260	1,000			
4	200			30	250	900			
4	500			20	180	700			
5	200				35	80	350	1,000	
5	500				30	70	300	900	
5	1,100				20	50	200	700	
6	350				25	50	200	400	1,300
6	620				15	30	125	300	1,100
6	960					24	100	250	1,000
6	1,900					20	70	200	700
8	600					50	150	500
8	1,400					40	100	400
8	2,200					30	80	350
8	3,600						25	60	250

Sec. 1014. SIZE AND LENGTH OF STACK-VENTS.—Stack-vents shall be of the same diameter as the soil or waste stack, if the soil or waste stack carries one-half or more of its permissible load by table 805 or has horizontal branches in more than two branch intervals. If the soil or waste stack carries less than one-half its permissible load and has horizontal branches in not more than two branch intervals, the stack-vent may be of a diameter not less and a length not greater than required by table 1013.

Sec. 1015. SIZE OF BACK VENTS AND RELIEF VENTS.—The nominal diameter of a back vent, when required, shall be not less than 1¼ inches nor less than one-half the diameter of the drain to which it is connected, and under conditions that require a relief vent for approved forms of group venting (see secs. 1007, 1008, and 1009), the sum of the cross sections of all vents installed on the horizontal branches in one branch interval shall be at least equal to that of either the main vent or the largest horizontal branch in the branch interval.

Sec. 1016. SIZE OF CIRCUIT AND LOOP VENTS.—(a) The nominal diameter of a circuit or loop vent and the first relief vent as required by section 1009(a) shall be not less than one-half the diameter of the horizontal branch thus vented. Under conditions that require a relief vent (see sec. 1009) the sum of the cross sections of the circuit or loop and relief vents shall be at least equal to that of either the main vent required or the horizontal branch. In determining the sum of cross sections for this requirement, all relief vents connected to the horizontal branch may be included.

(b) Additional relief vents, installed in compliance with section 1009(b), shall be not less in diameter than one-half that of the largest fixture branch connected to the horizontal branch.

Sec. 1017. RELIEF VENTS FOR OFFSETS.—The relief vent required for an offset, as prescribed by section 806(b), shall be installed either as a vertical continuation of the lower section of the soil or waste stack or as a side vent connected to the lower section of the soil or waste stack between the offset and the next fixture or horizontal branch below the offset. The size of the required relief vent shall be determined as follows:

(a) If the stack-vent from the upper section of the soil or waste stack is equal to that of the upper section, the relief vent shall not be smaller than the main vent of the stack system;

(b) If the stack-vent from the upper section of the soil or waste stack is smaller in diameter than that section, it may be the same diameter as the main vent required, in which case shall be equal to that of the lower section and shall be extended to the open air without reduction in size or may be connected to the main vent or stack-vent, provided the one to which it is connected is of equal or greater diameter.

If horizontal branches connect to any soil or waste stack between two offsets each offset shall be vented as required in this section.

Sec. 1018. FROST CLOSURE.—In cold climates adequate provision shall be made to guard against frost closure of vents.

Sec. 1019. LOCATION OF VENT TERMINALS.—(a) No vent terminal from the sanitary drainage system shall be within 12 feet of any door, window, or ventilating opening of the same or an adjacent building unless it is at least 3 feet higher than the top of such opening. Extensions of vent pipes through a roof shall terminate at least 1 foot above it and shall be properly flashed. Vent terminals extending through walls shall not terminate within 12 feet horizontally of any adjacent building line, shall be turned to provide a horizontal opening downward, shall be effectively screened, and shall be properly flashed, calked, or otherwise sealed.

(b) In the event that a structure is built higher than an existing structure, the owner of the structure shall not locate windows within 12 feet of any existing vent terminal on the lower structure, unless the owner of such higher structure shall defray the expenses of, or shall himself make, such alterations as are necessary to conform with the provisions of this section.

Sec. 1020. VENTS NOT REQUIRED.—(a) No vent shall be required for a leader trap, backwater trap, or subsoil catchbasin trap.

(b) No vent shall be required for the trap of a basement or cellar-floor drain or area drain, provided such drain branches into the building drain or a branch thereof at least 5 feet downstream from any soil or waste stack, the length and fall of the floor or area drain are within the limits of section 1005, the load on the building drain or any of its branches does not exceed the limits in table 807, and the building drain is not subject to backwater effects.

Sec. 1021. VENTS PROHIBITED.—(a) No back vent shall be installed within two pipe diameters of the trap weir.

(b) Except as permitted in sections 1006, 1007, 1008, 1009, and 1012, no wet vent shall be installed.

age system shall be at a temperature not higher than 140° F. Where higher temperatures exist proper cooling methods shall be provided.

CHAPTER XI. INDIRECT CONNECTIONS TO WASTE PIPES

Sec. 1101. INDIRECT WASTES.—Waste pipes from the following shall not connect directly with any building drain, soil, or waste pipe: a refrigerator, ice box, or other receptacle where food is stored; an appliance, device, or apparatus used in the preparation or processing of food or drink; an appliance, device, or apparatus using water as a cooling or heating medium; a sterilizer, water still, water-treatment device, or water-operated device.

Such waste pipes shall in all cases empty into, and above the flood level of, an open plumbing fixture or shall be connected indirectly to the inlet side of a fixture trap. Indirect waste connections shall not be located in inaccessible or unventilated cellars or other spaces. (See par. 1101, pt. III.)

Sec. 1102. SIZE OF REFRIGERATOR WASTES.—Refrigerator waste pipes shall be not less than 1¼ inches in diameter for one opening, 1½ inches for 2 or 3 openings, and 2 inches for 4 to 12 openings. Each opening shall have a trap and clean-out so installed as to permit proper flushing and cleaning of the waste pipe.

Sec. 1103. OVERFLOW PIPES.—Overflow pipes from a water-supply tank or exhaust pipes from a water lift shall not be directly connected with any building drain or with any soil or waste pipe, but shall discharge outside the building, or into an open fixture as provided in section 1101.

CHAPTER XII. MAINTENANCE

Sec. 1201. DEFECTIVE PLUMBING.—Any part of the plumbing system found defective or in an insanitary condition shall be repaired, renovated, replaced, or removed within 30 days upon written notice from the authority having jurisdiction over plumbing.

Sec. 1202. TEMPORARY TOILET FACILITIES.—Toilet facilities provided for the use of workmen during the construction of any building shall be maintained in a sanitary condition.

Sec. 1203. CONDENSATE AND BLOW-OFF CONNECTIONS.—No direct connection of a steam exhaust, boiler blow-off, or drip pipe shall be made with the building-drainage system. Waste water when discharged into the building-drain-

the time set for any inspection or test, the inspection or test shall be made by the plumber and the plumber required to file an affidavit with the authority having jurisdiction over plumbing and with the owner. The affidavit shall state that the work was installed in accordance with this manual and the approved plans and permit, that it was free from defects, and that the required tests were made and the system is free from leaks; also whether the owner or his authorized agent was present when such inspection or tests were made, or was duly notified.

Sec. 1304. LABOR AND EQUIPMENT FOR TESTS.—The equipment, material, power, and labor necessary for the inspection and test shall be furnished by the plumber, unless otherwise provided by the authority having jurisdiction over plumbing.

Sec. 1305. TESTS OF DRAINAGE SYSTEM.—(a) A water test may be applied to the system in its entirety or in sections. If applied to the entire system, all openings in the piping shall be tightly closed, except the highest opening, and the system filled with water to the point of overflow. If the system is tested in sections, each opening shall be tightly plugged (except the highest opening of the section under test) and the section shall be filled with water. In testing successive sections, at least the upper 10 feet of the next lower section shall be retested (except the uppermost 10 feet of the system) and shall have been subjected to at least a 10-foot head of water.

The water level shall remain constant without any further addition for sufficient time to inspect the entire section under test, but in no case less than 15 minutes.

(b) In place of the water test, an air test may be applied as follows: With all openings tightly closed, air shall be forced into the system until there is a uniform pressure sufficient to balance a column of mercury 10 inches in height (or 5 pounds per square inch) on the entire system or section under test. The air pressure shall be maintained on the system or section without any further addition of air for a sufficient time to determine tightness but in no case for less than 15 minutes. (See par. 1305 (b), p. III.)

Sec. 1306. FINAL TEST.—After all fixtures

CHAPTER XIII. INSPECTION AND TESTS

Sec. 1301. INSPECTION.—All piping, traps, and fixtures of a plumbing system shall be inspected by the authority having jurisdiction over plumbing to insure compliance with the requirements of this manual and the installation and construction of the system in accordance with the approved plans and the permit.

Sec. 1302. TESTS REQUIRED.—Every plumbing system shall be subjected to tests for tightness. The complete water-supply system of the building shall be subjected to a water or air-pressure test. The drainage system within or under the building shall be subjected to a water or air-pressure test before the pipes are concealed or the fixtures are set in place, and the sanitary-drainage and vent system shall be subjected to a final smoke or air-pressure test after the system has been completed and the fixture traps have been connected. The authority having jurisdiction over plumbing may require the removal of any plug or cap during the test to determine whether the pressure has reached all parts of the system. He may modify or change the order of any of the tests prescribed in sections 1305, 1306, and 1307, or may substitute a different test to meet special conditions; provided that the tests used are, in his opinion, as effective as those required in the sections enumerated.

Sec. 1303. NOTIFICATION FOR TEST.—(a) It shall be the duty of the plumber to notify the authority having jurisdiction over plumbing and the owner, or his authorized agent, orally, by telephone, or in writing, not less than one working day before the work is to be inspected or tested.

(b) It shall be the duty of the plumber to make sure that the work will stand the test prescribed before giving the above notification.

(c) If the authority having jurisdiction over plumbing finds that the work will not stand the test, the plumber shall be required to renotify the authority.

(d) If the authority having jurisdiction over plumbing fails to appear within 24 hours of

have been permanently connected and all trap seals filled with water, a smoke or air test under a pressure of approximately 1-inch water column shall be applied to the sanitary system.

In the case of a smoke test, a thick penetrating smoke produced by one or more smoke machines (not by chemical mixtures) shall be introduced into the entire system through a suitable opening. As the smoke appears at the stack openings, they shall be closed and a pressure equivalent to 1-inch water column shall be applied.

Sec. 1307. TESTS OF THE WATER-SUPPLY SYSTEM.—The water-supply system shall be tested in its entirety by filling the entire system with water under a pressure of at least 100 pounds per square inch, or by applying air pressure of at least 35 pounds per square inch (70 inches of mercury column) in case the water test is not feasible or not desirable. The test in either case shall be applied for sufficient time to determine tightness.

Sec. 1308. FINAL CONDITION.—All parts of the plumbing system and associated equipment shall be otherwise tested and adjusted to work properly and be left in good operating condition.

Sec. 1309. SEPARATE TESTS PERMITTED.—Tests may be made separately, as follows:

(a) The building sewer and all its branches from the property line to the building drain.

(b) The building drain and yard drains, including all piping to the height of 10 feet above the highest point on the house drain, except the exposed connections to fixtures.

(c) The soil, waste, vent, inside leader, and drainage pipes which would be covered up before the building is inclosed or ready for completion. The test required for (b) and (c) may be combined.

(d) The final test of the whole system.

After each of the above tests has been made and proved acceptable the authority having jurisdiction over plumbing shall issue a written approval.

Sec. 1310. COVERING OF WORK.—No drainage or plumbing system or part thereof shall be covered until it has been inspected, tested, and approved as prescribed in this chapter. If any building-drainage or plumbing system, or part thereof, is covered before being regularly inspected, tested, and approved, as prescribed in this chapter, it shall be uncovered upon the direction of the authority having jurisdiction over plumbing.

Sec. 1311. DEFECTIVE WORK.—If inspection or test shows defects, such defective work or material shall be replaced and inspection and the tests repeated.

All repairs to piping shall be made with new material. No calking on screwed joints, cracks, or holes will be acceptable.

Sec. 1312. TESTS OF LEADERS.—Leaders and their roof connections within the walls of buildings, or their branches on an outside system where such branches connect with the building drain or are less than 3 feet from the wall of the building, shall be tested by the water or air test. Branches on the outside system may be tested in connection with the house drain.

Sec. 1313. OUTBUILDINGS.—If a stable, barn, or other outbuilding or any part thereof is used for human habitation, the specified inspections and tests of the plumbing system shall be made. Otherwise, all drains shall be inspected, but need not be tested.

Sec. 1314. GARAGES.—For a garage or any part of a garage the specified tests and inspections of the plumbing system shall be made.

Sec. 1315. CERTIFICATE OF APPROVAL.—Upon the satisfactory completion and final test of the plumbing system a certificate of approval shall be issued by the authority having jurisdiction over plumbing to the plumber to be delivered to the owner.

Sec. 1316. TEST OF DEFECTIVE PLUMBING.—The smoke or air test shall be used in testing the sanitary condition of the plumbing system of a building where there is reason to believe that the system has become defective. In plumbing found defective by the authority having jurisdiction over plumbing the alterations required shall be considered as new plumbing.

Sec. 1317. INSPECTIONS AND TESTS NOT REQUIRED.—No tests or inspections shall be required where a plumbing system or part thereof is set up for exhibition purposes and is not used for toilet purposes and not directly connected to a sewerage system; nor after the repairing, or the replacement by a new one to be used for the same purpose, of an old fixture, faucet, or valve; nor after forcing out stoppages and repairing leaks.

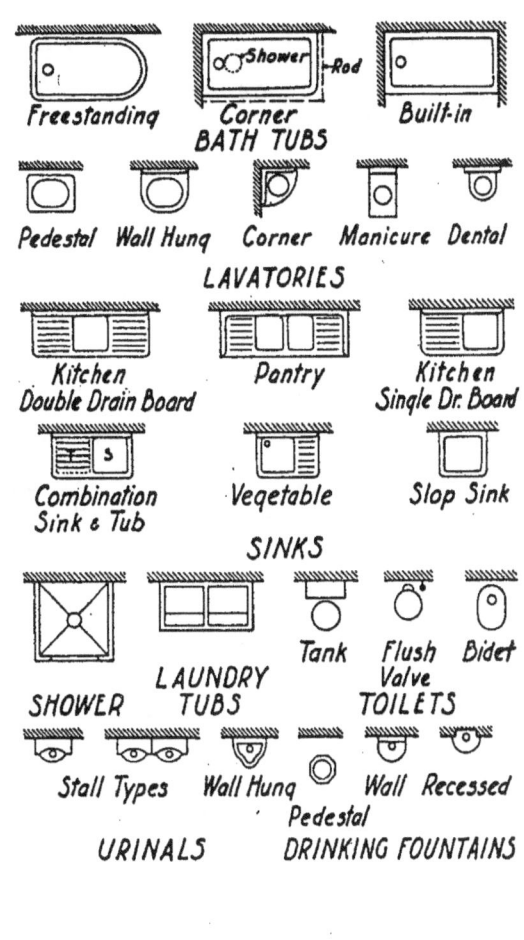

PLUMBING SYMBOLS			
Symbol	Plan	Initials	Item
———————	○	D.	Drainage Line
– – – – –	○	V.S.	Vent Line
———————	◎		Tile Pipe
—•—•—•—	○	C.W.	Cold Water Line
—••—••—	○	H.W.	Hot Water Line
— — — —	○	H.W.R.	Hot Water Return
—×—×—×—	⊗	G	Gas Pipe
—••—••—	○	D.W.	Ice Water Supply
—•••—•••—	○	D.R.	Ice Water Return
—/—/—/—	○	F.L.	Fire Line
—>—>—>—	⊕	I.W.	Indirect Waste
—I—I—I—	⊕	I.S.	Industrial Sewer
—\—\—\—	⊗	AW	Acid Waste
—○—○—	Ⓐ	A	Air Line
—oooo—oooo—	Ⓥ	V	Vacuum Line
—<—<—<—	Ⓡ	R	Refrigerator Waste
			Gate Valves
			Check Valves
—⌐CO ⌐CO		CO.	Cleanout
□ F.D		F.D.	Floor Drain
◎ R.D		R.D.	Roof Drain
◎ REF.		REF.	Refrigerator Drain
⌀		S.D.	Shower Drain
⊗		G.T.	Grease Trap
⊢S.C.		S.C.	Sill Cock
⊢G		G.	Gas Outlet
⊢VAC		VAC.	Vacuum Outlet
⊢Ⓜ⊣		M	Meter
[I×]			Hydrant
H.R.		H.R.	Hose Rack
H.R.		H.R.	Hose Rack-Built in
L		L.	Leader
Ⓗwt		H.W.T.	Hot Water Tank
Ⓦh		W.H.	Water Heater
Ⓦm		W.M.	Washing Machine
Ⓡb		R.B.	Range Boiler

FIGURE 1.—Standard plumbing symbols.

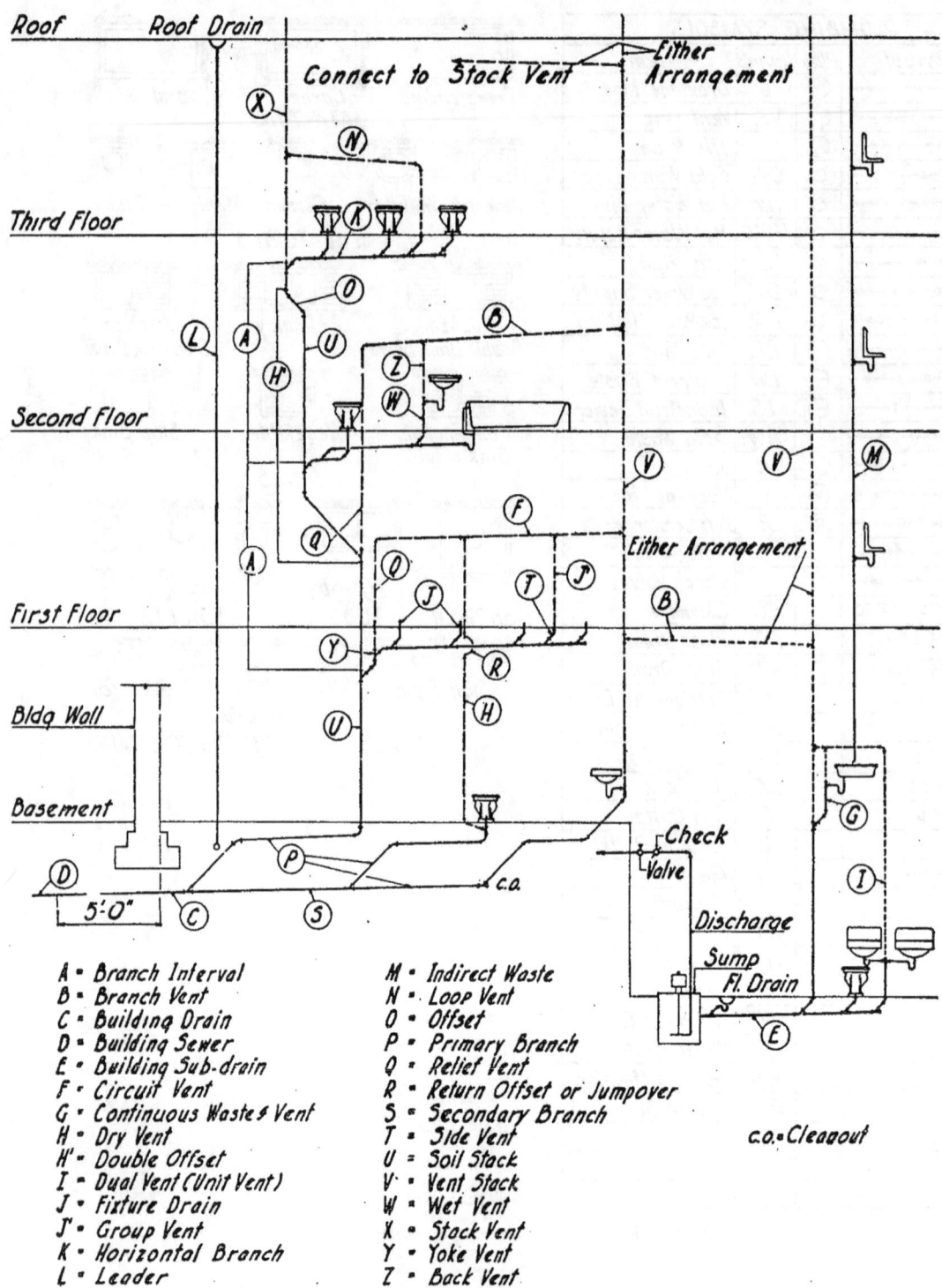

FIGURE 2.—Illustration of definitions.